ROUTLEDGE LIBRARY EDITIONS:
URBAN STUDIES

Volume 15

THE ROMANCE OF CULTURE IN AN URBAN CIVILIZATION

THE ROMANCE OF CULTURE IN AN URBAN CIVILIZATION

Robert E. Park on race and ethnic relations in cities

BARBARA BALLIS LAL

Routledge
Taylor & Francis Group

LONDON AND NEW YORK

First published in 1990 by Routledge

This edition first published in 2018
by Routledge
2 Park Square, Milton Park, Abingdon, Oxon OX14 4RN

and by Routledge
711 Third Avenue, New York, NY 10017

Routledge is an imprint of the Taylor & Francis Group, an informa business

British Library Cataloguing in Publication Data
A catalogue record for this book is available from the British Library

ISBN: 978-1-138-89482-2 (Set)
ISBN: 978-1-315-09987-3 (Set) (ebk)
ISBN: 978-1-138-03660-4 (Volume 15) (hbk)
ISBN: 978-1-138-03662-8 (Volume 15) (pbk)
ISBN: 978-1-315-17846-2 (Volume 15) (ebk)

Publisher's Note
The publisher has gone to great lengths to ensure the quality of this reprint but
points out that some imperfections in the original copies may be apparent.

Disclaimer
The publisher has made every effort to trace copyright holders and would welcome
correspondence from those they have been unable to trace.

THE ROMANCE OF CULTURE IN AN URBAN CIVILIZATION

Robert E. Park on race and ethnic relations in cities

BARBARA BALLIS LAL

ROUTLEDGE
LONDON AND NEW YORK

First published 1990
by Routledge
11 New Fetter Lane, London EC4P 4EE

Simultaneously published in the USA and Canada
by Routledge
a division of Routledge, Chapman and Hall, Inc.
29 West 35th Street, New York, NY 10001

Typeset by LaserScript Limited, Mitcham, Surrey
Printed and bound in Great Britain by
Biddles Ltd, Guildford and King's Lynn

British Library Cataloguing in Publication Data

Lal, Barbara Ballis, *1941–*
The romance of culture in an urban civilization: Robert E. Park on race
and ethnic relations in cities
1. United States. Race relations.
Theories of Park, Robert E.
I. Title
305.8'0092'4

Library of Congress Cataloging in Publication Data

Lal, Barbara Ballis, 1941–
The romance of culture in an urban civilization: Robert E. Park
on race and ethnic relations in cities / Barbara Ballis Lal.
p. cm.
Bibliography: p.
Includes index.
1. Park, Robert Ezra, 1864-1944. 2. Sociologists–United States–
Biography. 3. Chicago school of sociology–History. 4. Sociology,
Urban–United States–Study and teaching–History–20th century.
5. United States–Race relations–Study and teaching–
History–20th century. 6. United States–Ethnic relations–Study and
teaching–History–20th century. I. Title.
HM22.U6P344 1989
89–6198
305.8'00973–dc20
CIP

ISBN 0-415-02877-9

CONTENTS

Acknowledgements vii

Introduction 1

1 SOCIAL CONTEXT AND INDIVIDUAL BIOGRAPHY 11

2 CULTURE, COMMUNICATION, AND SOCIAL
CONTROL 27

3 PARK'S APPROACH TO RACE AND ETHNIC
RELATIONS 49

4 THE EMERGENCE OF AN ETHNOGRAPHIC
TRADITION 69

5 IMMIGRANTS AND THE 'ETHNICITY PARADOX' 92

6 'BRIGHT LIGHTS, IMPENDING SHADOWS': AFRO-
AMERICAN MIGRATION TO NORTHERN CITIES 124

7 GETTING IT TOGETHER: A SCHEME OF
INTERPRETATION 160

Notes 171

Bibliography 178

Name index 200

Subject index 205

To my mother, Ryer Ballis, and to the memory of my father,
Jack Ballis

ACKNOWLEDGEMENTS

Robert E. Park has been my constant companion for the last fifteen years. During this time, I have never tired of him, or the company of his mates. My children, Deepika and Akshay, felt otherwise, while my husband, Deepak, has threatened to name Park as the third party in unamicable divorce proceedings. My thanks to my children and my husband for managing to 'do without' on so many occasions.

My book started out as a research paper written for Robert Blauner while I was a graduate student at the University of California. Whilst at Berkeley, I studied with Herbert Blumer, a student of both Park and Mead. Blumer's gifts as a teacher and scholar, as well as his kindness, generosity, and integrity, recommended further study of the remarkable group of sociologists gathered at Chicago during the 1920s and 1930s. This I was able to do as a doctoral candidate writing my dissertation under the supervision of Troy Duster, Nathan Glazer, and Guy Benveniste. At various times this enterprise was funded by the Ford Foundation and by Goldsmiths' College. To the above, I owe thanks for their support.

I would like to also thank Martin Bulmer, John Lemley, Linda Levy Peck, and John Stone for reading parts of the manuscript and offering useful criticisms. My friend and colleague, Michael Levin, read the entire manuscript, offered invaluable comments, and shored me up with big doses of humour when this project threatened to overwhelm me. To him, I owe special thanks.

In addition, the following friends who provided cups of tea, collected children abandoned in the playground, and lent me a room to work in when my own house became more than usually noisy and chaotic, deserve thanks. These include Samuel Duval, Jancis Long, Jovencia Peralta, Maureen Shields, Annie Walker, and James Wood.

Leave of absence from my teaching duties, which was made available by Goldsmiths' College, and in particular, sponsored by Robert Pinker, Alan Little, Pat Thane, and John Stone, enabled me to enjoy periods of uninterrupted research. Iris Swain, Caren Catling, as well as Sacha Shaw, Pauline Ryall, and other members of the library staff at Goldsmiths', each contributed to this project in their special way. To all of the above, I owe my thanks.

John Rex and Chris Rojek, editorial adviser and editor at Routledge respectively, also deserve thanks for their initial help and later endurance. Thanks are also due to Paddi Taylor who typed this manuscript at unsociable hours.

Barbara Ballis Lal
London, February 1989

INTRODUCTION

Robert E. Park oriented thinking about race and ethnicity along modern lines. He did this by insisting that social research rather than speculation or populist wisdom inform social attitudes and public policy towards racial and ethnic minorities. He used research findings to subvert widespread denigrating stereotypes of minorities. Along with a handful of his contemporaries, he successfully challenged the pervasive racialist assumptions characteristic of the first half of the twentieth century.

In this book I present a general, critical overview of Park and the Chicago school of American sociology. I concentrate on the contribution that Park and those working within the Chicago school tradition have made to the area of urban race and ethnicity. I argue that the original perspective and the special style of social research developed by Park, along with W. I. Thomas and their students, are of equal importance in ensuring him a place among those social scientists whose ideas remain crucial to contemporary scholarship and current political and policy oriented debate. To conclude, I suggest how current thinking among sociologists, anthropologists, social historians, and social geographers might usefully be amalgamated with the ongoing tradition originating with Park at Chicago.

Along with W. I. Thomas, his friend and colleague at the University of Chicago, Park upheld the views of the anthropologist Franz Boas. He maintained that there was no indissoluble link between race and culture. Rather, he argued, culture is learned and transmitted through communication. Culture, he went on to note, is itself an adaptation to a physical environment and a historical setting. Park justified the inclusion of the study of ethnic

1

and racial minorities and their cultures as a distinct area of social investigation within sociology and as part of a university curriculum.

Park's interest in culture and communication contributed to the development of the perspective and method of the 'Chicago School' in the 1920s. Under Park's guidance, urban ethnography, the study of social behaviour in its 'natural setting', became the fulcrum of research at Chicago. Park encouraged his students to build upon the original study by Thomas and Florian Znaniecki, *The Polish Peasant in Europe and America* (1918-20), and to document the experience of immigrants, black migrants from the rural South, hobos, taxi-hall dancers, real-estate agents, juvenile delinquents, and other urbanites. Under his direction, students produced closely observed monographs which record how people lived in cities during the first half of the twentieth century. These monographs continue to be used by sociologists and social historians interested in reconstructing this earlier urban experience.

Sociologists who studied at Chicago during Park's tenure there include Herbert Blumer, Everett and Helen Hughes, E. Franklin Frazier, Charles Johnson, Edgar Thompson, Winifred Raushenbush, Louis Wirth, Jessie Steiner, Nels Anderson, Frederic Thrasher, Harvey Zorbaugh, Pauline Young, Horace Cayton, St Clair Drake, and Clifford Shaw. Erving Goffman, Howard Becker, Louis Killian, Ralph Turner, Joseph Gusfield, Tamotsu Shibutani, Arnold Rose, Anselm Strauss, Gregory Stone, Harvey Farberman, and Gerald Suttles are among the later sociologists contributing to this tradition.

Park's durability has been facilitated by the remarkably fruitful and prescient nature of his perspective on race and ethnicity. He was among the first of the Progressives to recognize the prophylactic qualities of all ethnic group cultures. Settlement house workers had commented upon the beneficial effects that foreign cultures seemed to have in aiding immigrants to adjust to the strains of urban life in America. With the exception of Jane Addams, the positive effects of a parallel development among black southern migrants to northern cities seemed to have escaped their consideration. Park, on the other hand, thought that the generic features of minority cultures, regardless of content, were of value – whether for immigrants or for black Americans.

2

Parochial minority cultures, he argued, fill universal human needs. Needs such as those for recognition, self-esteem, and solidarity with others could be met within the minority community. Local institutions such as the church and the foreign-language and black press provided both psychological support and practical information for immigrants and blacks making their way among xenophobic, colour-conscious, white, native-born Americans. Park's discovery, along with Thomas, of the 'ethnicity paradox' suggested that the development of separate social institutions and a distinct cultural identity among minority groups, rather than inhibiting greater participation in mainstream American life, facilitated such participation – especially in the face of opposition to greater participation by others.[1]

Park's observations predate current preoccupation with the question of how ethnic cultures, including Afro-American culture, support or depress the collective social mobility of the group as a whole, as this is measured by their share of resources such as income, education, health, and living accommodation (Glazer and Moynihan 1963; 1975; Light 1972; 1984; Lieberson 1980; Sowell 1981; Glazer 1975; 1983; 1988). He also asked whether effective political organization for minority groups, and in particular for Afro-Americans, required a prior commitment to 'cultural nationalism' (Carmichael and Hamilton 1967; Cruse 1967; Blauner 1972).

Park's interest in the value of maintaining separate ethnic and racial identities was voiced during the first decades of the twentieth century – a time when many intellectuals assumed that Americanization and 'Anglo-conformity' were the desirable end of acculturation and assimilation (Gossett 1963; Gordon 1964; Stocking 1968; Higham (1955) 1988). He, along with settlement house workers and social workers, addressed the question of whether American blacks were similar to immigrant groups in a pluralist society or whether they were 'a people apart' (Diner 1970: 393).

Park infused concepts such as 'social assimilation' and 'marginality' with a merited complexity and ambiguity (Park (1913b) 1950: 204-20; 1935a: 281-3; Higham 1984: 198-232). His discussion of these and related concepts reminds sociologists now, as in his own day, that they may not assume that a shared heritage, religion, skin colour, or historical memories of subordination and dominance become increasingly less important than social class in influencing collective action. Rather, Park believed that affective and sentimental cultural bonds, which may or may not be useful in furthering material interests, are persistent rather than fleeting, and that their importance varies with respect to the specific situation in which encounters occur.

In addition, Park, both in his work at the University of Chicago and in his roles as unofficial adviser to the Chicago Commission on Race Relations and as the first president of the Chicago Urban League (1916-18), initiated extensive programmes of empirical research using field-work and the analysis of 'human documents', as well as more conventional sources of data, to investigate the actual living conditions and the world-view of immigrants and Afro-Americans.

Why then, given his considerable achievements, has Park's work and that of his students fallen into disrepute?

Initially, in the 1940s and the 1950s, American sociologists committed to structural functional perspectives, challenged the analytical value of an ethnographic tradition which failed to consider the relations between social institutions and a notional social system (Parsons 1951; Merton 1957; Shils 1970). Later, in the 1970s, sociologists sympathetic to an increasingly influential Marxist-humanist critique of 'mainstream' sociology were inclined to question the adequacy of the Chicago school's approach on the grounds that it failed to locate social phenomena within the specific historical form of capitalism which determined the basic features of urban industrial life (Reynolds and Reynolds 1970; Colfax and Roach 1971; Reynolds and Henslin 1974; Schwendinger and Schwendinger 1974; Castells 1977; Pickvance 1976).

These broad attacks on the general perspective and method of Park and the Chicago school were complemented by criticisms of their contributions to specific areas of sociology, most notably, race and ethnic relations. The novelist and social critic Ralph Ellison characterized both the Chicago sociologists and the philanthropists who financed their research as hypocritical liberals more interested in devising methods of social control in the urban environment than in the pursuit of social justice (Ellison (1944) 1972: 303-17).

Sociologists routinely depicted Park as a naive liberal whose muddled essays on race and ethnicity contributed to a tradition that depicts black Americans as unlikely candidates for full participation in American life. Park, it is thought, supported the belief that Afro-Americans, unlike white immigrants (who also settled in cities before and during the first decades of this century), were unable to exploit their shared minority group status in order to build separate social institutions and to maintain both a supportive parochial culture and a positive collective identity. His unfortunate designation of Afro-Americans as 'the lady among the races' is repeatedly cited as evidence of his racialist conviction that blacks are the purveyors of an inferior cultural heritage which originated in slavery and which is ill-suited to the demands of a competitive urban civilization (Ellison (1944) 1972; Ladner 1973; Lyman 1973). Others attempted to reveal the hidden 'racist' agenda in Park's work and that of his students (Davidson 1973; Schwendinger and Schwendinger 1974).

The concept of a 'race relations cycle', in which the processes of 'competition', 'conflict', and 'accommodation' inevitably led to 'assimilation' between groups, became the focus for the discussion of what was wrong with Park's analysis of race and ethnic relations (Myrdal (1944) 1962: 1025-64; Cox (1948) 1970; Lyman 1973: 17-70; Bowker and Carrier 1976; Stone 1985: 24-5, 56; Persons 1987). Yet the race relations cycle is actually of minor significance when compared with Park's ideas about the social-psychological dimensions of race relations, race as an aspect of social stratification, the role of the media in influencing race relations, the functions of minority group cultures, and the character of ethnic boundaries in the urban environment (Lipset 1950; Matthews 1977). Park never intended his model of a race relations cycle to justify substituting speculation about race and ethnic relations in general for the detailed empirical study of specific cases.

Similarly, Park's supposed belief that blacks were just like another ethnic group has been cited as evidence of the analytical inadequacy of Park's approach to race and ethnic relations (Philpott 1978). Yet a careful reading of his books and essays suggests that he appreciated the importance of colour and the historical experience of slavery in differentiating the life chances of black Americans from those of newly arrived white Europeans. Park was aware that 'the chief obstacle to the assimilation of the Negro and the Oriental are not mental but physical traits' (Park (1913b) 1950: 208). Unlike white immigrants, the black American

5

'has had his separateness thrust upon him, because of his exclusion and forcible isolation from white society' (ibid.: 218).

Considering this hostile analysis as a whole, it seems clear that much of it stems from a mistaken view of Park's work and intentions. More specifically, much of this criticism is based upon a familiarity with only limited aspects of his writings. In addition, Park's political liberalism and the uses to which some of his ideas have been put by political conservatives have, quite wrongly, inhibited a fair appraisal of both the man and his ideas (Ovington (1947) 1970; Waskow 1967; Davidson 1973).

Recently, there has been a revival of interest in Park and the Chicago school, along with a renewed appreciation of their scholarship (Matthews 1977; Rock 1979; Diner 1980; Plummer 1983; Bulmer 1984; Kurtz 1984; Wacker 1985; Wiley 1986; Persons 1987; Smith 1988). This is a result of three factors. First, the rediscovery of 'subjectivist sociologies' as alternatives to 'sociological holism'. Holism was the major mode of sociological analysis that superseded the work of Park and the Chicago school during the late 1930s. Sociological work within this perspective concerns itself with the general features of whole societies, including conditions conducive to their stability and change. There are differences between varieties of sociological holism. The social systems model set out by the American sociologist Talcott Parsons at Harvard University (Parsons 1951) departs from the functionalist 'theories of the middle-range' constructed by his counterpart at Columbia University, Robert Merton (Merton 1957). Both of these schools are fundamentally different from Marxist and neo-Marxist models which represent yet a third type of sociological holism. However, what all of these varieties of holism share is a preference for sociological analysis which is based on social entities, such as social structures and social systems.

By the 1970s, the suspicion that social systems theories were deficient in generating knowledge about the way in which the social world works was becoming widespread (Gouldner 1971; Stone and Farberman 1970; Wiley 1979). Critics cited unduly deterministic models of social life in which an 'oversocialized man' was magically induced to conform to the needs of a notional social system at the expense of voluntarism and interpretative procedures in influencing social action (Wrong 1961; Blumer 1969). An over-emphasis upon social stability and a corresponding inability

6

to deal with social change and the reification of concepts such as class and social structure, rather than a concern with meaning, were alleged to contribute to deficient sociological work. Thus, for example, in an article citing the 'foibles of functional- ism', the American sociologist Marvin Scott complained that 'In the functional portrayal of man, the human comedy has become a comedy of insects' (Scott 1970: 28).

'Subjectivist' sociologies argue that the actor's point of view, together with the meanings that emerge from the situations he confronts with others, is central to sociological theory and method. The foundation of the social world is the culturally transmitted imagery that members of a group take into account in their everyday lives. Culture and social action have both a historical referent and an ecological dimension (Berger and Luckmann 1966; Berger and Berger 1976; Lal 1982).

The increasing salience of subjectivist perspectives initiated examination, both friendly and critical, of sociology at Chicago during the 1920s and 1930s. It also intensified interest in the ongoing work within the Chicago tradition after this time. In particular, Herbert Blumer and Everett Hughes found greater receptivity to their unsparing criticism of social systems theories, 'variable analysis', and the reliance upon quantitative methods in sociology. Blumer's cogent interpretation of the 'social behaviour-ism' of the Chicago philosopher George Herbert Mead, which is now known as 'symbolic interactionism', sought to reinstate ethnography and the investigation of social action from the actor's point of view as pre-eminent in sociology (Blumer 1969). Concurrently, Hughes demonstrated the value of the perspective and method developed at Chicago through his participation in empirical investigations of race relations, the professions, work, and higher education (Hughes 1971). Their students, Erving Goffman, Howard Becker, Louis Killian, Arnold Rose, Ralph Turner, and Tamotsu Shibutani made further theoretical contri-butions to the study of race and ethnic relations, deviance, col-lective behaviour, bureaucracies, and the mass media which were supported by ethnographic investigations.

In addition to sociologists within the Chicago school tradition, there were other groups of sociologists committed to subjectivist approaches who urged reconsideration of Park's work and that of his students. In particular, ethnomethodologists, although their work departs from that of the Chicago school in significant ways, have been instrumental in reviewing the basic premises and advantages of social psychological perspectives in sociology and in field-work as well as other ethnographic methods (Cicourel 1964; Garfinkel 1967; Douglas 1971; Filmer *et al.* 1972; Lal 1982).

A second factor contributing to renewed interest in Park and the Chicago school is the work of European sociologists and in particular social geographers. Ceri Peach, Vaughan Robinson, Susan Smith, and Hans van Amersfoort, among social geographers, have developed Park's concept of social interaction to explain patterns of minority concentration and dispersion in cities (Peach 1975; Jackson and Smith 1981; Amersfoort 1982; Peach *et al.* 1981). Among English sociologists, John Rex and Robert Moore used the work of the Chicago sociologists to understand racial conflict between minority groups in Birmingham in the 1960s (Rex and Moore 1967). More recently, Paul Rock, Kenneth Plummer, and Martin Bulmer have critically evaluated the use of human documents, field-work procedures, and the range of quantitative methods originating at Chicago (Rock 1979; Plummer 1983; Bulmer 1984). Criminologists outside the Chicago school tradition have also used concepts and methods associated with Park and his students (Phillipson 1971).

The increasing salience of practical problems having to do with race and ethnic relations, particularly in the 'inner city', is the third factor which has contributed to a resurgence of interest in Park and the Chicago school. In the United States and increasingly in Great Britain and the rest of western Europe, debate and investigation into urban race and ethnicity have run parallel to practical efforts to devise solutions to urgent problems such as minority underemployment, underachievement in schools, racial conflict, discrimination, and the erosion of confidence in the police (National Advisory Commission on Civil Disorders 1968; Scarman 1981; Glazer and Young 1983). These same problems had been discussed by Park and other sociologists within the Chicago school. Documents such as *The Negro in Chicago* (Chicago Commission on Race Relations (1922) 1968) and monographs such as *Black Metropolis* (Drake and Cayton (1945) 1962) and *The Negro Family in the United States* (Frazier (1939) 1966) are frequently acknowledged to shed light upon the past which might be useful in the present.

Chapter One, 'Social context and individual biography', consists of two parts. Part One argues that Park and his work rest comfortably within the linked traditions of political progressivism and philosophical pragmatism. 'The romance of culture in an urban civilization' provides thematic coherence to his sociology.

Park used the concept of culture to explore the paradoxes of life in cities. He, like many of his contemporaries, was ambivalent about the prospects for human happiness and social stability in the unfolding urban civilization. People in cities, he noted, were liberated from the conventions and prejudices of the isolated, rural settlements of the past. Geographical mobility and urbanization increased opportunities for individualism and for collective, social mobility. However, Park worried about the effects that the absence of constraining, affective social bonds would have for the socially emancipated individual. What, he wondered, were to be counted as effective mechanisms of self-control and social control in the urban environment?

Part Two of the first chapter consists of a brief summary of Park's life with special attention to the major events influencing his development as a sociologist and his career while at the University of Chicago.

Chapter Two, 'Culture, communication, and social control', clarifies what Park meant by these concepts and how they gave direction to his overall sociological perspective. It includes a discussion of Park's and Burgess's typology of social interaction and of Park's formulation of a sociology of 'collective behaviour'.

Chapter Three, 'Park's approach to race and ethnic relations', examines how his general perspective on culture, communication, and social control leads him to raise particular questions and to devise a distinctive outlook on race and ethnic relations. A critical examination of the most significant features of his approach concludes the chapter.

Chapter Four, 'The emergence of an ethnographic tradition', shows how the concepts of culture, communication, and social control lend themselves to the methods of urban ethnography. The development of field-work and the analysis of 'human documents' is considered in the context of the research into race and ethnic relations undertaken at Chicago. The usefulness of the procedures advocated by Park and Thomas is then assessed.

Chapter Five, 'Immigrants and the "ethnicity paradox"',

examines Park's and Thomas's studies of the attitudes and exper-
ience of immigrants and their adjustment to urban life in America.
It demonstrates how the monographs *Old World Traits Transplanted*
(Park and Miller (1921) 1969), *The Immigrant Press and Its Control*
(Park (1922) 1970), and Park's essays on immigrants utilize the
qualitative methods first advocated by Thomas in *Source Book for
Social Origins* (Thomas 1909), then successfully used in *The Polish
Peasant in Europe and America* (Thomas and Znaniecki 1918-20),
and later developed by Park and graduate students at Chicago.

The chapter concludes with a discussion of the remedies that
Park believed were available to overcome those features of urban
society which threatened both individual well-being and the social
cohesion of democratic polities.

Chapter Six, '"Bright lights, impending shadows": Afro-
American migration to northern cities', consists of two parts. The
first is based upon Park's comparison of race relations in the
periods before and after the Civil War (1861-65) in the American
South and contrasting of both with race relations in the North.
The second part deals with Park's views about the problems and
prospects of Afro-Americans in the northern cities to which they
migrated in large numbers after the turn of the century. It includes
a brief discussion of how Park's students have, through their own
research, evaluated and altered his approach and his insights into
urban race and ethnicity.

Chapter Seven, 'Getting it together: a scheme of interpretation', argues that during the last ten years fundamental changes
have occurred in the ways in which urban race and ethnicity have
been studied by social geographers, anthropologists, social
historians, and sociologists. These changes, while not directly due
to the influence of the Chicago school, have resulted in outlooks
that are in many ways similar to that developed by Park and sociologists working within this tradition. In this concluding chapter,
these new features of social research into race and ethnic relations
are integrated with the approach originating with Park and
developed by scholars working within the orbit of the Chicago
school.

Chapter One

SOCIAL CONTEXT AND INDIVIDUAL BIOGRAPHY

THE ROMANCE OF CULTURE IN AN URBAN CIVILIZATION

Park was a spokesman for a view and a tradition that may be identified as 'the romance of culture in an urban civilization'.[1] Civilization, he thought, tends to subvert and secularize cultures. 'Civilisation', Park observed, 'breaks down solidarity and results from the loss of culture. The growth of cities, the use of money, and the rationalisation of life activities are characteristic of the displacement of culture by civilisation.' Culture refers to a 'society' that has a 'moral order' while civilization 'is fundamentally a territorial affair' which comes about through trade and commerce. In this respect, while culture makes it possible for members of a group to act collectively on the basis of mutual understanding and a sense of solidarity, civilization consists of 'an aggregate of people who use the same artifacts and who have no solidarity at all' (Park 1950b: 15-23).

The instrumentalism of the market, Park believed, made urban institutions impervious to the requirements of the individual. These requirements include the need for self-identity, social recognition, self-esteem, social solidarity, and a degree of certainty about the nature of the 'objective' world. He thought that freedom for the individual revolved around shaping one's own destiny *within* the confines of the group and a regard for its general welfare rather than in the pursuit of unbridled self-interest.

In this regard, Park noted that civilization, which is governed by secular and universalistic principles of social organization, lacks the moral authority to regulate behaviour inherent in tradition and culture. Civilization releases individuals from traditional mechanisms of social control.

The American sociologist Edward Shils has pointed out that there are many different sources of social integration in modern, urban society, which are of greater or lesser importance in different situations. Personal and primordial attachments exist alongside interests and civic duty which integrate people into groups and knit groups together (or sunder them) (Shils 1957). However, Park's essays on race and ethnicity suggest that cultural and sentimental groups are the source of what is basic to individual identity and self-esteem.

Park's outlook lay within the orbit of the German debate about '*gemeinschaft*' and '*gesellschaft*' societies and the Durkheimian concern with the consequences of 'moral density' and the increasing division of labour in society. To be sure, he, like his former teacher at Frederich-Wilhelm University in Berlin, the German sociologist Georg Simmel, appreciated those aspects of urban civilization that were conducive to the flowering of individual talents and group genius. However, as was the case with Simmel, he also feared the toll that city life exacted from both the individual and the society. These costs seemed especially great when compared to the benefits of real or mythical small towns which were thought by Park, as well as by many of his contemporaries, to be repositories of an egalitarian culture common to all and encouraging full participation in civic institutions (Hofstadter 1955: 23-93; Quandt 1970: 3-20).

For example, in the city, freedom to 'pass quickly and easily from one moral milieu to another ... of living at the same time in several different contiguous, but otherwise totally separated worlds' had as its complement superficial, segmental role relationships. The 'obverse of this freedom' of movement was loneliness and distress (Park (1934c) 1955: 298).

Park saw culture as an antidote to those features of urban civilization that undermined the will and the capacity of members of increasingly large, anonymous, and heterogeneous social units to pursue common objectives. What was needed in cities, he thought, was a shared social heritage to integrate individuals into groups and to bind groups to each other. Foremost in importance within such a heritage was a world-view capable of imposing coherence upon diverse styles of life and imparting consistency to competing ideas and purposes.

12

Civilization sweeps away the shared heritage and taken-for-granted style of life characteristic of parochial groups. However, Park also nurtured a vision of cultural change and renewal within the civilizing process itself in which there is always the possibility of the emergence of new social groups creating for themselves a shared, coherent vision of the world and new conventions. Such groups are a source of cohesion for their members and boundary-maintaining entities with respect to larger, encompassing social units.

Park subscribed to a romantic belief in the 'redemptive nature of ethnic cultures' – a concept used by the historian Fred Matthews to describe the writings of Park's contemporaries Horace Kallen and Louis Adamic (Matthews 1984). His positive appraisal of immigrant heritages and of an emergent, urban 'black culture', discussed in Chapters Five and Six, remains an influential point of view in recent race and ethnic relations literature. However, 'the relative repudiation of the larger American society' (Matthews 1984: 73) through the celebration of ethnic cultures, displayed in the work of social critics as diverse in their political allegiances as Michael Novak and Harold Cruse, is not characteristic of Park's writing (Novak 1971; Cruse 1967; 1987). Instead, Park suggested that integration into parochial institutiions and pride in ethnic identity were of value, precisely because these increased life chances and facilitated participation in mainstream institutions and assimilation to a dominant American way of life.

A related reason for the modernity of the theme of the romance of culture in an urban civilization, has to do with current comment upon the role of the intellectual in discovering and honouring social bonds between people of the same origin and, in so doing, successfully heightening self-consciousness among members of different groups. Anthony Smith and Stephan Steinberg, for example, although writing from very different perspectives, emphasize the crucial role that intellectuals have had in defining a shared interest among people who themselves might feel less, rather than more, united on the basis of origin as opposed to factors such as social class (Smith 1981; Steinberg 1982). 'Ethnicity by consent' and 'compulsory ethnicity', discussed in Chapter Five, are two outcomes of this trend.

Progressive politics, pragmatic philosophy

1860 marked the beginning of rapid urbanization throughout the United States. Between 1860 and 1910, while the rural population doubled, the urban population increased sevenfold. Population increase tended to be greatest in the larger cities – Chicago more than doubled its population between 1880 and 1890.

Between 1865 and the First World War, in the absence of immigration restrictions, foreigners from southern and eastern Europe came to work in American industry, often doing the hardest and worst paying jobs. In numerous large cities in the North, White, Anglo-Saxon, Protestant Americans, many of them raised in small towns or rural homesteads, found themselves outnumbered by immigrants whose alien religions, foreign languages, and strange traditions made them a worrying presence. Some Americans concluded that the urban boss and the political machine, fostering patronage, corruption involving elected officials, the police, and purveyors of commercial vice, and malfeasance between government and business, were evidence of the infestation of cities by immigrants. Slums became the visible expression of the 'get-rich quick' mentality of a rising stratum of new men of economic and political power and the hapless foreigners that they exploited. Americans born in America began to wonder 'whether democracy, whose values descended from earlier and less complicated times in America, could survive the twentieth century' (Mann 1975:2).

Park, and many other intellectuals and reformers oscillated between a pessimistic appraisal of threatening social conditions and an optimistic belief in their ability to change these through the application by 'professionals' of scientific knowledge and through education for the masses. Their discovery of urban poverty and deprivation, business monopolies, exploited immigrants, and political corruption stimulated both civic action and social research (Lubove 1962; Carey 1975; Diner 1980).

Park combined the personal attributes associated with the Progressives. He was middle class, well educated, and a member of the professions. He shared the outlook that the American historian Richard Hofstadter identifies as 'the Progressive mind' which, the latter claims, was 'preeminently a Protestant mind . . . under which personal responsibility for the problems – and the morals –

14

of others could in fact often be assumed' (Hofstadter 1955: 204-5).[2]

While intrigued by the variety of political and ethical codes displayed by different social groups throughout the world, Park was wedded to a particular version of 'rightness' and morality in which order, efficient government by law, and democracy prevailed.

Park was also liberal. He believed that governments (as well as social reformers and sociologists) should concern themselves with setting out those conditions that enable individuals to make their own way *as they wish*. Thus, for example, Park thought that racial discrimination was objectionable because it was contrary to a democratic way of life in which each individual, regardless of colour, origin, or social class, is able to compete for wealth, jobs, and living space, on the basis of his own choice, effort, and merit. He agreed with liberal sentiment that business monopolies and political machines which inhibited individual choice and enterprise, and which interfered with a natural market in talent and effort, were antisocial and undesirable.

On the other hand, Park, again like many of his contemporaries, saw that the bountiful productivity unleashed by science and its application to technology had not rewarded members of the community equally; extremes of wealth and poverty, knowledge and ignorance, morality and vice were everywhere to be seen. Clergymen, journalists, social workers, and enlightened politicians, trade-unionists, and businessmen aimed to attend to those who were unable to make their own way and who were condemned to poverty, ill-health, and depravity. For this reason, the Progressives, unlike the 'Mugwumps' before them, acknowledged the limits of both *laissez-faire* economics and élite government, and eased the way for the coming of a welfare state supported by the (hopefully better-educated) masses (Hofstadter 1955).

Park saw no contradiction between the application of scientific knowledge to social and political life by élite groups and democratic government supported by the more numerous masses. Rather, he believed that the purpose of schools, settlement houses, and the media was to educate citizens so that they were able to use knowledge in order to reform themselves and improve their environment. Professionals, including social scientists, were needed to investigate social conditions and to recommend social

15

policies (Hofstadter 1955; Furner 1975; Diner 1980). However self-interested the support for reform among professionals, at least for some, like Park, enthusiasm for social betterment on the basis of specialist knowledge existed in coalition (albeit uneasily) with a belief in democratic government.

Pragmatism, also referred to as 'the Chicago school of philosophy', combined with the Progressive political mood and reinforced the drive to find scientific solutions to the social problems brought about by industrialization, urbanization, and immigration. In America pragmatism was the taken-for-granted outlook of the 'educated man' between the late nineteenth century and the middle of the twentieth century.

Pragmatism held out the hope of democratic 'reconstruction' of society. It contended that scientific 'truth' is always arrived at through activity in the world and that knowledge is a relationship between an idea and the activity of *any* group of knowledge – seeking human beings 'interacting contingently with each other and the larger natural world' (Hollinger 1980: 97). Pragmatism was, therefore, anti-élitist. It considered that knowledge of the social world, which was essential to intelligent self-government in a democracy, was accessible to the layman as an actor analogous to the scientist. Park's quip that sociology is 'just a little nicer and neater in its formulation than common sense' is in keeping with this view.

Pragmatism bridged the epistemological gap between mind and matter. The pragmatic philosophers John Dewey, George Herbert Mead, Edward Scribner Ames, James Angell, James Hayden Tufts, and Addison Webster Moore, both in their writing and in their public lives, debunked the distinction between the scholar and the man of action, between thinkers and doers (Rucker 1969). The trend towards professionalization of the social sciences reinforced a policy of 'enlightened interventionism'.

In this spirit, William Rainey Harper, the founding President of the University of Chicago, and his successors believed that great urban universities had a responsibility to produce scientific knowledge which could then be used in the public interest. Philanthropists who funded social research held the same view (Carey 1975; Diner 1980; Bulmer 1984).

Not surprisingly, sociologists at the University of Chicago anticipated that their research findings would be relevant to the

16

reform-minded public as well as to social scientists. This expectation was complemented by their participation in public service. Park himself served as the first president of the Chicago Urban League (1916-18) (Strickland 1966) and as president of the National Community Center (1922-24) (Matthews 1977: 177-8). He also influenced the research design and the report of the Illinois Commission on Race Relations' investigation of the 1919 race riots in Chicago (Chicago Commission on Race Relations (1922) 1968).

Park's colleagues engaged in similar public-spirited activities. The sociologist Louis Wirth presided over the University of Chicago 'Roundtable' radio broadcasts. The sociologist Ernest Burgess sought funding for the Institute for Juvenile Research whose publications by Clifford Shaw and Henry McKay significantly influenced juvenile justice policies (Carey 1975; Bulmer 1984).

Academics in other departments at the University of Chicago also participated in the city's civic life. The philosopher and social psychologist George Herbert Mead was president of the City Club, an organization whose purpose was to collect information, debate issues, and influence urban social policy. The political scientist Charles Merriam was elected to the Chicago city council and two years later was almost successful in his candidacy for mayor of Chicago (Diner 1980: 34-69).

Despite the range of his own civic activities and his commitment to a version of sociology in which ordinary human beings are depicted as being the agents of social change, Park insisted upon distancing sociologists from reformers. However, as the historian of sociology Anthony Oberschall points out, 'without the active support of various reform groups and favourable progressive public opinion, it is very doubtful that sociology as an autonomous academic discipline would have been established' (Oberschall 1972: 204).

Park's sociology took root and flourished in this scholarly and activist environment at the University of Chicago during the 1920s and 1930s. Additional factors that contributed to his view of sociology were his education and his career before beginning to teach at the University of Chicago in 1913 when he was almost fifty years old.[3] Once he was at the University of Chicago, the type of sociological thinking advocated by Albion Small, chairman of the

17

department of sociology/anthropology since its beginning in 1892, and the work of his colleague and collaborator W. I. Thomas were decisive in influencing the course he himself set for the development of sociology.

BIOGRAPHY

Park was born in 1864 in Harveyville, Luzerne County, Pennsylvania. His family moved to Red Wing, Minnesota, when his father, Hiram Asa Park, returned from serving in the Union Army. Park described Red Wing as a typical small town in which he had an ordinary childhood (quoted in Baker 1973).

In 1882, after graduating from high school, Park defied his father's wish that he enter the family grocery business and 'ran away' to study, first at the University of Minnesota and a year later at the University of Michigan. At Michigan, Park specialized in philosophy and German. He studied with John Dewey, whose view of the process of communication was to be of continuous interest to him throughout his life. He also met the journalist and writer Franklin Ford. Park acknowledged the influence of both Dewey and Ford in stimulating him to investigate the role of the newspaper in moulding public opinion in cities.

Between 1891 and 1898, Park worked as a reporter and as an editor on newspapers in Minneapolis, Detroit, New York, and Chicago. In an autobiographical note, Park suggested that his work as a reporter 'hunting down gambling houses and opium dens' was 'the beginning of my interest in sociology, although at that time I did not know the word' (quoted in Baker 1973: 254). In this same vein, the historian Fred Matthews points out that the newspaper reporter was an 'institutionalised voyeur', whose profession was analogous to 'the role of gossip filled by many citizens in the smaller community'. He goes on to reflect that, 'The city beat reporter from the first fulfilled the role of informal and intuitive sociologist, acting as eyes, ears, and moral censor for the audience removed by size and distance from the direct exercise of these traditional communal roles' (Matthews 1977: 10).

Towards the end of his life, Park reflected that his 'earliest conception of a sociologist' was as 'a kind of super-reporter', writing about what Ford called the 'Big News'. By the 'Big News' Ford meant 'the long-time trends which recorded what is actually going on rather than what, on the surface of things, merely seems to be going on' (Park 1950a: viii-ix).

Park's resolution to treat news and public opinion as an 'intellectual problem' led to his decision to stop working as a journalist and to pursue graduate studies at Harvard University where he studied with William James, Josiah Royce, George Santayana, and James Mark Baldwin, all of whom were influential contributors to the development of pragmatism, and with the psychologist Hugo Muensterberg. He obtained an MA in philosophy from Harvard.

Park then went on to study social psychology at Frederich-Wilhelm University in Berlin, Germany. Here he took courses with the sociologist Georg Simmel and with the philosopher Friedrich Paulson. While in Berlin Park read and was very much excited by a book on method, *Gesellschaft und das Einzelwesen (Society and the Individual Person)*, written by Thomas Kistiakowski, a student of the German folk psychologist Wilhelm Windelband. In order to study with Windelband he went first to Strasbourg and later, in 1902, to Heidelberg. At Strasbourg and Heidelberg universities, Park took courses in philosophy, geography, and political economy. Under Windelband's supervision he completed his doctoral dissertation, 'Crowd and public: a methodological and sociological inquiry'. His thesis was submitted to the philosophical faculty of Heidelberg in 1903 and published in Bern, Switzerland, in German, in 1904 (Raushenbush 1979: 34).

In the summer of 1903, Park returned to Harvard and became a teaching assistant in the department of philosophy. In 1904, he took on the additional job of publicity agent, and later of first secretary, to the Boston office of the Congo Reform Association. The purpose of this organization was to publicize the tyrannous exploitation of the African Congo by King Leopold of Belgium. In a letter to E. R. Morel, who worked for the Congo Reform Association in England, Park wrote that fighting against the inequity of 'slave labour in tropical Africa' was 'a great privilege'. He believed, he said, that his political work on behalf of the Association 'is the real business of human life' (quoted in Raushenbush 1979: 37).

Park's outrage at the 'forced production, extortion and organised system of plunder' in the Congo was conveyed in three articles published in *Everybody's Magazine* between November 1906 and

19

January 1907 (Park 1906a; 1906b; 1907). Here he reflected that the recent history of the Congo was an example of what happened 'whenever a sophisticated people invades the territories of a more primitive people in order to exploit their lands and, incidentally, to uplift and civilise them'. Park claimed that his work for the Congo Reform Association enabled him to know 'enough about civilisation' to realize that 'progress, as James once remarked, is a terrible thing. It is so destructive and wasteful' (Park 1950a: vii).

In his later sociological essays, Park viewed with concern the incorporation of previously isolated communities, in Africa or elsewhere, into the world economy in the absence of social and cultural integration. He urged that education be used to create a new cosmopolitanism in keeping with the economic interdependence between peoples. 'In the new and more inclusive society which is emerging', wrote Park, 'we shall be living ... in a new intimacy with all the peoples of the world.' Education, particularly through art and literature, should be used to 'communicate not ideas but sentiments' so that 'one's sense of mutual understanding and moral solidarity is enhanced' (Park (1943b) 1950: 327-30).

Park's interest in industrial education in Africa led him to correspond with the Afro-American leader and educationalist Booker T. Washington. Washington founded and was principal of Tuskegee Normal and Industrial Institute in Tuskegee, Alabama. Tuskegee Institute aimed to provide black Americans, and particularly black farmers most of whom were tenant farmers, with a practical, vocational education to enable them to better their lives. It offered southern blacks a chance to become educated in a region which otherwise offered them no instruction comparable to that available to whites. Washington's work included efforts to make white Americans, especially those in the more liberal North, shoulder some of the responsibility for black uplift through their financial support for Tuskegee (Harlan 1972 and 1983: passim).

In 1905 Park visited Tuskegee and shortly thereafter moved South to begin work as a ghost writer and press agent for Washington. He continued to work there until 1914, when he took up a full-time teaching post at the University of Chicago (Matthews 1977: 61-84).

Park wrote several books and articles which Washington published under his own name. Among these were *The Story of the*

Negro (Washington 1909) and *My Larger Education* (Washington 1911). Park also published articles about Washington and Tuskegee Institute under Washington's name (Washington-Park Correspondence, Booker T. Washington Papers). In 1912, *The Man Farthest Down* was published with Park cited as Washington's collaborator (Washington 1912). *The Man Farthest Down* was a description of a trip that Washington and Park took to Europe in the summer of 1910. In it, the authors described the social conditions and the prospects of peasants and other members of 'the poorer classes'. They compared European conditions unfavourably to the life and prospects of black tenant farmers in Alabama.

During the years that Park worked at Tuskegee, he was able to 'get acquainted with the actual and intimate life of the Negro in the South'. He travelled all over and 'poked ... into every corner where there was anything that seemed instructive and interesting', supplementing his field work with readings in black history (Park, cited in Baker 1973: 258). He collected all the references to black history that he could find, especially in libraries in New York City and Cambridge, Massachusetts, in order to build up the Tuskegee Library. When he left Tuskegee, Park claimed that he had 'a good many notions about the Negro and about race problems' (ibid.: 259).

Park appreciated the simplicity, dignity, and accomplishments of the black rural tenant farmers that he met. Yet he passionately advocated education and communication as ways to break down the cultural isolation that kept black people relatively helpless in confrontations with their white neighbours. Tuskegee Institute, he believed, provided a way of integrating blacks into the world of agriculture and business. Park's later analyses of Afro-American migration and urban life reflected this earlier concern with the impoverishment brought about by cultural isolation and his faith in education, communication, and organization in overcoming racial disadvantage and discrimination.

Park acknowledged the influence that both Washington and his experience at Tuskegee had upon his views about race relations. The influence that Park had upon Washington and Washington's able secretary, the historian and journalist Emmett J. Scott, is less well documented. For example, Raushenbush writes that, in their travels through Europe, Park was instrumental in getting Washington to consider political protest among the relatively powerless as an effective means for pursuing economic goals (Raushenbush 1979: 53-6).

In 1912, two significant events occurred in Park's life. First, he gave notice to Washington that he intended to leave Tuskegee so he could spend more time with his wife, Clara Cahill Park, and their four children who had continued to live in Massachusetts during Park's tenure at Tuskegee.[4] In his letter of resignation to Washington, Park noted that he had been very happy at Tuskegee and that he had learned much from his experience there. With characteristic sincerity and fervour, he wrote, 'I feel and shall always feel that I belong, in a sort of way, to the Negro race and shall continue to share, through good and evil, all its joys and sorrows' (quoted in Raushenbush 1979: 63).

The second significant event was Park's introduction to W. I. Thomas. In April of 1912, Park organized an 'International Conference on the Negro' at Tuskegee which was intended to facilitate a world-wide exchange of ideas. The theme of the conference was 'The Education of Primitive Man'. Among those invited were Afro-Americans, Afro-Caribbeans, and Africans. Thomas, who was then a professor at the department of sociology/ anthropology at the University of Chicago, gave a speech on 'Education and Cultural Traits'. 'I found in Thomas,' noted Park, 'almost for the first time, a man who seemed to speak the same language as myself' (cited in Baker 1973: 259). It was Thomas who invited Park to teach at the University of Chicago.

Park's career at Chicago

What is significant about Park's career is the continuity between his prolonged education, his earlier vocations, and his later career as an academic. His sociological interest in the newspaper and collective behaviour benefited from his work as a newspaper reporter and editor. His work as secretary of the Congo Reform Association and his European travels sensitized him to the international character of race and ethnic relations and of the effects of migration, conquest, and economic interdependence upon previously isolated people. His awareness of race relations was nurtured by his activities at Tuskegee as press agent, ghost-writer, and roving ambassador. Moreover, in the course of these earlier vocations, Park adopted an ethnographic style of social research which he subsequently set out as the rules of sociological method. His perseverance as both a teacher and an administrator at the University of Chicago, however, contrasts sharply with the peripatetic character of his working life before this time.

Park's first course at Chicago was entitled 'The Negro in America'. It was designed to analyse contacts between whites and blacks in the past with a view towards understanding race relations in the present. Park's course was 'one of the first dealing exclusively with black Americans to be given in any predominantly white university in the United States and may, indeed, have been the first such course' (Raushenbush 1979: 77). Two years later, in 1916, he taught three additional courses on 'The Newspaper', 'Crowd and Public', and 'The Survey' (Bulmer 1984: 67-72). By 1921 Park had added to his course offerings 'Research in the Field of Social Psychology', 'Race and Nationality', and 'Field Studies'. His course on field studies, according to one of its participants, 'proved so popular that it was given every year throughout the 1920s, not by Park alone, but by a group of faculty members' (ibid.: 96).

In March of 1915, Park published his influential essay, 'The city: suggestions for the investigation of human behaviour in the urban environment' in the *American Journal of Sociology* (Park (1915) 1952: 13-51). Taken together, the topics that Park posed as being suitable for an investigation of the city constituted an outline for a comprehensive community study. On the other hand, any single topic could be used as the basis for a case-study of a specialized area of social life. For example, under the heading of 'party politics and publicity', Park enumerated a set of problems about political behaviour and institutions which were subsequently investigated by the political scientist Harold Gosnell in his study, *Negro Politicians* (Gosnell (1935) 1967: passim).[5]

Between 1916 and its publication in 1921, in collaboration with his colleague Ernest Burgess, Park wrote and collected material for their textbook *An Introduction to the Science of Sociology* ((1921) 1969). The book was organized around headings such as 'Sociology and the social sciences', 'Human nature', 'Social control', and 'Collective behaviour'. Each of these headings introduced a discussion by the authors followed by the relevant readings and a bibliography citing additional readings.

The work of American sociologists such as Park, Thomas, William Graham Sumner, Thorstein Veblen, and Charles Horton

Cooley, as well as of European sociologists, notably Georg Simmel, Emile Durkheim, and Herbert Spencer, was represented in the readings. In addition, the writings of philosophers John Dewey and James Mark Baldwin, the biologists Charles Darwin and Eugenious Warming, and the historians W. E. H. Lecky and A. V. Dicey were also included.

The pragmatic point of view developed by Park and Burgess in this text is captured in the preface in which the authors point out that they have aimed to put together material that will 'appeal to the experience of the student', each of whom is 'invited to take an active part in the interpretation of the text' and to 'supplement classroom discussion by their personal observation' so that 'their whole attitude becomes active rather than passive'.

In 1918, Park took some time off from his teaching in order to do research on the foreign language newspaper. His investigation was one of ten 'Americanisation Studies' funded by the Carnegie Corporation, intended to dispel unwarranted fears about the subversive effect of immigrants upon traditional American values and institutions. With the assistance of Winifred Raushenbush, then a graduate student at Chicago, this project resulted in the publication in 1922 of *The Immigrant Press and Its Control* (Park (1922) 1970).

About this same time, Park was asked to complete a second Carnegie project on immigrant heritages which was started and then abandoned by his friend and professor of sociology at Oberlin, Herbert A. Miller. Park hired Thomas, then living in New York City, to work on this project with him. It resulted in the publication of *Old World Traits Transplanted* in 1921 (Park and Miller (1921) 1969). Although Thomas wrote much of this book, he was not listed as one of its authors. This was because of his involvement in a scandal which resulted in his forced resignation from the University of Chicago in 1918 (Volkart (1951) 1981).

In 1919, with Park's help, Charles S. Johnson, one of Park's graduate students, was appointed as Director of Research for the Chicago Commission on Race Relations. The Commission's task was to investigate the race riot that had occurred that summer. The resultant report, *The Negro in Chicago* (1922), was comprehensive, innovative, and very much influenced by Park himself. It dealt with topics that Park considered important such as the role of newspapers in moulding public opinion, and the role of rumour in fomenting riots. It also used methods popularized by Park and Thomas, such as the analysis of newspapers and letters, to arrive at its conclusions (Chicago Commission on Race Relations (1922) 1968).

Between the autumn of 1923 and spring 1924, Park directed a survey of race relations on the Pacific Coast with particular emphasis upon tensions involving Japanese- and Chinese-Americans. As a result of the Japanese Exclusion Act in May 1924, this investigation was abruptly terminated. Two very interesting publications that resulted from this partially completed study were 'Our racial frontier on the Pacific' and 'Behind our masks' both of which were included in a special issue of the magazine *Survey Graphic* which was devoted to East-West issues (Park (1926a) 1950: 138-51; (1926b) 1950: 244-55; Raushenbush 1979: 107-18).

Park had a voracious appetite for travel. Beginning in 1925, he visited most countries in Asia and Africa. Throughout his travels he pursued his interest in the process of race conflict and cultural fusion, the marginal man, the personality traits of racial hybrids, and other aspects of race and ethnic relations. He predicted that 'race consciousness' would emerge on an international basis as a result of race and culture contacts in the modern world (Raushenbush 1979: 127-40).

In the summer of 1933, Park formally retired from the University of Chicago but continued to teach there in one capacity or another for several more years. In the autumn of 1936, at the suggestion of Charles Johnson, now head of the social science department at Fisk (and its future president), Park and his family moved to Nashville, Tennessee, so that he could begin teaching at Fisk University.

Park prompted and successfully promoted social research. He supported and edited the University of Chicago Sociological Series, which published monographs written by graduate students at Chicago. Among these monographs were Nels Anderson's *The Hobo* (1923) and Louis Wirth's *The Ghetto* (1928). He also helped establish the Local Community Research Committee which sponsored inter-disciplinary research projects in Chicago (Bulmer 1984: 129-50).

In 1925, Park served as President of the American Sociological Society (later called the American Sociological Association).

Park was an inspired sociologist precisely because his life

complemented the sociological concepts to which he was attached. He viewed sociology as a means whereby strangers could communicate their experience and the meanings they attached to their lives to each other. As such, sociology, like other forms of symbolic social interaction, was a matter of creating and sustaining a shared culture. Together with his colleagues and students, he used the city of Chicago as 'a social laboratory' in which to study conflict and personal and social disorganization, as well as to discover the conditions contributing to cohesion and order (Park (1929b) 1952: 72-87). He integrated descriptions of a fragmented, morally indifferent social world with an inspired, always successful search for sources of redress and regeneration. Nowhere is this rhythm of description and redress more evident than in his writing about race, ethnicity, and collective behaviour in cities.

Park enjoined sociologists to study the city as 'a spatial pattern' and as 'a moral order'. He noted the absurdity existing in twentieth-century American cities, such as Chicago, which combined increasing 'physical propinquity' with increasing 'social isolation' (Park (1926c) 1952: 165-77). He concluded that the 'social problem' of the concerned citizen was identical to the 'sociological problem': the answer to both was to create a new cultural consensus and to find new sources of social control, which would bring about 'a social order in the city equivalent to that which grew up naturally in the family, the clan and the tribe' (Park (1929b) 1952: 74).[6]

Chapter Two

CULTURE, COMMUNICATION, AND SOCIAL CONTROL

The concepts of culture, communication, and social control are crucial to Park's overall sociological perspective which in its turn influenced how he approached the investigation of race and ethnic relations. His ideas about culture and communication also led to the development of a style of social research based upon urban ethnography, the case study approach, and the analysis of human documents discussed in Chapter Four. For these reasons, it is essential to clarify what Park meant by culture, communication, and social control and to understand the theoretical significance that he attributed to these concepts.

Park thought that culture is the property that differentiates human 'society' from non-human forms of association. In his essay 'Sociology and the social sciences', Park wrote,

> The same social forces which are found organised in public opinion, in religious symbols, in social convention, in fashion, and in science ... are constantly recreating the old order, making new heroes, overthrowing old gods, creating new myths, and imposing new ideals. And this is the nature of the cultural process of which sociology is a description and an explanation.
>
> (Park (1920-21) 1955)

The essence of culture is the understanding made possible through the process of communication.[1] 'Culture', noted Park, 'includes all that is communicable [and] its fundamental components' consist of the 'forms and symbols' that embody the understanding shared members of a group (Park (1938) 1950: 39). Shared meanings are linked to a life-style and both generate a sense of common identity.

Park used the analytical distinction between the objective or external aspects of a culture and its subjective meaning made by the anthropologists Clark Wissler and W. H. R. Rivers. The objective aspects of a group's culture consist of 'its arts', 'its ceremonial', 'its tools', and all other observable forms through which its subjective meaning is displayed. The closely related subjective aspects of culture include 'the core of ideas and beliefs' based upon the group's 'memories', 'traditions', and 'relatively unorganised social experience'. The subjective elements of culture are expressed as ways of thinking as well as in ways of acting and in the group's artefacts (Park (1925a) 1950; (1938) 1950).

Given his focus upon culture, communication, and the subjective dimension of social action, it seems surprising that Park has often been treated as an exponent of human ecology. According to Park, human 'society', as opposed to plant and animal 'communities', exists on two levels: 'the biotic' and 'the cultural'. These levels can be presented analytically as 'a spatial pattern' and a 'cultural' or 'moral order' (Park (1926c) 1952).[2] Human ecology deals with the 'biotic' (e.g., biological and geographical) aspects of group life while sociology investigates 'culture' and the subjectively motivated activities of 'persons'. The 'cultural order' is imposed upon and modifies the 'ecological order' (Park (1938) 1950).

Human ecology charts the spatial distribution of groups, institutions, and activities as well as examining the distribution of a population in an occupational order. Spatial and occupational distributions result from 'competition' among individuals and groups for both living space and an economic niche. Competition in turn results in 'symbiosis' defined by Park as 'the living together of distinct and dissimilar species, especially when the relationship is mutually beneficial'. Symbiosis is a condition in which there is co-operation sufficient to maintain a common economy, but no communication and no consensus sufficient to ensure collective action. Competition is a type of 'non-social' interaction because there is neither communication nor the reciprocal adjustment of activity in pursuit of a common goal.

Ecological processes such as competition, 'succession', and 'dominance' describe observable, aggregate properties of a group. Ecological explanations are not concerned with the actor's point of view.

Human ecology used maps and graphic representations, and promoted both the collection of numerical data and the development of statistical analysis.

Park's contributions to human ecology have captured the interest of social geographers as well as sociologists. His interest in 'colonies and segregated areas' of the city predate contemporary studies of patterns of residential concentration and dispersion. Moreover, many of his insights into the consequences of such patterns have been discovered anew. For example, Park noted that an outcome of segregation in cities was to promote the social cohesion of ethnic and racial groups in neighbourhoods. He anticipated the finding of sociologists Nathan Glazer and Daniel Moynihan that 'where individuals of the same race or of the same vocation live together in segregated groups, neighbourhood and sentiment tend to fuse together with racial antagonisms and class interests' (Park (1916) 1952:20; Glazer and Moynihan 1963: 1-23).

Park never confused sociology, whose objective is to study culture and communication, with human ecology. Society is by definition a cultural unit of association, made possible by socialization and 'based on communication and consensus'. Society entails 'a kind of solidarity based on participation in a common enterprise and involving the more or less complete subordination of individuals to the intent and purpose of the group as a whole' (Park (1939b) 1952: 244). Human ecology, as Park conceived it, was of interest because social relations were often reflected in spatial patterns and 'social distances' were frequently expressed as physical distances. As Park's student Louis Wirth later pointed out, human ecology 'is not a substitute for, but a supplement to, other frames of reference and methods of social investigation' (Wirth (1945) 1964: 188).[3]

Methods such as the social mapping of numerical data were always considered by Park to be of little importance in understanding human society when compared to those research strategies that aimed to reveal the subjective world of the actor's experience. Thus, in a controversy over method in the department of sociology at Chicago in the late 1920s, Park defended the case-study, field-work, and the analysis of 'human documents' as basic to sociological research on the grounds that these methods captured subjective processes and the symbolic nature of group life (Bulmer 1984: 151-89).

There are three theoretical approaches generally attributed to the development of sociology at Chicago, namely, human ecology – already discussed, the formal sociology of social interaction which has its roots in the work of Georg Simmel, and 'symbolic interactionism'.

Robert Faris noted that, in the 1920s, students at Chicago 'never heard the term "symbolic interactionism" applied to their social psychological tradition and no member of the department either attempted to name it or encouraged such naming' (Faris (1967) 1970: 88). However, systematic examination of the essays and research monographs produced at Chicago leads me to support Herbert Blumer's contention that the perspective and method of symbolic interactionism 'was implicit in what was being done under Park's direction at Chicago' (Blumer, personal conversation, 6 August 1979). Furthermore, rather than considering symbolic interactionism appropriate to social psychology alone, this perspective is, and was always intended to be, a framework appropriate to the study of large-scale social phenomena, such as race and ethnic relations, revolution, urbanization, and collective behaviour.

The neologism 'symbolic interactionism' was coined by Blumer in 1937 to stand for the sociological approach based upon philosophical pragmatism and particularly influenced by George Herbert Mead (Blumer 1969:1). In addition to Mead, other philosophical pragmatists at the University of Chicago included John Dewey, James Hayden Tufts, Edward Scribner Ames, James Angell, and Addison Webster Moore.

An important factor accounting for the way in which sociology developed at Chicago was the frequent contact between scholars in different disciplines within the university (Diner 1975: 544). However, so great was the influence of Mead that the department of sociology (called the department of sociology and anthropology before 1929 when it was split into two departments) was sometimes referred to as 'an outpost of George Herbert Mead' (Rucker (1969) 1971).

Park's intellectual indebtedness to his contemporaries should not obscure either his own original contributions to sociological theory or his leadership in the development of a particularly fruitful style of social research (discussed in Chapter Four). He, along with W. I. Thomas, was the first to apply the emergent sociological perspective greatly influenced by pragmatism to the study of race, ethnicity, and collective behaviour in cities. In particular, Park introduced a new way of looking at race and ethnic conflict (discussed below and in Chapters Three, Five, and Six). Those publications in which he dealt with specific subjects, such as the immigrant press, race literature, and the personality of the 'marginal man', reveal the depth of his theoretical inventiveness and the scope of his knowledge.

PARK'S OVERALL THEORETICAL PERSPECTIVE

THE SIGNIFICANCE OF CULTURE AND COMMUNICATION FOR SOCIAL LIFE

Society exists in and through communication
(Dewey cited in Park (1938) 1950: 37)

Evolution itself, as this process was understood by Park and his contemporaries, supported his conviction that culture and communication are what differentiate 'society' from plant and non-human animal 'communities'.[4]

In the process of evolution, human beings acquired the capacity to use symbols, the most important of which were linguistic symbols. Language allows the person to think in abstractions, to make perceptual 'objects' of himself, and to 'take the role of the other'.[5] It underpins reflection and self-restraint.

According to Park, language and all other forms of communication are 'not a form of interstimulation only'. Communication, he noted, 'would not apply to two individuals who by occupying the same bed kept each other warm'. Rather, communication 'involves an interpretation by A of the stimulus coming from B, and a reference of that interpretation back to the person of whose sentiment or attitude it assumes to be an expression' (Park (1938) 1950: 37-8). In the process of interpretation the individual evaluates the situation that he confronts, taking into account his goals as well as the activities and the projected activities of others. He sees himself and his behaviour from the point of view of particular others actually present in the situation, and from the point of view of the expectations of specific others and the group as a whole existing in imagination.

Human conduct has a social dimension in so far as each individual 'gesture' is a statement of future intention which calls forth a similar response from others. This is what Park meant when he noted that 'The individual in society lives a more or less public existence, in which all his acts are anticipated, inhibited, or modified by the gestures and intentions of his fellows.' Park concluded that 'Not only is it true that we all participate directly or indirectly in making up the minds and determining the overt acts of our fellows, but *the craving for this participation in a common life ...* is one of the *fundamental* traits of human nature' (Park (1927) 1955: 18-20; my emphasis). Hence, Park suggested that human beings exist as 'public' persons *and that they seek to participate in groups in which they are subject to constraints.*

Put slightly differently, Park observed that all social forms of association and collective activity are *social* precisely because participants reflect upon their own actions and adjust these by taking into account what they think will be the likely response of others. Reflection, adjustment, negotiation, and restraint – these are the defining characteristics of *social* activity. Communication is thus a form of *social* interaction.

Those aspects of culture that act as mechanisms of restraint, whether self-imposed and generated through the use of language, or externally secured, for example by way of the law and policing or etiquette and convention, are what Park meant by mechanisms of 'social control'. This natural identification with culture is implicit in Park's definition of social control as 'the conscious participation in a common purpose and a common life, rendered possible by the fact of speech and the existence of a fund of symbols and meanings' (Park (1927) 1955: 17). Here, and elsewhere, Park contends that membership in social groups requires that the individual becomes 'conscious of rights and duties and more or less concerned about the welfare of the group to which he belongs' (Park (1931d) 1950: 359). Park argues that individuals, despite a certain degree of 'reserve', rather than resisting the claims of others, more often than not willingly submit to mutually agreed upon and negotiated restraints. For him then, the concept of social control and that of the social group or society entail a co-operative process in which individual egoism is voluntarily submerged in the interest of social harmony. According to this view, an individual's self-interest is not antagonistic to, but complements the welfare of the group.

Thus, for example, demoralization among immigrants or the disorganization of a community is a consequence of a lack of commitment to the traditions, values, and objectives of a group (Park and Miller (1921) 1969). In this respect Park noted that 'mental distress' seemed to be due 'less to the rigour with which the tribal mores and the family discipline are enforced than to the general lack of direction and the new responsibilities which have come in with the new freedom, that is to say, with the individualisation of the person, the secularisation of social life' (Park (1931d) 1950: 364). Similarly, the misery or 'deracination' unease suffered by the 'marginal man' stems from his being psychologically located in the interstices of two cultures rather than being firmly attached to one of them (Park (1931d) 1950; (1937c) 1950).

Park lodged the fulcrum of social control in self-constraint, and in particular in the individual's symbolic environment, including language. His idea of social control is close in spirit to Mead's suggestion that 'social control depends ... upon the degree to which individuals in society are able to assume the attitudes of others who are involved with them in common endeavours' (Mead (1924-5) 1964: 291). Park thus avoided the holistic presumption that social control refers to 'the capacity of the society to regulate itself according to desired principles and values' which the sociologist Morris Janowitz claims was fundamental to this concept as used by early American sociologists including those at Chicago (Janowitz 1980: 29).

The process of communication, and in particular language and education, transmutes the experience of the group into the subjective world of meaning and value which directs individual effort. 'The lower animals', commented Park, 'have neither words nor symbols; nothing has for them what we may describe as meaning' (Park (19267 1955: 17).

Language transmits shared imagery of what the empirical or objective world is like by specifying 'social objects'. A social object 'is an artifact; something made; or a ceremony, custom, ritual, words; anything which, like a word, has a meaning and is not just what it seems'. Social objects 'are symbolic expressions of the common life' whose meanings are revealed 'by observing the ways in which they are used' (Park (1929a) 1952: 202). What imbues social objects with reality is not their existence; rather, 'the significance of objects for men and women is, in the final analysis, what gives them the character of reality' (Park (1931b) 1955: 284).

The study of 'the etiquette of race relations' (Park (1937b) 1950; Doyle (1937) 1971), 'collective definitions' (Blumer and Duster 1980), and 'racial discourse' (Reeves 1983) is an effort to uncover the meanings which blacks have as social objects and how this might direct the behaviour of both blacks and whites in specific historical contexts. In his introduction to Bertram Doyle's monograph on the etiquette of race relations in the South, Park noted the anomalies arising when white Southerners 'retain the intimate and familiar forms of address such as "uncle", "auntie", and "boy", which were appropriate to the ante-bellum South'. 'Negroes', he went on to say, 'are more and more disposed to reject any terms or any racial distinctions that reflect and tend to preserve the memories of an earlier inferior status' (ibid.: 187-8).[6] More recently slogans such as 'black is beautiful' and 'black power' redefine the meaning of blacks as social objects in new ways.

Past meanings underlie social interaction but new meanings may emerge in present and in future interaction. 'What anything means to anyone at any time', commented Park, 'is substantially what it means, has meant, or will mean to someone else' (Park (1938) 1950: 44). Park's interest in the role of race leadership and the mass media in the resolution of racial conflict, such as race riots, reflected his conviction of the importance of both in recasting meanings that are initially expressed as public opinion and that are later institutionalized as norms, conventions, and patterns of social interaction. Thus, for example, the Chicago Commission on Race Relations recommended that 'in view of the recognised responsibility of the press in its influence upon public opinion concerning Negroes' there be more frequent news of the 'creditable achievements' of blacks, of improvements in their 'cultural and social life' as well as the physical condition of their neighbourhoods and houses, of their lawfulness as opposed to lawlessness. The Commission also suggested 'the capitalisation of the word "Negro" in racial designation, and avoidance of the word "nigger", as contemptuous and needlessly provocative' (Chicago Commission on Race Relations (1922) 1968: 650).

Communication and any instances of social interaction in which objects and their meanings are reinforced, changed, or abandoned always take place in 'situations'. These situations themselves have a historical and cultural referent. For example, Park pointed out that in the rural American South, slavery, legally ended in 1865, achieved continuity through the institutionaliz-ation of 'caste'. Caste relationships were not endemic to the cultural order of northern cities. Therefore, in the North, the image of Afro-Americans, patterns of interaction with whites, and 'definitions of the situation' differed in kind, variety, and stability from that characteristic of the rural South (Park (1928b) 1950; (1937b) 1950).

Objective situations and what W. I. Thomas called 'definitions of the situation' represent constraints upon activity. 'Preliminary to any self-determined act of behaviour', observed Thomas, 'there is always a stage of examination and deliberation which we may call the definition of the situation. And actually, not only concrete acts are dependent on the definition of the situation, but gradually a whole life-policy and the personality of the individual himself follow from a series of such definitions' (Thomas (1923) 1969). Park and Thomas cited 'the "shall nots" of the Ten Command-ments' as an example of a definition of the situation (Park and Miller (1921) 1969: 60). Later Thomas summarized his view of 'situational analysis' in his observation that 'If men define situations as real, they are real in their consequences' (Thomas and Thomas (1928) 1966: xi).

Situations may offer new opportunities for the emergence of novel ways of seeing and acting in the world as well as reinforcing conventional interpretations (Park and Miller (1921) 1969: 60-2). These novel ways of seeing and acting may themselves become part of a group's culture. For example, Park considered social insti-tutions to be time-honoured solutions to the past problems encountered by groups. But in periods of crisis, social institutions may be changed or abandoned in response to the perception of new needs and objectives (Park (1932) 1955; (1941a) 1955).

Socialization consists of the transmission of a relevant world of social objects to a new member of the group. 'Man is not born human', observed Park. He only becomes human when he is able to participate in appropriate ways in ongoing group life. This requires access to the shared meanings that are a part of the group's culture. This is especially important since familiar objects may have different meanings for different groups. Consider, for example, 'the cross' and 'what different meanings it has had, and still has, for devout Christians and orthodox Jews' (Park (1929a) 1952: 202). Park was among the first to point out, as the sociologists Gregory Stone and Harvey Farberman put it at a later time, that the apprehension of the 'objective world' is available to members of a group in its 'social transformation' through shared meanings and images learned in the process of socialization (Stone and Farberman 1970: 147-53).

Communication is central to the cultural order because it enables shared understandings to exist between members of a group, as well as transmitting these inter-generationally. Understanding based upon a world of shared meanings (i.e., a common culture) in turn makes collective action possible. Paradoxically, however, the process of interpretation or thinking which is made possible by language and which represents the culture and the constraints inherent in group life, *also* facilitates the emergence of human individuality and social change within the group.

'Mind' and 'intelligence' which originate in communication and self-deliberation – which is another term for thinking – are adaptations to the requirement that individuals live in groups (Shibutani 1961: 13-14). Communication, thinking, mind, and intelligence enable individuals to manipulate their social and their physical environments rather than merely responding to these in identical and predetermined ways as do non-human animals. Human beings 'have first to learn through experience how to react to various stimuli' (Park (1904) 1972: 40).

However, once having done so, the socialized individual can, through the process of self-deliberation, check his impulses, come up with new ideas, and construct novel plans of action which may contradict the prevailing meanings, beliefs, and traditions of the group. For this reason Park was certain that while 'the customs of the group impose themselves upon the individual, and his habits are consciously formed in conformity with them', it is also the case that changes in individual experience, which result in changes in personal outlook and habit, may 'eventually undermine custom and destroy its influence and authority' (Park (1931a) 1955: 254-5).

This is exemplified in Park's observation that racial and nationalist movements are often precipitated by 'a purely personal sense of injury' arising out of an occasion in which an 'exceptional' individual experiences 'in his own person the ignominy and the wrong' to which the less fortunate among his fellows are subjected daily and who then decides to make their cause his own. He cites the Indian nationalist leader Gandhi as an instance of this (Park (1931d) 1950: 367).

The sources of new experience for the individual include communication with others, whether verbal or written, because, as Park noted, communication always 'involves a transformation in the individuals who communicate' and 'this transformation goes on unceasingly in individual minds' (Park (1926c) 1952: 174). Park's belief in the efficacy of communication to change individual and collective imagery for example, as this has to do with racial stereotypes, underlies his assessment of the role of face-to-face encounters and the role of the mass media, and especially the newspaper, in mitigating race conflict.

Park also linked the inevitability of human individuality to locomotion. 'The fact that every individual is capable of movement in space insures him an experience which is private and peculiar to himself, and this experience ... affords him, insofar as it is unique, a point of view for independent and individual action.' Moreover, it is because 'the experience of every individual differs from that of his fellow men, that the meaning of the outside world is different for every individual' (Park (1904) 1972: 40). This specialness of experience and outlook contributes to the emergence of the individual as a 'person' capable of transcending group constraints and initiating social and cultural changes (Park (1926c) 1952: 175).

Another fundamental way in which individuals differ from non-human animals is in having 'self-concepts' or 'selves' and in being 'self-conscious' – an attribute which is also dependent upon language. Park's concept of 'the self' was influenced by the ideas of his teacher, the philosopher William James, as well as by Charles Horton Cooley's 'looking glass self' and Mead's elaboration of the genesis of 'the self' in the process of childhood socialization (James (1892) 1970: 189-226; Cooley (1902) 1964; Mead (1934) 1962: 135-226). According to their collective view, the self is the kind of object that a person makes of himself on the basis of seeing

himself from the point of view of others (what Mead called 'taking
the role of the other'). The way in which the individual sees
himself arises out of the process of communication. Of particular
significance is interaction with important figures, such as parents,
during childhood.

The self-concept, however, while it refers to the past is also a
response to the type of social interaction that takes place in
situations in the present. While the psychological concept of
'personality' presumes 'an organised set of persistent and
characteristic patterns of individual behaviour' which reflect a
constant sense of personal identity, the self-concept, because it is
rooted in ongoing processes of social interaction (i.e., communication) which take place in different situations, must emphasize
the variability in the ways in which the individual sees himself and
is, consequently, prepared to act towards himself (Stone and
Farberman 1970: 367). This is why Mead insisted that the self be
seen as a process and not a structure. It also underlies the later
observation of sociologist Erving Goffman that, in a sense, the self
is 'on loan' from society and the anthropologist Sandra Wallman's
concept of 'identity options' (Goffman (1956) 1969; Wallman
1983). The idea of 'labelling' developed in Howard Becker's essays
on deviance also emphasizes the importance of others in
influencing changes in personal identity, such as learning to see
oneself as 'deviant' on the basis of the appraisals of police and
social workers (Becker 1964).

Park suggested that the variability of the self-concept lies in the
number of different 'statuses' that the individual occupies in
modern life. What Park meant by status is position within a group.
An individual, he noted, 'may have many "selves" according to the
groups to which he belongs and the extent to which each of these
groups is isolated from others'. Also, the individual 'is influenced
in differing degrees and in a specific manner by the different types
of groups of which he is a member' (Park (1920-21) (1921-22)
1955: 240).

The marginal man, for example, both experiences personal
discomfort and confounds the expectations of others because he
is a member of two conflicting status groups (Park (1928a) 1950;
(1937c) 1950: 372-6). Everett Hughes developed this insight in his
discussion of the 'dilemmas and contradictions of status' which

occur when the incumbent of two discordant statuses communicates with others. He cited Afro-American doctors and female engineers as examples (Hughes (1945) 1971: 141-50).

The dynamic aspect of status is role. In this regard Park noted that 'everyone is always and everywhere, more or less consciously, playing a role. We are parents and children, masters and servants, teachers and students, clients and professional men, Gentiles and Jews.' That the self, status, and role overlap is evident from Park's conclusion that '[i]t is in these roles that we know each other; it is in these roles that we know ourselves' (Park (1926b) 1950: 249).

The status of a group relative to other groups and the role that its members play is the outcome of a historical past which has become embedded in the culture of the society. For this reason, any effort to change the status of a group relative to other groups and the role traditionally associated with a particular status is difficult to initiate and is likely to encounter resistance. This is especially true for relatively undifferentiated societies and for racially and ethnically stratified societies. In the latter case individuals can be located with respect to one preponderant status group on the basis of physical appearance, language, or nationality, rather than having to be dealt with on the basis of membership in a variety of status-conferring groups.

In general, Park insisted that efforts to change the position, status, and role of social groups, as these had been woven into a culture as a result of a historical run of events, must result in group consciousness, prejudice, and conflict. This is expressed in his analysis of race and ethnic relations in the United States, as well as in his consideration of the causes of nationalist conflict in Europe suggested in *The Man Farthest Down* (Washington and Park 1912), both of which are further discussed in Chapters Three, Five, and Six.

As the above discussion should suggest, the self and personal identity refer not only to group membership but also to its evaluation. A person's 'self-esteem', which is a measure of how much he values himself, is influenced by his status within the social groups of which he is a member *and* the relative position of these groups to other groups (Park and Miller (1921) 1969: 47-59; Park (1926a) 1950; (1928b) 1950; (1931d) 1950). This evaluative aspect of the self is what makes it a moral concept. [These observations resonate in the Afro-American novelist James Baldwin's quip that the purpose the black man serves in America is to tell white people where the bottom is!]

Park located the self and self-esteem in status groups and their relationship to one another. Solidarity between members of status groups stems from a shared culture and what Herbert Blumer later called a sense of 'group position'. Group position includes the elements of domination and subordination, privilege, obligation, deference, social distance, and monopolization of or exclusion from certain types of activities (Blumer 1958).

Taking all of the above into consideration, Park concluded that status groups, rather than social classes, are the most likely basis for collective action in general and for social conflict in particular.

> It is in the effort to maintain this status or improve it; to defend personality, enlarge its possessions, extend its privileges, and maintain its prestige that conflicts arise ... This applies to all conflicts, whether they are personal or party squabbles, sectarian differences or national and patriotic wars, for the personality of the individual is invariably bound up with the interests and order of his group and clan, that in a struggle he makes the group cause his own. (Park and Burgess (1921) 1969: 238)

Park went on to note in this vein that

> much has been said and written about the economic causes of war, but whatever may be the ultimate sources of our sentiments, it is probably true that men never go to war for economic reasons merely. It is because wealth and possessions are bound up with prestige, honour and position in the world, that men and nations fight about them. (ibid.)

It is important to note, in anticipation of further discussion of Park's analysis of race and ethnicity, the significance that he attributed to the concept of status. As suggested above, this stems from two sources. First, his belief that the relative position of status groups, as well as the person's position within each group, influences the collective consciousness of the group as well as personal identity and self-esteem. Second, Park suggested that considerations of status motivate individuals to act and groups to act collectively. Status influences the willingness of groups to engage in social conflict.

In heterogeneous societies like the United States, race and ethnicity are bases of status group formation and the source of self-identification and self-esteem. In these circumstances, there is almost bound to be conflict between racial and ethnic groups. Antagonism expressed as a 'conflict of cultures' is an outcome of the monopolization strategies of dominant status groups unwilling 'to compete on equal terms with a people of a lower status' (ibid.: 240). While non-human animals and plants may 'compete' for scarce resources, only human beings can enter into social conflict over them.

TYPOLOGY OF SOCIAL INTERACTION

Park's typology of social interaction is a way of analytically designating the types of communication characteristic of distinct spheres of social life which demand particular subjective orientations to action. 'Conflict' corresponds to 'the political order', 'accommodation' relates to 'social organization', and 'assimilation' to 'personality and the cultural heritage'. Conflict, accommodation, and assimilation are features of the cultural order because, unlike the non-social process of competition characteristic of the ecological order, these processes are part of a socially controlled collective activity (i.e., activity negotiated through reciprocal pressures, needs, and demands of individuals and groups). In each of these processes, the mutual adjustment of lines actively proceeds on the basis of 'taking the role of the other'. This implies, of course, that 'the other' is both rational and co-operative. Consensus and co-operation, even in situations of conflict, are always features of social interaction and communication.

Park's typology of social interaction has been confused with his 'race relations cycle'. His critics are correct to refute Park's observation that 'The race relations cycle, contact, competition, accommodation and assimilation – is apparently progressive and irreversible' (Park (1926b) 1950: 138). However, the race relations cycle is an unimportant feature of his analysis of race and ethnicity (Lipset 1950: 475-9; Matthews 1977: 157-93; Lal 1986) and these same critics err in overlooking the more legitimate ways in which

Park used the concepts of competition, conflict, accommodation, and assimilation (Myrdal (1944) 1962: 1025-64; Cox (1948) 1970: 462-77; Lyman 1973: 27-70; Persons 1987; Smith 1988).

Below it is argued that Park's typology of social interaction, very much influenced by Georg Simmel, was intended to differentiate among the range of collective action that actually exists in all sorts of combinations and in a variety of time sequences in the social world (Simmel (1950) 1964; 1971).

'Social contact' initiates each type of social interaction. What Park meant by social contact was minds mutually influencing one another as a result of communication through language, letters, and the printed page, as well as through 'the medium of the telephone, telegraph, radio and moving picture' (Park and Burgess (1921) 1969: 121, 187).

Conflict occurs when people define the pursuit of their interests and the successful execution of their plans as limited by the objectives and activities of others rather than as a result of inadequate individual effort, fate, or a natural order of some sort. Conflict is 'conscious competition' in which 'competitors are transformed into rivals and enemies' (ibid.).

As already noted above, Park differentiated between the goals of competition, which are economic and material advantages, and the objectives of conflict, which are status and privilege. He maintained that status, which has to do with self-conception and self-esteem, is of greater importance than the enhancement of material well-being in influencing collective action in general and conflict in particular. 'Competition', he noted, 'determines the position of the individual in the community; conflict fixes his place in society. Location, position, ecological interdependence – these are the characteristics of community. Status, subordination, and superordination, control – these are the distinctive marks of a society' (ibid.: 236-7).

Conflict requires consensus concerning the way in which social interaction between rivals or enemies should be resolved. Thus, after noting that an enemy may arouse fear, animosity, and jealousy, Park added that 'it is always possible to come to terms with an enemy whom one knows and with whom one can communicate'. He concluded that with the passage of time, such communication 'brings with it a more profound understanding, the result of which is to humanise social relations' (Park (1938)

1950: 43). Park, then, subscribed to the optimistic, even paradoxical, view that one of the effects of conflict is the humanizing of social relationships. This idea is expressed in one of his earlier essays when he reflected that conflict, 'and particularly cultural conflict ... inevitably increases our knowledge not merely of ourselves but of our fellows, since the attitudes and sentiments we find in ourselves we are able to appreciate and understand, no matter how indirectly expressed, when we find them in the minds of others' (Park (1904) 1972: 49-50).

A related beneficial effect of conflict is to heighten self-consciousness, thus bringing to 'the surface and into clear consciousness sentiments and attitudes that otherwise would escape rational criticism and interpretation' (ibid.: 49-50). For example, arguing with adversaries might result in the discovery of the untenable or undesirable aspects of one's own views. On the other hand, it could reinforce a belief in both the correctness of one's own outlook and the flawed vision of one's antagonists. In either of these cases, the forced re-evaluation of beliefs ends in either abandoning or pursuing with greater conviction a particular course of action.

Park's positive attitude towards particular kinds of race conflict must be considered in the light of his perception of the beneficial outcomes of social conflict in general.

The 'natural outcome' of conflict is social accommodation. Park meant by this 'an organization of elements more or less antagonistic to each other but united for the moment, at least, by an arrangement which defines the reciprocal relations and respective spheres of action of each ... [a]ccommodation, while it is maintained, secures for the individual or group a recognised status' (Park and Burgess (1921) 1969: 360). Social accommodation enables people 'of divergent interests and types' to carry on their activities together on the basis of consensus about relative group position and what constitutes appropriate behaviour for each group. A social heritage, including stratification arrangements, customs, and laws, represents the resolution of past conflict.

Within the individual, social accommodation is expressed in attitudes of dominance and deference. Conventions and etiquette are also internalized and regulate social distances.

Park suggested that beliefs, conventions, and etiquette – all aspects of social heritage – rather than force or 'false conscious-ness' maintained the stability of stratified societies. Thus, a highly differentiated society in which inequality is a norm need not be 'disharmonious' (Béteille 1971; Dumont 1970). For example, he noted that '[e]ven where accommodation has been imposed, as in the case of slavery, by force, the personal relations of master and slave are invariably supported by appropriate attitudes and sentiments'. He further emphasized the point: 'sentiments of subordination which have grown up in conformity with an accepted position eventually become the basis of a life-philosophy of the person' (Park and Burgess (1921) 1969: 308-9).

Park's assessment of the stability of the ante-bellum plantation demonstrates the importance that he attributed to subjective factors in legitimating inequality.

Accommodation may be relatively permanent, it may fall apart in conflict or resolve itself by assimilation. Only when assimilation occurs is the latent antagonism inherent in accommodation 'wholly dissolved'.

In the process of assimilation, social distances are overcome through participation in a *common cultural life* that includes access to the range of experience offered within a society. There exists a sense of social solidarity based on membership in a 'we-group'. Assimilation, then, 'is a process of interpenetration and fusion in which persons and groups acquire the memories, sentiments, and attitudes of other persons and groups, and by sharing their experience and history are incorporated with them in a common cultural life' (ibid.: 360-2). A prerequisite to assimilation is a common language.

Initial social contacts influence whether or not, and with what degree of rapidity, assimilation will occur. Unlike accommodation, in which changes in social relationships and subjective orient-ations may occur with great rapidity, assimilation generally takes place gradually and often unconsciously, as 'the unreflective responses to new experiences'. Assimilation is most likely to occur within the primary group where the transmission of attitudes and participation in a common life occur on a day-to-day basis.

In the process of assimilation people see each other as morally equivalent. Social cohesion is not founded on like-mindedness or on a division of labour but rather is 'a unity of experience and of orientation out of which may develop a community of purpose and action' (ibid.: 362). But it is not clear whether assimilation necessarily entails *social* equality. In an early essay, for example, Park offered the southern ante-bellum plantation and the relationship between master and house slave as an example of assimilation (Park (1913b) 1950; (1928b) 1950).

Park's typology of social interaction is best considered in the context of his more general analysis of communication, social control, and the cultural order. He contrasted these *social* processes with 'collective behaviour' – defined by the absence of communication, negotiation, and social control.

COLLECTIVE BEHAVIOUR: CROWDS AND PUBLICS, SOCIAL MOVEMENTS, AND SECTS

Initially, Park conceived of the crowd and the public as alternatives to the types of associations in which individuals routinely act to accomplish their ends. The crowd and the public are arenas of 'collective behaviour' but not of 'collective action'. This is because collective behaviour does not require that participants self-consciously adjust their activities on the basis of the gestures and actions of others, bringing into play self-deliberation, restraint, and the negotiation which are aspects of culture, communication, and social interaction. Instead, collective behaviour springs from 'impulse' and individuals act 'under the influence of a mood or state of mind' which is 'unconscious' and in which 'collective attention is intensified' (Park (1904) 1972: 45-62; Park and Burgess (1921) 1969: 381).

Collective behaviour is an expression of 'social unrest' precipitated by a change in the environment or of a perception of a deficiency in the environment. A 'crisis' ensues when such change or perception of inadequacy results in a breakdown in some aspect of the design for living prescribed by the group's culture and, in particular, when its moral code or normative order is challenged. The 'more or less disruptive and revolutionary crowd ... seldom arises where there is social stability and where customs have deep roots', remarked Park. However, 'where social bonds are removed and old institutions weakened, great crowd movements develop more easily and forcefully' (Park (1904) 1972: 47).

In instances of collective *behaviour*, unlike that of collective *action*, people act together in the absence of traditions and the normal mechanisms of social control inherent in a shared culture, individual habit, and extant social arrangements. Social movements and sects require that members sever their attachments to conventional groups and customary styles of life in order to enter into new associations with unsettled social and cultural parameters and uncertain futures (ibid.: 46-7; Levine 1972: x-xxv). Demoralized individuals, unattached to already existing groups, form a reservoir for membership. Park included an abridged version of the nineteenth-century historian William Lecky's account of the rise of Methodism as an illustration of this (Lecky (1892), abridged in Park and Burgess (1921) 1969: 431-40).

Ironically, collective behaviour is an antidote to social disorganization in so far as it induces individuals who had withdrawn from social groups to act. Here it is pertinent to note that, for Park and Thomas, the defining characteristic of 'social disorganization' is non-participation, rather than deviance from social norms per se.[7]

There are two kinds of crowds. The 'organized crowd' is 'controlled by a common purpose and acts to achieve, no matter how vaguely it is defined, a common end'. The lynch mob and the 'storming' of the Bastille are examples of this type of crowd. The 'ecstatic', 'expressive crowd' enables individuals to 'relieve their feelings'. Holy Rollers, Convulsionaries, and other such religious groups whose demonstrations are aimed inward rather than towards objects in the external environment are examples of expressive crowds (ibid.: 387-92).

If not dispersed in 'a panic', organized crowds generate a set of norms, leadership, and other features of mass movements and 'finally crystallise in institutions'. 'The history of almost any single social movement – women's suffrage, prohibition, Protestantism', noted Park, 'exhibits in a general way, if not in detail, this progressive change in character' (ibid.: 390). Park went on to observe that 'There is first a vague general discontent and distress. Then a violent, confused and disorderly, but enthusiastic and popular movement arises. Finally, the movement takes form; develops leadership, organization; formulates doctrines and dogmas. Eventually, it is accepted, established, legalised. The movement dies, but the institution remains' (ibid.: 390). Herbert

Blumer developed Park's ideas in his depiction of the 'generative character of social unrest' (Blumer 1978).

In *An Introduction to the Science of Sociology*, published in 1921, and in Park's other work published after *The Crowd and the Public* in 1904, it becomes increasingly clear that the public does not conform to the properties defining the crowd *or* collective behaviour. The public consists of groups representing divergent points of view and goals. Among and between these groups there exists a shared 'universe of discourse' and a sufficient community of interest to ensure conflict resolution. The public is a forum for critical discussion, the outcome of which is compromise – a final agreement 'qualified by all the different opinions that cooperate to form its judgment'. Thus public opinion is never an 'unmediated expression of emotion, as in the crowd' (Park and Burgess (1921) 1969: 376).

Publics, public opinion, and political conflict represent rational processes of change in which communication and social control depend upon individuals and groups self-consciously adjusting their behaviour to one another. 'It is this fact of conflict, in the form of discussion', noted Park, 'that introduces into the control exercised by public opinion the elements of rationality and of fact.'

The products of public opinion are the 'mores'. Unlike 'custom and the folkways', which Park likened to habit in the individual and which are 'a mere residuum of past practices', mores are judgments upon matters which were probably once live issues but that have been 'settled and forgotten' (ibid.: 376).

Park believed that political discussion on the part of publics is an attempt to substitute an advanced form of political action for a more elementary form, namely, the use of force. When views or interests are irreconcilable, however, force may be resorted to.

By and large, Park tended to overlook the role of force in either maintaining social order or precipitating social change.

The sociologist Leon Bramson points out that Park's analysis of collective behaviour contradicts the pessimistic predictions about 'mass society' and the crowd put forward by Jose Ortega y Gasset, Karl Mannheim, Gustav LeBon, Gabriel Tarde, and Scipio Sighele because he thought that the 'organized crowd' was a potentially creative approach to modifying unsatisfactory social conditions

(Bramson 1961: 62-72). Thus, Park noted that in cities, 'where the population is unstable, where parents and children are employed out of the house and often in distant parts of the city, where thousands of people live side by side for years without so much as bowing acquaintance', there may arise 'new and strange political and religious movements ... which represent the groping of men for a new social order' (Park (1915) 1952: 32-46; Park and Burgess (1921) 1969: 383). Bramson also observes that, unlike these Europeans, Park did not assume that social classes are necessarily the basis for crowd behaviour and political discontent.

Bramson's conclusion, however, overlooks the evidence leading to the conclusion that Park saw the public and political conflict as the preferable and rational way to achieve social change in modern urban society.

The above discussion of culture, communication, and social control provides the analytical framework for a consideration of Park's perspective on race and ethnicity in Chapter Three. In Chapter Four, 'The emergence of an ethnographic tradition', the research methodology that complemented Park's perspective is discussed.

Chapter Three

PARK'S APPROACH TO RACE AND ETHNIC RELATIONS

What, then, are the significant features of Park's perspective on culture, communication, and social control for the study of urban race and ethnicity? What differentiates his approach from others?

THE SUBJECTIVE ASPECTS OF COLLECTIVE ACTION AND THE SYMBOLIC NATURE OF GROUP LIFE

Park, along with W. I. Thomas, was an early advocate of the view that the subjective dimension of human behaviour must be included in sociological investigation. Subjective factors such as attitudes, motives, and meanings are derived from individual experience but also reflect the culture and the history of social groups. The acquisition of culture, which plays the crucial role of orienting the individual in his activities by transmitting to him 'a pattern of symbolic meanings through which the members of a collectivity grasp their world', is available only through communication within society and 'social' forms of association (Higham 1984: xi).

The importance placed upon the subjective aspects of action and the symbolic dimension of group life urges scrutiny of the mass media, art, and literature. It also requires the examination of the statements of politicians and civic leaders on behalf of dominant and subordinate groups and of the 'process of collective definition' that makes public opinion, scientific belief, ideologies, and mythologies available to members of a society. (The process of 'collective definition' is discussed in Chapter Seven.)

Park's and Thomas's second significant contribution was to require that the sociologist know the culture and the history of social groups in order to interpret the experience and the world view of its members accurately. The sociologist was responsible for recognizing the coherence (or dissonance) between ideas, activities, and institutions.

Thus, for example, Park's field-work in the South while working at Tuskegee in Alabama and his knowledge of both southern culture and history led him to discount popular racial theories of his contemporaries, which viewed race prejudice as a reflection of an instinctual dislike between different races. Instead, Park noted that contemporary southern culture and southern history were replete with situations of intimacy between blacks and whites belying theories of race prejudice based on instinct. Racial etiquette, he thought, was intended to *enforce* social distances rather than reflecting a natural, instinctual dislike between races (Park (1928b) 1950: 230-4; Park (1937b) 1950).

Third, Park's concern with culture, history, and the subjective world of meaning led him to conclude that men are not always motivated by 'interest' – whether self-interest or class interest. Under certain conditions, ideas and passions, rather than either material interests, such as that of social class, or even ideal interests having to do with status and privilege, become the most important factors in the explanation of action.[1] Human beings, he believed, 'live in the world of imagination' and are able to entertain ideas and feel emotions which may lead them to act over against what *appears to the sociologist* to be in their self-interest. Empathy, which Park considered a concomitant of communication and collective action, may result in altruistic behaviour. According to Park, both empathy and altruism are normal features of social life.

The sociology of race and ethnicity abounds with examples of the substitution of interest-oriented explanations framed by the investigator for explanations that take the *prima facie* ideas and explanations of the actor seriously. For example, the writer Harold Cruse, in his study *The Crisis of the Negro Intellectual*, suggests that an adequate explanation of the 'relationship between groups in America, and on the international plane' is that they 'are actuated by power principles and not by morality and compassion for the underdog classes' (Cruse 1967: 494). This leads him to expunge ideas of morality and compassion from his explanations of race and ethnic relations.

Similarly, in her otherwise excellent study, *In the Almost Promised*

Land: American Jews and Blacks, 1915-1935, the historian Hasia Diner argues that 'for many Jewish leaders, black issues provided a forum in which to work out certain tensions of acculturation' and to pursue 'Jewish ends'. However, the material in her book lends itself equally well to alternative interpretations which take the motives acknowledged by Jewish leaders at the time at their face value. Her decision to pit alleged Jewish self-interest against 'genuine' but none the less 'overstated and unrealistic' sentiments, such as empathy with blacks and the pursuit of elementary justice, is an example of the logic of procedure that follows from an interest-oriented approach to race and ethnic relations (Diner 1977).

An interest in 'hidden interests' may also result in looking behind the avowed motives of analysts of race and ethnicity. Ralph Ellison's denunciation of Park is the classic example of the substitution of the observer's agenda of hidden interest-oriented motives for the *prima facie* ideas of the sociologist. Ellison condemns the work of the sociologists at the University of Chicago during the 1920s and 1930s on the grounds that it was financed by guilt-ridden, white, northern philanthropists of a liberal political bent who had an interest in the continued subordination of black American labourers. Nowhere does Ellison address himself to the question of either the analytical usefulness of the approach developed by the Chicago scholars or the adequacy of their description of race relations in the United States (Ellison (1944) 1972: 303-17). In a similar vein, Cruse asks, 'Just what is *behind* Nathan Glazer's fervent insistence that Negroes be integrated as fast as possible, and by any means?' (Cruse 1967: 494-7).

Park assumed that there is a range of experience available to members of the same social class, both within and between racial and ethnic groups. The sources of experience and subjective meaning – including beliefs about what the world 'is really like' – include communication within associations as disparate as the immediate family, kin, the church, trade unions, professional societies, and neighbours. The school and the mass media are also purveyors of cultural imagery and sources of belief. Why should a unitary class interest emerge and become of greatest importance in influencing behaviour given such variety?

(Park's concept of the 'marginal man' is based on the idea of a social world in which there are multiple sources of imagery and

51

meaning, and underscores the diversity – and in some sense idio-syncratic range – of experience available to individuals and groups in modern urban societies (Park (1928a) 1950; (1931d) 1950; (1937c) 1950: 372-6; Stonequist (1937) 1961).)

Park's preference, as already pointed out, was to link interest to status groups. However, his vision of the multiplicity of sources of experience and meaning in urban life led him to advocate that the attribution of motive be an outcome of empirical investigation. This last point directs attention to the advantages of research strategies that take the actor seriously as a source of knowledge about his own activities – a point further discussed in Chapter Four.[2]

STATUS GROUPS AND SOCIAL CONFLICT

Park's conclusion that social conflict is most often the outcome of the efforts of status groups to enhance or preserve their position relative to others is another important component of his approach to race and ethnicity that follows from his general perspective on group life. In American society, race, and, to a lesser extent, ethnicity are among the major bases of status group formation. According to Park, conflicts between native-born white Americans, Afro-Americans, and immigrants had to do with relative group position, style of life, and corresponding beliefs about deference, obligation, identity, and self-worth.

Here it is crucial to remember that Park stretched the concepts of culture and society, communication and collective action to include a corresponding social psychological theory that related these concepts both to individual needs, such as the need for recognition, esteem, and identity, and to the needs of social groups for cohesion and morale.

Park's conviction of the importance of status groups in the explanation of social conflict opposes the view that attributes such as colour, national origin, language, religion, and gender mask the fundamental cleavages around which 'genuine' groups, motivated by 'real' shared concerns, should cohere (Castles and Kosack 1973; Phizacklea and Miles 1980; Stone 1985: 62-82). The latter influential strand of thought assumes that social conflict between racial and ethnic groups, as opposed to social classes, is a manifestation of false consciousness arising from the cynical manipulation of the proletariat or the have-nots at the hands of a ruling class and their representatives in government, the media, and the schools. In the United States, it is argued, racism itself 'is built into the structure of modern capitalism' (Sherman and Wood 1979: 96).

Yet, studies of slavery, immigration, nationalism, and contemporary race relations contain examples of groups who have acted to preserve a set of social relationships from which they do not appear to have gained much. Thus, for example, in the debate about the causes of the American Civil War the historian Kenneth Stampp points out that only one-quarter of free whites in the antebellum South owned slaves and, among this number, only a small percentage owned more than fifty slaves (Stampp 1956). Moreover, even among slave owners, plantations were not always profitable. How then to explain the persistence of slavery and a civil war which was supported by non-slaveholding white Southerners?

This question is posed and answered by Eugene Genovese, himself a Marxist social historian, who points out in a discussion of materialistic and idealistic interpretations of slavery, that members of a dominant racial group may become committed to a style of life, or a set of beliefs and a mythology, which motivates them to act in ways that are not economically rational, politically expedient, nor likely to result in their own prosperity (Genovese (1966) 1972: 23-52).

Park placed status groups and the study of conflict at the centre of his approach to the sociology of race and ethnicity because he took the view that racial and ethnic studies had to do with the interactions between cultural groups. In addition, his appraisal of the importance of status groups and, in particular, of their role in influencing individual stability suggests that he was fundamentally convinced that human beings survive and succeed when they are incorporated into 'sentimental groups'.[3] Sentimental groups, as conceived here, are based upon a shared culture, social solidarity, and affective relationships between members.

Sentimental groups share some of the properties of primary groups. However, they do not necessarily have an ecological basis such that members participate in 'intimate, face-to-face association' over a long period of time and in many different role relationships (Cooley (1909) 1962: 23-31). Along with other types of associations, they are the purveyors of values and ideals.

Sentimental groups may limit membership on the basis of characteristics, such as race, nationality, and gender. On the other hand, the concept of 'ethnicity by consent' (discussed in Chapter Five) suggests that sentimental groups may consist of volunteers who share a mystical or mythical connection and participate in a newly created culture.

Sentimental groups may or may not further interests and perform 'functions'. For example, ethnically based fraternal lodges fostered solidarity and identity while at the same time performing useful services such as the provision of social insurance. Events such as dinners, dances, and picnics, while not of instrumental value, provided individuals with psychological and social support. The 'storefront' church established by Afro-American migrants from the South represented their attempt 'to re-establish a type of church in the urban environment ... in which they were known as people' (Frazier (1963) 1974: 58).

Recent events and current social analysis impart credibility to what twenty years ago might have been evaluated as Park's naive vision of the needs of human beings and the basis of an orderly society. Thus, for example, the growth of fundamentalist, born-again Christian sects, as well as a renaissance in Jewish orthodoxy, has not escaped the notice of contemporary social scientists. Why, it is asked (although not necessarily answered), do people seek to give up the liberty and freedom from authoritarian social institutions so recently won? Of equal significance in this respect is the growth of organizations such as Weight Watchers Anonymous and Debtors Anonymous which foster the belief that the group and its teaching will enable individuals to attain values which are impervious to unaided individual effort. Each of these instances affirms the necessity for sentimental bonds whether of ancient or relatively recent origin.

SOCIAL CONTROL

As already pointed out above, Park supported efforts to integrate individuals into groups which provided them with a coherent vision of the world, a notion of desirable behaviour, and affective ties to others. Such groups, whether parochial minority groups, sentimental groups, or sects, were a source of social control.

Traditionally, a shared culture and, in particular, informal mechanisms of social control lodged within language, as well as primary groups and local institutions such as the church and school, worked to restrain individual impulse and unbridled egoism. More recently, Park thought, urbanization, the predominance of secondary associations, and an ethic of individualism eroded these mechanisms of social control and sanctioned in their place unbridled self-expression and gratification, both of which contributed to demoralization.

Park and Thomas believed that in twentieth-century urban America the social sciences could also promote socially controlled behaviour by increasing an awareness of the interdependence and reciprocal obligations between individuals and groups. As Thomas pointed out,

> if we recognize that social control is to be reached through the study of behaviour, and that its technique is to consist in the creation of attitudes appropriate to desired values, then I suggest that the most essential attitude at the present moment is a public attitude of hospitality toward all forms of research in the social world, such as it has gained toward all forms of research in the physical world.
>
> (Thomas (1917) 1981: 38)

Park and Thomas hoped to use sociological findings to resurrect a citizenry of 'character'. Character, according to the political scientist James Wilson, is based on 'virtue', that is, 'habits of moderate action; more specifically, acting with due restraint on one's impulses, due regard for the rights of others, and reasonable concern for distant consequences' (Wilson 1985: 15).

The concept of social control is no longer fashionable among sociologists. Nor has the idea of character gained much of a hearing. However, social disruption stemming from drug misuse, child abuse and neglect, broken families, crime and violence, all press for a response from sociologists. Solutions to these problems may involve greater reliance upon formal mechanisms of social control initiated by the state, such as more effective policing, greater numbers of social workers, and subsidies to community-care facilities. Park and Thomas, however, pinned their hope upon education, including greater knowledge about the social world, and increased communication, as the ways to encourage the growth of informal mechanisms of social control which relied upon self-restraint rather than externally imposed regulation for its effectiveness. They endorsed movement towards a society based upon 'voluntary cooperation' in which 'consent' rather than 'force' predominated (Fisher and Strauss 1979: 465).

Park's positive attitude towards informal mechanisms of social control based upon self-restraint and consensus complemented his belief that Afro-Americans and immigrants should be integrated into urban America mostly as a result of their own voluntary efforts. In particular, effective mechanisms of social control among blacks and foreigners were those based upon the internal discipline imposed by the minority group and internalized by by the individual rather than a result of efforts by a dominant group to force acquiescence to a particular style of life deemed to be beneficial. Park's liberal vision of social control, which was to be achieved through education and self-help within the community, contradicted the programmes of racists and Americanizers who argued that both the black community and the immigrants required externally imposed programmes to enforce conformity to a prescribed way of life.

THREE MODELS OF SOCIAL CHANGE

Park presented three models of social change, each of which has implications for his analysis of race and ethnic relations and his prognosis of the future of minorities. The first model emphasizes the process of social conflict and is characterized by the rational adjustment of activities among a plurality of groups on the basis of negotiation and the reconciliation of conflicting interests. Communication between contentious groups, either through the mass media, art, and literature or within the framework of political institutions such as elections, is the activity that typifies this mode of social change. The public, consisting of a variety of self-interested groups, is the form of association exemplifying this model.

Park's hope for the future rested with the efforts of a 'democratic public' to alter its own destiny on the basis of public opinion, education, and socially controlled conflict. He held this view despite his acknowledgement that politics, social reform, and planning often resulted in unanticipated and undesired outcomes because they are as subject to the limitations imposed by human nature as they are to the resistance of aggrieved groups.[4]

Fisher and Strauss draw attention to the connection between Park's vision of 'a democratic public' and the incorporation of minorities into the mainstream of American life. 'This public', they note,

> required the supportive social conditions and a level of general education that enabled communication over what provincial peoples might see as insuperable barriers ... The problem of democracy was: under what conditions would who be able to speak to whom? The difficulties of the American attempt to build a variable nation-state were linked to the reality that so many barriers to communication existed. Racial and ethnic groupings constituted the foremost barriers.
>
> (Fisher and Strauss 1979: 466)

Park's second model of social change is based upon collective behaviour and, more specifically, the transformation of social unrest into crowds or into social movements which generate leadership and culminate in new social institutions. This second model is based upon the initially irrational response of isolated, socially disconnected individuals to a collective unease brought about by a dimly perceived deficiency in the environment. The religious sect, for example, represents the efforts of people to adapt their religious beliefs and their church to a new environment.

The Montgomery bus boycott organized by Martin Luther King and the emergent Southern Christian Leadership Conference is one example of how relatively unorganized protest may be transformed into a coherent social movement capable of mobilizing the energy of an oppressed group, of jogging the sensibilities of a minority of liberal whites, and eventually bringing about significant changes in racial stratification in the American South.

Other examples of the collective behaviour model of social change are the 'ghetto revolts' in major American cities during the

1960s and the related rise of the Black Muslims under the leadership of Muhammed Ali and Malcolm X at about this same time. In both of these instances, angry groups of Afro-Americans were able to call attention to what they perceived to be the inequities of racial stratification in America through popular appeals made without benefit of great financial resources or access to the usual avenues of political change.

As already pointed out in Chapter Two, Park departed from the conventional wisdom of many European social theorists and took an optimistic view of the creative potential of crowds rather than emphasizing their mindless, destructive capabilities. Although he does not himself suggest it, this second model of social change based upon collective behaviour is the poor man's alternative to social change based upon publics and access to resources such as the mass media, influence, and political organization. Park did not advocate ghetto revolt as a way of bringing about social equality. None the less, his second model of change remains a useful way of understanding how aggrieved groups that are relatively impoverished may use numbers and disruption as weapons to protest and change existing social arrangements.

Park's third model of social change is based upon cyclical processes, such as a race relations cycle or a 'natural history', in which a series of transformations occur as a result of the properties inherent in phenomena or events or on the basis of 'social forces'. Since social forces are treated as analytically separable from conscious human volition, the outcome of this type of social change is not directly effected by the values or desires of individuals and groups.

The 'social forces' model is the most metaphysical and least persuasive model of change. It contradicts Park's own account of cognizant individuals directing their activities in a cultural order. Instead, this model of unpremeditated change is most suitable when used to describe ecological processes such as that of succession and dominance. It is of less interest as a model of specifically *social* processes.

The numerous criticisms of the race relations cycle highlight the deficiencies of this model of social change (Cox (1948) 1970; Lyman 1973; Persons 1987; Smith 1988).

FLIES IN THE BUTTERMILK

In order to set out the basic features of a viable approach to the study of race and ethnicity which builds upon the strengths of Park's contributions, it is now necessary to consider the problematic features of his approach. By and large, objections revolve around Park's undue emphasis upon the volitional elements in group life and his unwillingness to acknowledge the constraints inherent in the environment in which individuals and groups construct their activities and in which cultures flourish, are transformed, and disappear.

STATUS GROUPS WITHOUT SOCIAL CLASSES

Park considered status groups, such as racial and ethnic minorities and occupational groupings, to be more important than social classes in the analysis of collective action.[5] But relegating social class to the periphery of sociological investigation leads Park to overlook the fragmentation of status groups along the dimension of social class. The consequence of such neglect was to overestimate social cohesion and social consciousness among minority group members.

Thus, for example, Park predicted that an embryonic, aspiring black middle class would provide leadership among Afro-Americans. Moreover, he assumed that the 'bi-racial organization' of businessmen and professionals would eventually predispose members of different racial groups to act together on the basis of a shared world-view stemming from similarities in education, occupation, and life-styles.

In his monograph *Black Bourgeoisie* published in 1957, Park's student E. Franklin Frazier studied the black middle class identified earlier by Drake and Cayton in their study of Chicago. Frazier established that the black middle class was fundamentally different from the white middle class because it had no foundation in the larger American economy and therefore exercised power and influence only on the basis of holding strategic positions in segregated institutions within the Afro-American community. This resulted in the emergence of an opportunistic middle class who claimed to speak for the black community as a whole but whose retention of power was dependent upon residential segregation and real and symbolic separation rather than integration into mainstream American life.

Frazier's study suggested differentiating members of the black community along the line of social classes rather than assuming that race obliterated differences within this population. Moreover, he challenged Park's assumption that the black middle class would be more or less equivalent to its white counterpart in a bi-racially organized society. Finally, Frazier's study noted the ways in which the different constituencies of white and black leaders effected the reconciliation of an interest in retaining power with the adequate representation of the objectives of their supporters.

It is also clear that Park overlooked the extent to which class influenced both the kinds of situations in which different class strata within each racial group experience each other and the variety of meanings within each racial group brought into play in their resolution. Thus, for example, in their comparison of upper-class blacks who comprise 5 per cent of Bronzeville's population and lower-class blacks making up 65 per cent of this group, Drake and Cayton pointed out that the former, in 'carrying the responsibilities of the major Negro institutions', are likely to find themselves 'cooperating with sympathetic and liberal whites who give them financial and moral support' such that 'this Negro upper class becomes symbolic of racial potentialities'. However, the lower social classes, '[n]ot alone by choice but tossed by the deep economic tides of the modern world', are 'pressed and moulded by an unusually indifferent and occasionally unkind white world' (Drake and Cayton (1945) 1962: 522-3).

The puzzle of where the balance between status interests and class interests lies, both from the point of view of the sociologist and from the point of view of those being studied, underlies the often vitriolic debate about the significance of class strata among both Afro-Americans in the United States and Afro-Caribbeans in Great Britain today. It also lies behind the quarrel about the relative importance of cultural differences based upon country of origin among 'non-whites' or 'blacks' in the USA and Britain (Modood 1988).

Thus, for example, the American sociologist William Julius Wilson suggests that in general the influence of race on minority class stratification has decreased and 'class takes on greater importance in determining the life chances of minority individuals'. Wilson points out that

> whether one focuses on the way race relations was structured by the system of production or the polity or both, racial oppression (ranging from the exploitation of black labour by the business class to the elimination of black competition for economic, social and political resources by the white masses) was a characteristic and important phenomenon in both the pre-industrial and industrial periods of American race relations.
>
> (Wilson 1978: 149)

He goes on to assert that in the 'modern industrial period', beginning after the Second World War, the significance of race has yielded its pre-eminence to social class. 'As race declined in importance in the economic sector,' observes Wilson, 'the Negro class structure became more differentiated and black life chances became increasingly a consequence of class affiliation' (Wilson ibid.: 153).

Wilson's argument is not that race is insignificant in influencing the life chances, of Afro-Americans but that the effect of race upon education, job placement, and occupational mobility has declined. He is careful to note the possibility of white resistance in eroding such hard-won gains in the future.

The problem, in Park's day as now, is to differentiate between those aspects of living in which being black limits choice, diminishes life chances and constitutes a disability shared by all blacks from situations in which the differential distribution of resources, such as wealth, education, and market position, means that at least for some members of the group, race is no longer the predominant constraint upon choice and range of available options. For example, the *de jure* abolition of restrictive covenants in northern cities in the USA as a result of the 1968 Civil Rights Act resulted in middle-class blacks being able to exercise the option of living in suburbs even in the face of the resistance of their white residents.

Park had little more to say about the effects of the formation of social classes among Afro-Americans than his observations concerning the impact of the new middle class in cities. Surprisingly, in an era punctuated by conflict between labour and big business, the socialist revolution in Russia, discussion of the ideals of socialism and of the welfare state, Park was relatively silent about the importance of social class divisions among and between native-born American whites and immigrants, as well as Afro-Americans.

Clearly for Park the barriers of race and, to a lesser extent, of ethnicity were the crucial factors dividing Americans from one another, inhibiting communication, and threatening the durability of democracy in urban America. His use of the concepts of class and class conflict is incidental to his analyses in which cultural conflict between status groups predominates.[6]

SOCIAL CONFLICT WITHOUT TEARS AND SOCIAL CONTROL WITHOUT FORCE

According to Park, in most cases, the resolution of social conflict involves negotiation and adjustment through the process of communication. He suggested that there are few conflicts between groups that cannot be solved through greater efforts by members to scrutinize their own position and to better understand their opponent's point of view. Thus, for example, when Park dealt with industrial disputes he, like Durkheim, found the source of conflict in a lack of understanding between workers and management. He concluded that 'The ills from which civilisation is suffering are not fundamentally political; they are cultural ills that can be cured not by legislation but by concert, collective action and leadership.' He endorsed the industrial psychologist Elton Mayo's suggestion that what was needed was an 'administrative élite' trained to improve 'worker morale' (Park (1934c) 1955: 299).

Park's vision of the peaceful, rational nature of social conflict was also sustained in his belief in the efficacy of communication and personal friendship in undermining racial antagonism (Park (1939a) 1950).

Park's interpretation of social conflict and his relative lack of interest in the concepts of power and of force are inherent in his view of social control and in his overall perspective on group life. As already noted in Chapter Two, Park believed that understanding and self-restraint are the bonds that hold groups and society together. He also argued that a shared heritage and language – both of which are aspects of culture – rather than force and coercion lead people to identify with the interest of the group or the society as a whole, rather than to pursue unrestrained self-interest or self-expression.

In short, Park's imagery of the co-operative nature of individuals and the consensual basis of society recognized no necessity for coercion, force, and the predominance of formal mechanisms of social control in the analysis of social life. This view underlies his analysis of social conflict.

In addition, Park's interest in the symbolic nature of group life led him to examine the point of view of individuals and social groups and to pay less attention than warranted to the constraints within which subjective orientations are expressed and social processes unfold. Park did not wish to reduce historical events to a social psychology of inter-subjective orientations. However, he sometimes seemed to forget that slavery, discrimination, and segregation stand for relationships which consist of more than just the subjective orientations of groups towards one another.

This bias in the direction of social-psychological reductionism – which Park hoped to avoid – also led him to overestimate the role of communication and empathy in mitigating racial injustice. It is a major element in his romantic vision of what Vidich and Lyman identify as a 'moral brotherhood' (Vidich and Lyman 1985: 195-208).

Finally, Park's interpretation of social control as essentially self-control emphasized the volitional aspects of action and deflected interest away from the limitations arising from the differential distribution of resources, and in particular economic and political power. For example, Park emphasized social ritual and etiquette rather than legislation – such as the Black Codes and physical abuse, including torture and death – in ensuring compliance with the requirements of chattel slavery. In a similar way, a natural history approach to the dispersion and concentration of minorities neglected the role of restricted covenants and unlawful methods of harassment in ensuring residential segregation in cities (Park (1929a) 1952).

SOCIAL PROCESS WITHOUT SOCIAL STRUCTURE

Some social critics have argued that Park's lack of interest in social class, and in the role of power and force in influencing race and

63

ethnic relations, is an inevitable consequence of the omission of a concept of social structure from his general perspective (Gordon 1958; Cox (1948) 1970; Berger and Luckmann 1966; Collins and Makowsky 1972; Smith 1988). In order to evaluate such criticism, it is necessary, first, to explore the theoretical grounds for Park's preference for concepts based upon social process rather than social structure and, second, to indicate how scholars working from *within* the Chicago school tradition reformulated Park's ideas in order to take social class and political and economic power into account.

Overall, Park's perspective and method are antagonistic to the idea that group life can be conceived of in the orderly and predictable way that the concept of a social structure implies. This is so for the following reasons. First, the actor's definition of the situation and his plan of action are in some sense always tentative and emergent since they are contingent upon, among other things, social interaction – real or imagined – which can never itself be predetermined. Second, the process of interpretation enables people to behave in routine and conventional ways as well as in novel and unexpected ways. Third, it cannot be assumed that notions of social reality are the same for individuals and groups even if they share the same 'objective' social location. According to this view, group life consists of 'the recurrent adjustment and cooperation of associated persons through which action patterns of all kinds are formed, sustained, modified, evaded, or contravened' so that what sociologists think of as society 'might best be regarded as an ongoing process, a *becoming*, rather than a being' (Shibutani 1961: 174; emphasis is his. See also Chapter Two, above). The passage of time and changes in flow of situations confronted by actors require analytical concepts and a set of procedures sensitive to shifts in the symbolic nature of group life.

Structural analysis tends to be a substitute for the difficult task of describing the actual process in which action is constructed by purposeful individuals and groups in historically specific settings. Moreover, this approach often over-emphasizes what is common to social phenomena and neglects what is significant and historically unique or culturally specific to them.

Park's depiction of the role of communication and culture in the construction of action makes it incompatible with any theoretical scheme or methodological procedure which explains behaviour on the basis of 'variables' which are lodged outside the actor or group in a notional social structure or a social system and which, it is suggested, 'produce' behaviour (Blumer (1956) 1969: 127-30). Therefore, for example, Park's work is antagonistic to the type of structural analyses advocated by scholars such as Talcott Parsons and Seymour Martin Lipset in which a 'cultural system' in the guise of institutionalized norms and values is presumed to underlie regularized patterns of behaviour that constitute social structure (Parsons 1951; Lipset 1976).

Writing from within the tradition established by Park, Herbert Blumer responded to Park's neglect of the effect of political power upon the fate of racial minorities by including it in his own scheme of interpretation. Park, it should be recalled, was sceptical about the efficacy of the government to effect changes in attitudes and morality regarding racial stratification. Blumer, on the other hand, while taking into account all of the features of race relations emphasized by Park, such as the process of collective definitions inherent in the history and culture of social groups, also included in his discussion the role of the state and especially its ability to enforce legislation despite the resistance of dominant groups. Race relations, argued Blumer, are influenced by the inter-subjective orientations of individuals and groups which must themselves always be considered in the context of objective social conditions, including the activities of government and political interest groups (Blumer 1955; 1958; Blumer and Duster 1980). By way of illustration, in an essay published in 1965, Blumer argued that the federal government in the USA, acting in the national interest, might launch a 'massive attack' 'to improve the economic and community position of the urban Negro' (Blumer 1965a: 334). Similarly, in an essay on the effects of industrialization, he observed that the role of the state was crucial in determining change in any prevailing racial order (Blumer 1965b).

Howard Becker, a student of both Hughes and Blumer, although himself not concerned with race relations, extended the Chicago school perspective, through his discussion of 'labelling theory', to demonstrate explicitly how the differential distribution of power between social groups influences both existing and emergent definitions of the situation and the activities of relatively disadvantaged groups within the society to whose activities these definitions and their attendant sanctions are applied (Becker (1963) 1966; 1964; 1971).

Other scholars working within the Chicago school tradition have added social class and social structure to the battery of concepts used in their discussion of race relations.

There is a fundamental difference between those sociologists working from within the Chicago school tradition and most influenced by Blumer, and those Chicago sociologists more influenced by another of Park's students, Everett Hughes. This divergence lies in the reluctance of the former to adopt any set of concepts or set of procedures which relies upon the static notion of social structure implicit in 'variable analysis' or the 'social systems' approach (Blumer (1956) 1969). Blumer, like Park, stressed the uncertainties inherent in social relationships because these are influenced by unpredictable historical events as well as by the personal histories of individuals which give rise to idiosyncratic interpretations of the social world. Following Park, Blumer cautioned against any form of sociological determinism. He subscribed to Park's view that 'The world is an open one, and the ceaseless round of group encounters and conflicts demonstrates as much' (Fisher and Strauss 1979: 478).

On the other hand, Hughes and Morris Janowitz, among others, depict social life as an essentially orderly set of social arrangements which exist almost apart from human volition. For example, Hughes's discussion of institutions as 'going concerns' shares the functionalist fallacy of reifying social relationships (Hughes (1962) 1971: 52-64).

In some respects, Erving Goffman, also trained at Chicago, bridges the interrelated positions of Park/Blumer and Park/ Hughes. Goffman placed the volitional, interpretive elements involved in the construction of action in the 'self'. His concept is of an idiosyncratic self which reflects a person's life experience as well as the larger culture in which he participates. The self, according to Goffman, is inventive and not only responds to the expectations inherent in 'interactional rules' or in the wishes and beliefs of powerful others, but is also able to manipulate elements in its environment in order to satisfy personal goals *despite* the constraints social institutions present (Goffman (1961) 1968).

In a parallel way, Goffman applied the concepts of 'stigma' and

66

'social identity' to race relations and demonstrated the limitations imposed by existing images and conventional patterns of interaction between groups as well as the opportunities subordinate groups have to avoid or to change some features of ongoing social relationships.

Stigma, noted Goffman, refers to 'an attribute', like colour, 'that is deeply discrediting' such that 'an individual who might have been received easily in ordinary social intercourse possesses a trait that can obtrude itself upon attention and turn those of us whom he meets away from him, breaking the claim that his other attributes have upon us' (Goffman 1963: 5). As Park had pointed out earlier, the external mark of colour results in exclusion and segregation such that the Japanese, Chinese, and blacks cannot move among Americans with the same freedom as members of other white minority groups (Park (1917) 1950: 228).

The set of 'disabling' attributes attached to Afro-Americans constitutes a definition of the situation which sets the parameters for interaction between themselves and whites. Ideologies arise to explain putative inferiority and 'exclusion which limits life chances' for those bearing 'the tribal stigma of race'. However, the stigmatized individual or group, like Goffman's self, is not a passive victim of outside forces or variables. Instead, Goffman introduces ideas about 'information control' and 'group alignment and ego identity' which suggest the ways in which those stigmatized may manipulate dominant groups and use their spoiled identity to their best advantage.

Goffman's investigation of stigma in conjunction with his work on 'total institutions', however, contradicts Park's overly optimistic view of the role of human volition and group effort in overcoming the limitations upon human freedom that ongoing institutional arrangements necessarily impose. Goffman identified 'total institutions' as settings in which individuals live out their daily round of activities segregated from the outside world and to which inmates are confined with or without their own consent. Rules govern activities and limit the types of permissible interaction among inmates and between inmates and staff. The use of regulations and prohibitions enables staff to standardize behaviour and to mould a uniform type of inmate out of the diverse personalities who initially come to live within the institution's confines. Total institutions restrain but do not prevent the emergence of particular clandestine types of selves more attuned to the outside world and at odds with the requirements of the institution (Goffman (1961) 1968: 13-115).

Although Goffman does not make this point explicitly, total institutions, such as mental hospitals and prisons, are extreme versions of the whole range of bureaucratic organizations that predominate in urban industrial societies. Bureaucracies co-ordinate and coerce individuals to act collectively in order to complete a range of complex, interrelated tasks.

Park was clear about the beneficial effects of particularistic, minority group cultures and parochial group affiliations in enhancing individual self-esteem, social cohesion, and group morale. He was less explicit about how bureaucratic organization undermines these and re-creates the need for particularistic cultures and parochial group affiliations in urban societies.

CONCLUSION

Park's relative lack of interest in social class and social structure, and in the role of power in influencing race and ethnic relations, stemmed from his emphasis upon the volitional aspects of human group life. It resulted in his unwillingness to consider the constraints which frustrate the realization of individual wants and which influence the ways in which social processes unfold. The problem intrinsic to the analysis of race relations is to find the balance between imposed constraints, on the one hand, and self-generated possibilities, on the other.

Park's students resolved this problem of balance in a variety of ways. Clearly, however, as Blumer's work suggests, a scheme of interpretation which emphasizes the subjective features of action and social processes, rather than social structures of 'variables', need not result in studies that ignore the macroscopic character of group life.

Chapter Four

THE EMERGENCE OF AN
ETHNOGRAPHIC TRADITION

FIELD-WORK AND HUMAN DOCUMENTS

Every sociological theory generates its own methodology. The significance that Park attributed to the concepts of culture, communication, and social control led him to develop a research methodology that relied upon field-work and the collection of 'human documents' as its mainstays. He fostered a vision of sociology as a kind of urban anthropology.

The concept of culture, which had served the anthropologists Franz Boas, Edward Sapir, W. Pitt Rivers, F. Lowie, and Robert Redfield so well in their investigations of small, non-industrial, agricultural societies, recommended itself as a useful approach to the study of 'strangers', such as immigrants and Afro-Americans living in cities in the United States but perceived to be on the margin of mainstream American society. In addition, as the sociologist Norbert Wiley points out, the 'interlocking concepts, culture, symbol, self and interaction' resulted in 'an important alliance between cultural anthropology, at least in its ascendant Boasian variety, and the pragmatic, interactive sociology', and differentiated social science from biologically rooted explanations of social life (Wiley 1986:27).

Case-studies investigating 'man in his habitat and under the conditions in which he actually lives' (Park (1929b) 1952: 75) had already been used by Jane Addams, Edith Abbott, and Sophinisba Breckenridge in the Hull House papers documenting immigrant life in Chicago and published as early as 1908. Accounts of group life based upon observation also continued the plan for social research initiated by Park's friend and colleague at the University of Chicago, W. I. Thomas.

69

Park summarized his point of view in his often quoted introduction to St Clair Drake and Horace Cayton's study, *Black Metropolis* – an investigation which itself vindicated the research strategy Park proposed (Drake and Cayton (1945) 1962). Park wrote:

> Anthropology, the science of man, has been mainly concerned up to the present with the study of primitive peoples. But civilized man is quite as interesting an object of investigation, and at the same time, his life is more open to observation and study. Urban life and culture are more varied, subtle, and complicated, but the fundamental motives are in both instances the same. The same patient methods of observation which anthropologists like Boas and Lowie have expended on the study of the life and manners of the North American Indian might be even more fruitfully employed in the investigation of the customs, beliefs, social practices, and general conceptions of life prevalent in Little Italy on the lower North Side of Chicago, or in recording the more sophisticated folkways of the inhabitants of Greenwich Village and the neighbourhood of Washington Square, New York.
>
> (Park (1915) 1952: 15)

'Classic Chicago' fostered a special style of 'sociological ethnography' whose major emphasis was upon 'actually getting out and observing life as it is going on' (Herbert Blumer quoted in Lofland 1980:261). Park's interest in experience and the subjective point of view of the actor was reflected in the development of this type of research and the analysis of 'human documents' (discussed later). Both ethnography and the analysis of human documents followed from his perspective on the construction of collective action (discussed in Chapter Two).

'Sociological ethnography' refers to the systematic description of the experience of a social group as this unfolds in its natural setting. It includes accounts of the group's activities, its world-view – especially as this is conveyed through its language and imagery and its artefacts; in other words, sociological ethnography is a description of collective action and group culture in a specific setting.

Participant observation is the predominant research technique used by sociological ethnographers. It requires that the investigator participate in the activities of the group under study, either in the role of researcher or in some disguised role. Participant observation facilitates both understanding events from the point of view of members of the group and constructing explanations that take into account the shared understandings around which their action is organized.

Park assumed that within the same society, even a society in which people share a common language and participate in the same major institutional arrangements, such as the United States, there are smaller, often overlapping, culture-bearing groups organized around parochial commitments, shared life chances, or shared ethnic and racial origins. In Chicago, participant observation enabled Park and his students to enter into the different social worlds of groups as culturally distinct from one another as hobos living in Hobohemia, Jewish immigrants on Maxwell Street, selling 'odd sizes of shoes long out of style ... copper kettles for brewing beer ... second hand pants', and Afro-Americans from the rural South seeking a better life for themselves in northern cities (Wirth (1928) 1956: 231-40). Later sociologists working within this tradition emphasize the necessity of getting at 'collective definitions' as these influence the construction of action within and between different culture-bearing groups (Blumer and Duster 1980; see also Chapter Seven).[1]

In his argument in favour of field-work, Herbert Blumer called attention to the methodological consequences of acknowledging that the same 'objective' empirical world may have a variety of different meanings for different social groups within the same community. Blumer noted that there is a 'persistent tendency of human beings in their collective life to build up separate worlds, marked by an operating milieu of different life situations and conceptions for handling these situations'. He concluded that in order to study group life adequately 'one has to know these worlds and to know the worlds one has to examine them closely. No theorising, however ingenious, and no observation of scientific protocol, however meticulous, are substitutes for developing a familiarity with what is actually going on in the sphere of life under study' (Blumer 1969: 38-9).

The adequacy of the interpretations resulting from participant observation depend upon the ethnographer's skill in 'taking the role of the other'. Taking the role of the other, which is inherent in both the logic of field-work and the analysis of human documents, is also pivotal to Mead's social behaviourism and Park's perspective on the construction of collective action (see Chapter Two). Taking the role of the other supposes that the sociologist, like any other human being, is able to empathize with those with whom he interacts despite differences in age, education, social class, ethnicity, or experience.[2]

Moreover, informed by the pragmatic perspective on scientific knowledge discussed below, advocates of field-work insist that what passes for sociological 'truth' must always be tested by recourse to 'the world of brute fact' and 'to the beliefs of others that are not of its own making' (Mills 1966:160). Sociological findings must be subjected to empirical negation or what Karl Popper calls 'falsification' (Popper 1957).

Field-work supports the view that knowledge is available to the sociologist in the same way that it is available to the ordinary actor, that is, on the basis of trying out one's ideas in the world. The difference between the sociological attitude and that of the ordinary actor hinges on the first being committed to having his images of the social world changed in the process of social interaction, while the ordinary actor does not usually strive for evidence of disconfirmation of his view of the world. For example, religious beliefs and ideologies are not usually subject to attempts at falsification.

A second major contribution of the Chicago scholars to the development of sociological method was to encourage the collection and analysis of 'human documents'. Human documents are sometimes called 'life history materials'. These consist of 'any sort of record or document ... which tend to throw light on the subjective behaviour of individuals or of groups'. Human documents vary from being 'a mere record of obvious and external events to that of a confession' (Park (1931a) 1955: 256-8). Court hearings, case histories of social agencies, sermons, political party tracts, newspapers, biographies, letters, and autobiographies are different types of human documents. However, Park did suggest that the collection of materials revealing the subjective life of the actor from his own point of view, such as autobiographies and letters, were more useful than biographies, social agency records, and other material that presented the actor's subjective life from the point of view of an outside investigator.

Park cited William James's essay, 'A certain blindness in human beings' and his Gifford lectures, *The Varieties of Religious Experience*, as 'among the earliest perhaps the very first attempts to study attitudes on the basis of personal documents' (James (1899) 1958; (1902) 1961; Park (1934b) 1950). The 'blindness in human beings' to which James referred 'is the blindness with which we are afflicted in regard to the feelings of creatures and people different from ourselves'. James went on to note that every human being is concerned with his own 'vital secrets' and treats others with neither the curiosity nor the sympathy they deserve. 'Hence,' concluded James, 'the stupidity and injustice of our opinions, so far as they deal with the significance of alien lives' or the 'value of other persons' conditions or ideals' (James (1899) 1958: 149). Park endorsed James's 'conception of human nature and knowledge' and its usefulness for studies of people 'who live, to be sure, within the political boundaries of the United States but nevertheless on the margins of our culture' (Park (1934b) 1950: 67).

Human documents were used by Thomas and Znaniecki in their study *The Polish Peasant in Europe and America* (Thomas and Znaniecki 1918-20) and subsequently used by Park in *Old World Traits Transplanted* (Park and Miller (1921) 1969) and *The Immigrant Press and Its Control* (Park (1922) 1970). Park also collected letters and newspaper clippings which were written before and after the emancipation of slaves in 1865, and which revealed attitudes of white Southerners and Afro-Americans towards slavery and freedom (Park and Washington 1922).

Park's monograph *The Immigrant Press and Its Control*, written with the help of Winifred Raushenbush, is based primarily on one sort of human document, namely, newspapers (Park (1922) 1970). Park studied the foreign-language press in relation to the process of 'Americanization' among immigrants. He used advertisements in the press to gain insight into the institutional arrangements of ethnic enclaves. For example, he reprinted an advertisement that revealed attitudes towards marriage from the *Jewish Morning Journal*, written in Yiddish, and published in New York. Under the heading 'MARRIAGE WANTED', it reads: 'Wanted – A lovely rabbi's or scholar's daughter. She must be tall and young, sympathetic, religious, idealistic, and interested in Zionism and Jewish interests....Money is not required and a Lithuanian girl is preferred ...' (Park (1922) 1970: 125).

Park also used the foreign-language press as a way of discovering the 'vital secrets' mentioned by James. For example, he collected items from the Japanese press to illustrate 'the new race consciousness' among the Japanese and their bitter feelings towards white native-born Americans. Among the documents cited are an excerpt from the *Tacoma Japanese Times* published in Washington in which the writer noted that 'in general, the Japanese are not liked in America by Americans. This natural dislike finds expression in the unjust and oppressive anti-Japanese movements. To complain of the injustice of the Americans in granting to Europeans the right to naturalisation and refusing the same right to Japanese is futile. Americans don't like us and are saying so' (Park 1922) 1970: 162).

Unfortunately, neither *Old World Traits Transplanted* nor *The Immigrant Press and Its Control* includes a methodological note. Therefore, the scope and representativeness of the human documents presented remains a question.

The analysis of human documents required the investigation of historical events and cultural contexts that are sources of experience and the subjective world of meaning. For example, Park believed that the sociologist must have a sense of the immigrant's past in order to appreciate his present situation as this is revealed in human documents. With this in mind, he suggested that the despondence expressed in immigrant autobiography stemmed from the immigrant's futile efforts to re-establish his status in urban America on the basis of rural peasant cultural values left behind in his country of origin. Thus, an immigrant compared 'the pride with which my breast had heaved as a "learned man" among my kindred' in Europe with his mortification in the United States 'which did not seem to take immediate notice of my worth' (A. M. Rihbany, *A Far Journey*, cited in Park and Miller (1921) 1969: 54).

Park explained the popularity of the immigrant press itself in terms of the immigrants' prior European experience. For example, he explained the significance of the widely subscribed to socialist Yiddish press as a result of the emergence of a Jewish urban proletariat as well as opportunities available for learning in the United States. Unlike in Europe, 'through the medium of the popular press the learning which had been the privilege of the few became the possession of the many.' The Yiddish socialist press, he noted, was primarily 'an instrument of general culture' in which 'the intimate, human, and practical problems of the life of the common man' were aired (Park (1922) 1970: 108-9).

'Subjectivist' sociologies argue that the actor's point of view and the meanings that emerge from the situations he confronts are central to sociological theory and method. The foundation of the social world is the culturally transmitted imagery that members of a group take into account, or create anew, in their everyday lives. The media are a particularly important source of symbolic meaning.

Park, Thomas, and like-minded sociologists at Chicago generated research strategies that aimed to discover the culturally transmitted imagery that members of a group take into account, or create anew, in their everyday lives. Not surprisingly, Park rejected the work of his colleague at Chicago, the behaviourist psychologist L. L. Thurstone, on the grounds that he attempted 'to apply to the study of human conduct the methods of investigation first employed in the study of animal behaviour'. 'Consciousness', Park noted, differentiates human 'conduct' from non-human animal behaviour and is therefore of crucial import to the description and explanation of social processes (Park (1927) 1955).

Field-work and the analysis of human documents were intended to capture the subjective point of view of the actor and the variety of social realities generated by the processes of social interaction. In particular, participant observation over a long period of time and covering many different situations was conducive to getting at the subjective and symbolic features of group life as these appear, disappear, shift, and change in response to changing events and long-term historical trends.

What makes the Chicago community studies fascinating reading and what gives them stature as sociological studies has as much to do with the preservation of the experience and point of view of the people of Chicago during the first part of the century, as it has to do with theoretical insight, methodological innovations, and the subsequent development of sociology.[3] Well before Studs Turkel (1967) took to recording the experiences and opinions on Division Street, and before oral history projects became fashionable in universities, sociologists at the University of Chicago took to the streets, scanned newspapers and institutional records, recorded interviews, collected letters and diaries, and preserved for all who were interested a social history, an anthropological field-study, and a sociological interpretation of life and times in the city of Chicago. These activities followed from Park's observation that,

> The city ... is something more than a congeries of individual men and of social conveniences – street buildings, electric lights, tramways, and telephones, etc.; something more, also, than a mere constellation of institutions and administrative devices – courts, hospitals, schools, police and civil function- aries of various sorts. The city is, rather, a state of mind, a body of customs and traditions, and of the organised attitudes and sentiments that inhere in those customs, and are transmitted with this tradition.
>
> (Park (1915) 1952: 13)

Park wanted to understand the dislocations brought about by urbanization, migration, and immigration, with respect to 'the conduct of concrete personalities in specific situations' (Hinkle 1963: 710). In this respect, the work of the Chicago school was similar not only to anthropology but to that of the naturalistic novelists writing at about the same time, such as Theodore Dreiser, Upton Sinclair, Frank Norris, and Richard Wright (Kramer 1966).

Thus far, discussion has concentrated upon field-work and the collection of human documents. These procedures answer to Park's insistence that sociologists take into account the subjective point of view of the actor, the particular culture of a group, and the ethos of a historical period. Yet it is clear from the kinds of questions that Park posed that he sought additional kinds of data about the social world and countenanced other research strat- egies. These, however, were meant to complement, rather than replace, ethnography and the analysis of human documents.

Park's essay, 'The city: suggestions for the investigation of human behaviour in the urban environment', published in 1915, is suggestive of the rich diversity of topics he thought urban sociologists needed to consider (Park (1915) 1952). For example, under the heading 'The city plan', Park asks: 'What are the sources

76

of the city's population?' 'What part of its population growth is normal, i.e., due to excess of births over deaths?' 'What part is due to migration (a) of native stocks? (b) of foreign stocks?' 'What are the outstanding "natural" areas, i.e., areas of population segregation?' 'How is distribution of population within the city area affected by (a) economic interests, i.e., land values? (b) by sentimental interest, race? vocation, etc.?' Under the heading 'The neighbourhood' he asks, 'What part of the population is floating?' 'Of what elements, i.e., races, classes, etc., is this population composed?' 'How many people live in hotels, apartments, and tenements?' 'How many people own their own homes?' 'What proportion of the population consists of nomads, hobos, gypsies?' Under the heading 'Colonies and segregated areas', he lists questions about 'the age, sex and social condition of the people'.

Each of these questions required the collection and analysis of quantitative data. Statistics on land use, land value, population concentration, population movement, and the magnitude and distribution of vital statistics were recorded and used to chart changes in the growth, land use, and patterns of activities within and between cities.

Park also wanted sociologists to find out about the history of the city and of its various neighbourhoods. To this end he posed questions such as 'What is there in the subconsciousness in the forgotten or dimly remembered experiences of this neighbourhood which determines its sentiments and attitudes?'

However, as previously noted, statistical data and historical documentation are significant for Park because they contribute to a description and explanation of the cultural order. Information about population and neighbourhood history were sought in the context of his overriding concern with questions about residents' sentiments, attitudes, and doctrines, what they regarded as fact, and what they regarded as news, their models of behaviour and whether these were endogamous or exogenous to the group, social ritual, leadership, interests, and methods of social control.

Similarly, in an article outlining the research requirements for a survey of race relations on the Pacific Coast, Park included the collection of human documents consisting of 'letters, narratives of personal experiences, newspaper clippings, detailed descriptions of individuals' cases, i.e., case histories, autobiographical materials and life histories' *as well as* 'official reports, monograph studies, statistics' and interviews 'recorded as far as possible in the language' and reflecting 'the accent and emphasis of the person interviewed'. He also required information 'to suggest the general social and historical setting'.

Park concluded that his proposed survey of race relations

> requires the materials that a historian might want, fifty or a hundred years hence, if he were to give a lively, intimate and authentic picture of the relations of the immigrant races and the native population of the present day. Such a picture would tell us not merely what took place, but how the people felt about the matter, and why.
>
> (Park (1923c) 1950: 158-65)

CRITICS' CHOICE: ISSUES OF METHODOLOGY

Park viewed sociology as an empirical science. He promoted the development of a perspective and methodology which aimed to investigate ongoing group life as this could be observed through field-work and in the analysis of human documents. The value of sociological explanations was related to the extent to which these captured the experience and expressed the perceptions of people. Yet few of Park's critics have applied themselves to the task of evaluating his work and that of the Chicago school with respect to their success in attaining verifiable knowledge about the empirical world through the development of those methods and the analytical concepts to which they correspond. Instead, criticism of Park and the style of social research originating at Chicago tends to be organized around alleged deficiencies which are themselves considered to be the converse of the strengths of sociological holism and its complementary methodology.

First, the Chicago school studies are thought to lack both historical and comparative dimensions. Second, reminiscent of the earlier criticism of Karl Mannheim, their approach is believed to have resulted in studies which are trivial because they failed to locate social phenomena with respect to American society as a whole (Mannheim (1932) 1953; Mills (1941) 1963; Friedrichs 1970; Gouldner 1971: 440-5; Reynolds and Reynolds 1970; Schwendinger and Schwendinger 1974; Colfax and Roach 1971; Zeitlin 1973).

Such complaints are not crucial to an evaluation of Park and the Chicago school because they are either based on a conception of sociological theory and research which was not shared by scholars in the Chicago school tradition or they are based upon misconstrued notions of this tradition. None the less, this section on the issues which Park's style of social research raises will begin with a brief discussion of these old complaints. Discussion will then move on to more critical questions arising from the methods developed at Chicago among those who agree that these constitute acceptable sociological practice.

Comment upon the use of qualitative as opposed to quantitative techniques in sociology is omitted from discussion for two reasons. First, because this would require extensive examination of quantitative procedures and would therefore shift the focus of analysis from the task of evaluating the research strategy developed at Chicago with regard to its own criteria of methodological adequacy. Second, because there are already numerous discussions of this broad area of debate – many of them excellent (Blumer 1939; 1969; Becker 1971; Denzin 1978; Bulmer 1977; Shipman 1988).

A review of the old complaints

Lack of a historical dimension

The alleged ahistoricity of Park's work and that of the Chicago school has already been disclaimed (see Chapter Two). It was pointed out that, far from eschewing the study of past events, Park believed that history made a group's style of life, institutions, and beliefs intelligible in the same way that biography renders an individual's actions and world-views understandable. Thus, for example, both *Old World Traits Transplanted* and *The Immigrant Press and Its Control,* following the precedent set in Thomas's and Znaniecki's *The Polish Peasant in Europe and America,* analyse the immigrant and his community in American cities in the context of his rural life in his country of origin (Thomas and Znaniecki 1918-20; Park and Miller (1921) 1969; Park (1922) 1970).

Similarly, Pauline Young's study, *The Pilgrims of Russian-Town,* traces the Molokan community in Los Angeles at the turn of this century back to its emergence as a sect in Russia during the fifteenth century. Young locates the origin and growth of Molokan institutions, such as the 'brotherhood' and the family, in the oppressive Russian rural hinterland. She argues that the historical experience of centuries of adversity remains living memory for older members of the community now relocated in the United States. Young, therefore, is able effectively to depict the changes in the brotherhood and the family, and the tensions that beset the community, and in particular, intergenerational conflict in terms of the community's transition from a hierarchical, rural, religious society to a democratic, urban, secular one (Young 1932).

Lack of a comparative dimension

Park appreciated the usefulness of comparison. Written in conjunction with Booker T. Washington, *The Man Farthest Down* compared the poorer peasants and working classes in Europe with black agricultural workers in the rural South. Their purpose, claimed the authors, was to 'get first-hand information about the European'. as distinguished from the American 'race problem' (Washington and Park 1912: 3-20). In addition, both *Old World Traits Transplanted* and *The Immigrant Press and Its Control* include comparisons between immigrant communities and social institutions in America (Park and Miller (1921) 1969; Park (1922) 1970). Similarly, in his essay, 'The city as a social laboratory', Park suggested that research findings in the city of Chicago would offer insights into urban processes as these occurred in other cities throughout the United States (Park (1929b) 1952: 73-87). His colleague Ernest Burgess's 'concentric zone' theory was intended to be a description and explanation of city growth patterns and is perhaps the most well-known outcome of efforts to construct a comparative urban sociology (Burgess (1924) 1967).

Park also encouraged comparative analysis in the work of his students. For example, in his introduction to Charles Johnson's *Shadow of the Plantation*, he noted the need for a 'world-wide and comparative study of the cotton plantation not merely as an economic and industrial but as a cultural unit' – 'a comparative study of the actual conditions of the world in which people on the plantation live' (Park (1934b) 1950: 76). His student Edgar Thompson was among those who undertook this task (Thompson 1975). Case studies such as *The Ghetto* (which compares the Jewish ghetto at different points in time and in different historical settings), *The Pilgrims of Russian-Town, Shadow of the Plantation, Black Metropolis, The Negro Family in Chicago, Black Bourgeoisie, The Etiquette of Race Relations, Negroes in Brazil,* and *French Canada in Transition* are themselves units of analysis in the comparative study of race and ethnic relations (Wirth (1928) 1956; Young 1932; Johnson 1934; Drake and Cayton (1945) 1962; Frazier 1932; 1957; Doyle (1937) 1971; Pierson (1942) 1967; Hughes (1943) 1963).

Absence of a view of American society as a whole

The ethnographic case-study and the analysis of human documents did not result in the description and analysis of unconnected fragments of social reality. Rather, the case-study was intended to be a searchlight which illuminated an area of sociological interest by shedding light on some aspect of it. Thus, Park remarked in his introduction to *The Immigrant Press and Its Control*, 'The immigrant press is interesting from many points of view, but mainly from the light which its history and its content throw upon the inner life of immigrant peoples and their efforts to adjust themselves to a new cultural environment' (Park (1922) 1970: xix).

Park saw himself, and his students and colleagues, as contributing each of their specific case-studies to a larger research effort. 'It was this collective enterprise as a whole, and not its individual parts, that was intended to represent a picture of social reality' (Becker 1971: 67-73).

No concept of social structure

The objection that Park's analysis faltered in the absence of an adequate concept of social structure has already ben discussed at some length in Chapter 3 (pp. 64-8). However, a further example from the race relations literature of the pitfalls inherent in the use of over-simplifying structural analyses is found in the numerous studies that predict the automatic displacement of racial hierarchy by social classes as an outcome of the process of industrialization. Such flawed explanations fail to gather together the strands of culture, history, and leadership which, along with the 'technological imperatives' of industrialization, influence whether stratification based upon race remains or that of social class emerges. As this example suggests, a preference for categories which emphasize social processes need not result in studies that ignore the macroscopic character of group life (Blumer (1956) 1969).

SIGNIFICANT OBJECTIONS

Whose social world is it anyway? Discrepancies between the actor's point of view and that of the sociologist

Park, Thomas, and their students believed that the investigation of any social group required that its culture, and, in particular, the set of common understandings around which collective action is organized, be sought out and incorporated into sociological explanations. Yet studies generated from within this tradition demonstrate that the researcher has often sought to explain social life in terms that are not necessarily those employed by members of the group investigated. Erving Goffman's essay 'The moral career of a mental patient' illustrates the conceptual gap between the sociological investigator and his informants as did earlier studies, such as E. Franklin Frazier's *Black Bourgeoisie* (Frazier 1957; Goffman (1961) 1968).

Holistic theorists, structural functionalist and Marxist alike, are generally unconcerned about the possible discrepancies between the actor's point of view and that of the sociologist. Instead, holistic theorists assume that explanations gleaned from their own professional culture provide them with adequate interpretations of social events. Their explanations, regardless of plausibility or predictability, violate the integrity of the actor by assuming either that he knows not what he does or that the actor's everyday understandings are of less importance than those of the sociologist familiar with the requirements of a notional social system or of a society organized around a particular mode of economic production. Sociological holism considers individual purpose and experience as properties of transcendent entities such as class, status, and functional prerequisite, and is not conducive to those research strategies which aim to discover and take seriously the meanings which people bring to bear on the construction of their activities in specifiable situations, as well as the great range of their behaviour even in similar circumstances.

Among sociologists sympathetic to Park's perspective there is disagreement as to how to treat the actor's conceptual framework and his explanations of the events in which he participates. Jim Thomas cites 'naive realism' as a pitfall displayed in much of the social ethnography originating at Chicago. According to Thomas, naive realism is based upon the assumption that there is a simple relationship between the meanings or explanations of events as these are reported by informants and the empirical social world in which these events are located and which these explanations are presumed to reflect (Thomas 1982: 129; 1983: 479-84).

On the other hand, Aron Cicourel, in his discussion of the methodology appropriate to ethnomethodology, argues that sociological ethnographers must work only within conceptual frameworks which are understood and used by those people whom he studies. Cicourel notes that 'the researcher's model of the actor must rest on interpretive procedures common to both the actor's and the observer's methods for evaluating and generating appropriate courses of action' (Cicourel 1973: 11).

The issue here should not be one of choosing the actor's explanation *or* that of the sociologist. What is of concern is the adequacy of explanations which *disregard* the conceptual framework or explanations offered by the actor in favour of those of the sociologist. Informants may share common understandings which distort the nature of the empirical world – at least from the point of view of what passes for sociological or scientific knowledge. However, these very distortions and 'illusions of the epoch', because they influence the collective activity of the group, must be taken seriously by the social researcher. For example, the belief that culture was learned behaviour rather than biologically transmitted differentiated Park's perspective on race from that of the southern whites among whom he worked and about whom he wrote. Yet, as both he and Booker T. Washington knew, in order to understand race relations in the South it was essential to acknowledge that this misconception about the relationship between race and culture existed and influenced social interaction between the races.

The serious consequences of ignoring the actor's point of view are discussed by the American anthropologist Charles Valentine. Valentine suggests that the 'culture of poverty' concept, as this was developed in the work of E. Franklin Frazier, Oscar Lewis, Nathan Glazer, and Daniel Moynihan, supposes that underclass Afro-Americans were committed to a 'pathological' style of life and sought values which differentiated this group from mainstream white middle-class people. On the basis of his own field-work Valentine offers evidence that members of the black underclass are, by and large, attached to the same images of success and support the same sought after values as those that dominate middle-class America (Valentine 1968; Valentine and Valentine (1970) 1975). He argues that proponents of the concept of the poverty of culture mistake 'situational adaptations' for culture. Situational adaptations consist of behaviour and a style of life based upon what the respondent believes to be a realistic but not necessarily desirable course of action given the opportunities available to him in the situation he confronts. Culture, contends Valentine, stands for a style of life and an identity positively valued and preferred by members of a group. Underclass blacks do not value low educational achievement, unemployment, and family instability.

Subsequent field-studies support Valentine's critique. For example, in Lee Rainwater's investigation of Afro-Americans in St Louis, informants' conversations demonstrate the discrepancy between values such as steady work and a stable family life, and their perception of their probable futures given limited opportunities in education and employment and discrimination in the encompassing white society (Rainwater 1971). In addition, Sandra Wallman's study of South London records diversity within ethnically similar households which renders suspect the concept of a culture of poverty purporting to embrace all members of a particular socio-economic group of shared ethnic origins (Wallman 1984).

The inclusion of techniques of oral history and the analysis of human documents by historians is further evidence of an increasing awareness of the need to take the point of view of the actor seriously (Henretta 1983). For example, Gilbert Osofsky noted that many of the successful attempts of slaves to divert their masters from a particular course of action by playing the fool were subsequently interpreted as evidence of biologically determined stupidity by their owners *and* by historians sympathetic to slavery (Osofsky 1969).

In conclusion, the sociologist must be permitted to develop generic concepts and to construct explanations which transcend the actor's understandings *as long as* these understandings are always taken into account. For example, the analytic utility of a concept such as that of race prejudice as a sense of group position does not hinge upon its acceptability to those to whom it refers (Blumer 1958: 3-7; 1969a: 21-47).

Particularity or generality: the case-study confronts the typology, model, and general law

Advocates of naturalistic inquiry are often required to explore the issue of the level of generality to which explanations in sociology should aspire. Discussion is sometimes couched in terms of a contrast between sociology as fulfilling a 'nomothetic (or generalizing) function' rather than an 'idiographic (or nongeneralizing) function' (Meltzer and Petras 1970: 6).

Naturalistic inquiry, the case-study approach, the analysis of human documents, and a perspective emphasizing the processes of group life argue against a nomothetic function on the grounds that high-level generalizations simplify and distort the complex nature of inter-group relations which are themselves anchored to specific situations and subject to change over time. In opposition to this point of view, it is argued that idiographic explanations run the risk of inducing 'a completely relativistic account of social interaction, in which episodes are elevated to the status of the prime unit of methodological and theoretical interest' (Brittan 1973: 200-2).

The methods of urban ethnography, the analysis of human documents, and the case-study approach represent a set of constraints upon generalization and the construction of very abstract models, typologies, and 'laws' in sociology (Plummer 1983). These constraints are absent in speculations about social systems in which concepts such as social structure are intended to enable the sociologist to locate a particular event or episode with respect to a representative social type. Constraints upon generaliz-ation are also less compelling in the statistical manipulation of quantitative data based upon surveys in which the sociologist himself selects issues and images to which members of a sample respond.

Park did not seem to see any contradiction between the ethnographic style of social research that he advanced and the generalizing objective of sociology that he advocated. He ignored the tension inherent in employing a perspective and method that sought to respect the variety and complexity of group life while at the same time endeavouring to generate more universal explanations of social processes. 'The historian', noted Park, 'is interested in ... generalizations about human nature in so far as they enable him to determine just what actually happened in a given place at a given time. The sociologist is interested in the particular experience only in so far as it enables him to say something about human nature in general, irrespective of any particular time or place.' 'The sociologist', he concluded, 'classifies experience and so explains it' (Park (1924b) 1950: 155).

Park's model of a 'race relations cycle' illustrates very well the inconsistency between capturing the unique characteristics of a social phenomenon and at the same time submerging what is special about this event in the interest of depicting a general or representative type. Consider, for example, the Chicago race riot in 1919. The history of race relations in the United States, the migration of Afro-Americans to Chicago from the rural South and their confrontation with immigrants and native-born white Americans seeking to preserve actual and symbolic 'territory', the role of the press in defining the nature of racial conflict before and during the riot, were all factors that combined to make this event occur when and as it did (Chicago Commission on Race Relations (1922) 1968). The race relations cycle does not enumerate all the conditions that together precipitated this conflict nor was it of very much use in anticipating the events which followed the riot; these were outcomes of often contested public policies and party politics as well as large-scale events, such as economic depression and the Second World War.

Subsequently, Herbert Blumer and Troy Duster have tried to resolve the opposition between the general and the 'particular' in their extension of Park's discussion of race prejudice and its reformulation as a theory of the process of 'collective definition' (Blumer and Duster 1980). For further discussion see Chapter Seven.

The view taken here is that accuracy of sociological reporting should take precedence over concern about the level of generality of sociological concepts and explanations. A careful picture of how social groups make choices, plan and carry out their activities in the actual conditions that they face (which may limit choices), and how this changes over time is basic to sociological research. Such an enterprise is very time consuming. Its advantage is that it has the best chance of capturing the complex, often contradictory ways in which people view the situations that they confront, the gaps which frequently exist between their views and their behaviour, and the inconsistencies in both outlook and activity with respect to the context in which action occurs.

In line with this conclusion, advocates of naturalistic inquiry and those working within the Chicago school tradition do not try to explain social life through the discovery of general laws of behaviour or by constructing universal hypotheses upon which to base predictions about the future. 'The city as a spatial pattern and a moral order', 'the marginal man', 'race prejudice as a sense of group position' are 'sensitising concepts' or 'mini-concepts' (Blumer 1969; Lofland 1970). They are used to suggest patterns of association between social groups which are tied to actual instances of 'racial experiencing' (Blumer and Duster 1980).

In the area of race and ethnic relations, social surveys tend to generate structural models based upon 'categorical markers' such as colour, religion, birthplace, or other such attributes, or 'a once-for-all typology of people' which presents a 'tidier than life' account of social reality in which questions such as 'whether, when and how far the actor identifies with those who share the same categorical status' are never posed (Wallman 1986: 233-4). Ethnographic studies which emphasize social process are less likely to oversimplify social interaction because the ethnographer is constantly confronted by inconvenient confusions.

Ethnographic case-studies need not result in research fragments. Rather, as Sandra Wallman argues on the basis of her research in two inner London areas, urban ethnography based upon a 'process view' of social interaction may contribute to both a single theoretical framework and a body of knowledge relevant to public policy (Wallman 1984; 1986).[4]

Wallman's theory of 'ethnic boundary processes', which draws on the earlier work of Fredrik Barth, Raymond Firth, and other anthropologists, is compatible with the Chicago school tradition in so far as both are committed to the methods of urban ethnography, along with the investigation of the history and ecological setting in which ethnic relations exist (Barth 1981; Wallman 1984;

1986). Both endeavour to reconstruct the *context* in which inter-group relations, based upon opportunities and choices, and felt identity, get played out. For Wallman, as for Park and Thomas, the actor's point of view is critical, as are the variety of situations that he encounters in his everyday life and changes in these situations over time.[5]

As already argued, the justification for sociological research need look no further than the presentation of carefully observed accounts. Park thought that urbanites in cities such as Chicago existed in 'physical propinquity and moral isolation' (Park (1926c) 1952: 165-77). What he meant was that an important characteristic of modern urban society was that people share the same physical space but have no notion of how their neighbours organize their lives or view their shared environment. 'Humanist sociology', which took root in Chicago, aims to remedy this ignorance and indifference and to relate the lives of strangers who are also neighbours to one another (Lee 1973). Ethnographic monographs such as *The Negro Family in Chicago* (Frazier 1932), *Black Bourgeoisie* (Frazier 1957), *Black Metropolis* (Drake and Cayton 1945), and, more recently, *Tally's Corner* (Liebow 1967), *Soulside* (Hannerz 1971), *Behind Ghetto Walls* (Rainwater 1971), *All Our Kin* (Stack 1975), and *Eight London Households* (Wallman 1984) present accounts of 'alien' lives to sociologists, anthropologists, social policy analysts, politicians, and to a general public of neighbours.

The transience of knowledge and the permanence of method, the influence of philosophical pragmatism

Park acknowledged that pragmatism was fundamental to 'the particular type of research that has been identified with the "Chicago School"', and which, he claimed, was embodied in the Society for Social Research at the University of Chicago. W. I. Thomas's approach, noted Park, 'became a logical scheme for a disinterested investigation of the origin and function of social institutions as they everywhere existed, and was in substance an application to society and social life of the pragmatic point of view which Dewey and Mead had already popularised in the department of philosophy' (Park (1939c) cited in Kurtz 1982: 336).

Park's genius lay in taking ideas that originated with the philosophical pragmatists and applying them to the *empirical* study of social life. Basic to pragmatism was the view that inquiry directed by scientific method uncovered knowledge and 'truths' about the physical and social worlds which could then be used to alter these worlds. Knowledge was the outcome of the activity of a community of practitioners at a particular time and place. Knowledge, and for that matter truth, were, therefore, transient and plural. In contrast, scientific method was itself the source of stability in an ever-changing world of experience (Hollinger 1980). Philosophical pragmatism, therefore, predicts the supersession of taken-for-granted certainties to which the theories and methods of social research give rise. In other words, it is to be expected that what passes for sociological knowledge will change because sociological method is both a constant source of discovery *and* a source of disconfirmation about the social world.

More specifically, urban ethnography, the case-study, and the analysis of human documents are based upon a respect for the 'obdurate character of the empirical world – its ability to talk back' and to contradict the sociologist's conceptions and images about social life (Blumer 1969: 22-3). It assumes that sociological concepts and findings must be confronted with an independent social world. In this way, sociology at Chicago differs from more recent relativist sociologies such as ethnomethodology, which view 'discourse' as the only reality science apprehends. The assumption of an independent social world also separates the Chicago approach from Marxist perspectives which equate social theory with ideologies that legitimate a ruling class and its interests (Lal 1982).

CONCLUSION

Field-work, the case-study, and the analysis of human documents together constituted the special style of social research associated with the Chicago school. However, scholarly commitment to intellectual excellence ensured that individual innovation was encouraged and that conformity to a prevailing orthodoxy was inhibited (Faris (1967) 1970: 80; Bulmer 1984: 6). There were, therefore, differences in the way in which sociological problems were framed and investigated by sociologists between 1915 (when Park joined the faculty) and 1934 (when Park retired to Fisk University in Tennessee). Yet, despite increasing diversity, the predominance of the research strategy that emerged during Park's tenure at Chicago and the sense of 'community' among staff and students, who believed themselves to be consciously engaged in 'collaborative research' with a 'common goal', justified calling the sociologists at Chicago a 'school' of sociology (Wiley 1979; Bulmer 1984: 1-11; Blumer, personal conversation, 1979).[6]

With Park's retirement in 1934, however, this collective sociological effort began to break down. Its demise was also hastened by the increasing influence of newer staff members in the department of sociology, most notably William Ogburn, appointed professor in 1927, and his student Samuel Stouffer. Ogburn and Stouffer were committed to the collection of numerical data and statistical procedures in sociology. Outside the department, the psychologist L. L. Thurstone also contributed towards the development of quantitative methods in social science research (Oberschall 1972; Lengermann 1979; Bulmer 1984: 172-89).

Park firmly believed that the objective of sociology is to study culture, communication, and social control. Society is by definition a cultural unit of association, made possible by socialization and 'based on communication and consensus', entailing 'a kind of solidarity based on participation in a common enterprise' (Park (1939b) 1952: 244). The social mapping of numerical data and statistical methods were considered by him to be of less importance in understanding human society than those research strategies that aimed to reveal the subjective world of the actor's experience. Thus, in a controversy over method in the department of sociology at Chicago in the late 1920s, Park defended the case-study, field-work, and the analysis of human documents as basic to sociological research on the grounds that these methods captured subjective processes and the symbolic nature of group life (Bulmer 1984: 151-89).

The antagonism that arose between representatives of the earlier 'Chicago School' organized around the work of Park, Thomas, and Ellsworth Faris, and exemplified by the case-study approach, field-work, and the analysis of human documents, and the later quantitatively oriented sociologists, who adopted

Ogburn's preference for social surveys, the collection of numerical data, and statistical procedures, has continued to be central to the discipline. Despite this debate and an ever-increasing reliance on quantification, the research tradition established by Park, Thomas, and their students continues to be influential among sociologists intent upon examining social life in all of its complexity, first-hand.

Chapter Five

IMMIGRANTS AND THE
'ETHNICITY PARADOX'

What, if anything, do ethnic cultures do for individuals and groups? Is it the particular and variable content of a culture (for example, its attitude towards the family, the status that it accords to women, or its evaluation of education) that influences the life chances of its membership? Or are the generic properties of all ethnic groups such as the maintenance of 'ethnic boundaries' and the identity-bestowing features of membership, of greater significance in influencing individual behaviour and the destiny of the group? Are ethnic groups that support parochial, minority-group cultures anachronisms in an urban industrial civilization?

These issues, which Park and his colleague W. I. Thomas raised in their monographs and essays on immigration and its effect upon American life, have a remarkably modern ring to them. Since the 1960s, sociologists, historians, anthropologists, social geographers, and economists have raised similar sorts of topics for discussion. The more recent analyses of the 'character' and the effects of an ethnically diverse population tend to be written with a sharp appreciation of the policy implications of the data and of the interpretations presented.

There are two significant ways in which later scholars differ from Park, Thomas, and intellectuals writing before the Second World War. First, later generations of scholars explicitly compare the fate of immigrants who came to the United States from southern, central, and eastern Europe between 1880 and 1924 – when restrictive immigration legislation was enacted – with the achievements of black Americans. Sociologists, economists, political scientists, and others are concerned about the 'gap' in the 'average positions' in American society that blacks and the descendants of post-1880 immigrants now occupy. Their investigations differ with respect to the data presented and the reasons which they give for differences in group mobility where these are alleged to exist. Their studies support contradictory social policies in areas as diverse as aid to female-headed households, school busing, affirmative action programmes, and priorities in trans-racial adoptions.

A second and related difference between Park, and his colleagues, and later scholars is in the use of the concept of an 'opportunity structure' to explain relative achievement in education, income, occupation, political power, and other social indicators of individual and group well-being. Park emphasized the ways in which immigrants, blacks, and other newcomers to cities could better their individual and collective lot. Despite periodic depression, sustained economic growth between 1860 and 1922 led him to conclude that opportunity for those willing to work was a staple of American life. This optimistic prognosis was shattered by the Great Depression of the 1930s when the promise of social mobility as a result of individual effort was contradicted by the realization that life chances had more to do with international economic markets and political events outside individual control. A proliferation of welfare policies during the 1930s expanded the role of the state and acknowledged the responsibility of society as a whole for its constituents.

Between 1880 and 1930, approximately twenty-five million immigrants arrived in the United States. The influx was greatest during the decades 1901-10, in which 8,795,386 immigrants arrived, and 1911-20, when 5,735,811 came.

Prior to the 1880s, immigrants came primarily from western Europe and were generally assumed to be suitable material for integration into white, Protestant, English-speaking, Anglo-Saxon, American society. However, the period of 'second immigration' consisted of population movement from southern and eastern Europe and Mexico. Over three million Catholic Italians, three million or more Slavs, two million East European Jews, over one million Mexicans, and 'hundreds of thousands of Orientals, Hungarians, Greeks, Armenians, Syrians, Turks, Arabs, Bulgarians, Latin Americans, Portuguese, and French Canadians' arrived in America (Dinnerstein *et al.* 1979: 121-5). For many native-born Americans, the predominant linguistic, religious, and institutional hegemony seemed threatened by the arrival of newcomers so patently at odds with both themselves and the descendants of earlier immigrants from western Europe. During the first two decades of the twentieth century, 'confident faith in the natural easy melting of many peoples into one' gave way to demands for 'Americanization' and later for the exclusion of foreigners (Higham 1984: 234).

The expansion of industry in the United States offered new opportunities for earning a living. In addition, political revolution and social upheaval in Europe and the revival of racist and nationalist sentiments there resulted in both the emergence and repression of ethnic, linguistic, and religious minorities. While many immigrants, such as eastern European Jews, came as settlers, others planned to make enough money in the United States to return home. For example, among 1.8 million Hungarians who arrived in the USA between 1880 and the First World War, 64 per cent subsequently returned to Hungary.

In Chicago in 1900, immigrants and their children constituted about 80 per cent (2,701,150) of a total population of 3,376,438 (Philpott 1978: 116-17). Thirty-five per cent of the foreign population was German, 17 per cent Irish, 14 per cent Scandinavian. By the 1920s, 'colonies' of Persians, Poles, Czechs, Serbo-Croatians, Lithuanians, Greeks, Jews, Slovaks, and blacks further increased ethnic diversity (Dinnerstein et al. 1979: 127). Immigrants found employment as unskilled and semi-skilled workers on the railroads, in the grain and lumber trade, livestock processing and meat packing, breweries, iron and steel mills, and garment manufacturing. Wages, working conditions, and housing were often inadequate. Yet Chicago's population continued to swell as labour always seemed in short supply.

Park did not share the xenophobia of American nativists. Neither, however, did he feel a sense of guilt about exploitation of foreigners since he retained an optimistic belief in the increased range of opportunities which American society offered newcomers, despite their initial privation. In 1918, in the face of growing restrictionist sentiment among Americans, he endorsed the National Committee for Constructive Immigration Legislation, 'the one real effort on the part of liberals to define a clear-cut alternative to the main draft of postwar restriction' (Higham (1955) 1988: 302). Other sponsors included James Harvey

Robinson, Vida D. Scudder, Oswald Garrison Villard (one of the founders of the National Association for the Advancement of Colored People as well as a one-time sponsor of Tuskegee), and Lillian D. Wald. Park's position reflected two views general among liberals active on the immigrants' behalf. These were either that the immigrant problem was already in the process of disappearing or that the problems immigrants faced were a reflection of the need to alter post-First World War American society, if not in its entirety then at least to make it more receptive to the preservation of valuable cultural differences among various groups (Higham (1975) 1984: 214-20; Matthews 1970). Park believed that the assimilation of immigrants was inevitable although subject to inhibiting factors (Park and Miller (1921) 1969: 308).

The uniqueness of the contributions of Park and Thomas lies in their integrating their views and hypotheses about immigration and ethnic relations with a sense of what it must be like to be an Italian, Jew, Pole, Japanese, or other foreigner in a new and not always welcoming country. Their object was to describe and explain immigration and its effects on American society, taking into account the experience of the immigrant, as well as the parameters of his community and its institutional arrangements.

Park argued that the problems of the immigrant (and of the Afro-American) are related to the movement of isolated and provincial people 'out of a society based on primary relationships' to 'the looser, freer and less controlled existence of life in great cities' (Park (1920-21) (1921-22) 1955: 241). Migration and contact between cultures has a dual aspect: 'the breakdown of tradition and custom' of the group transplanted to a new environment, and a corresponding change in the habits and attitudes of the individual.[1] These alterations in individual 'habit and outlook' then go on to subvert the immigrant's traditional heritage. Park and Thomas describe changes in both 'objective cultural elements', such as the traditional family and other immigrant institutions, and 'subjective characteristics of the members of the social group' such as habits and attitudes.

The Immigrant Press and Its Control (1922), *Old World Traits Transplanted* (1921), and Park's essays on ethnic relations deal with the process of immigration and the immigrant on several different levels. First, there are data on the size, shape, and history of the 'communities and cultural institutions which immigrant people have created' in the United States. (This corresponds to 'objective cultural elements'.) Second, his studies contain accounts of the immigrant's experience from the immigrant's own point of view. Third, there is an attempt to see both the immigrant community and immigrant experience in terms of *ethnic relations*.

Part One of this chapter argues that Park identified the 'ethnicity paradox': that is, that participation in separate immigrant institutions increased the effectiveness with which immigrant groups were able to compete for resources in the wider American community and ultimately to achieve fuller integration into its dominant institutions.[2] A discussion of two new concepts, 'ethnicity by consent' and 'compulsory ethnicity', conclude this section.[3]

Part Two examines Park's resolution of the ethnicity paradox and locates him with respect to theories of cultural pluralism.[4] It considers Fred Matthews's suggestion that, for many American intellectuals, 'alienated romanticism', by which Matthews means disillusionment with American society and what it has to offer, 'created not xenophobia but xenophilia' in the belief that 'fundamental meaning and protection from the psychic terror of alienation could come only from membership in historic national communities developed through centuries of shared experience' (Matthews 1970: 9).

THE ETHNICITY PARADOX

'It is participation rather than submission or conformity that makes Americans of foreign-born peoples' (Park (1922) 1970: 88). Park and Thomas argued that the immigrants' participation in the corporate activity of the larger community was an essential condition for maintaining the American 'system of life, ideal and political as well as economic' (Park and Miller (1921) 1969: 264). 'Our state system', they pointed out, 'is based on the participation of every member and assumes in all the wish and the ability to participate; for in the last analysis what we mean by democracy is participation by all, both practically and imaginatively, in the common life of the community' (ibid.: 261).

Park and Thomas found that immigration often had the effect of raising nationalist feelings for the home country, left behind in most instances voluntarily. 'Loneliness and an unfamiliar environment turn the wanderer's thoughts and affections back upon his native land. The strangeness of the new surroundings emphasize his kinship with those he has left' (Park (1922) 1970: 49).

The immigrants' efforts to preserve their foreign languages had to do with their wish to keep alive old world memories and heritages. Park noted that 'When schools in the native language were closed in Europe, they were opened in America. When the vernacular press was being slowly extirpated by a hostile censorship in the old country, it flourished so much the more in the new, where the government did not seem to know that it existed' (ibid.). Park reached the ironic conclusion that through the preservation of vernacular language the new world offered the possibility of celebrating the old.

To begin with, Park and Thomas suggested that it was both natural and beneficial for the newly arrived immigrant who 'does not know how to live except as a member of a group' to locate himself in the midst of those of his fellow-nationals who preceded him to America. Within the immigrant group, a shared language, as well as shared memories and a common cultural heritage, enabled the immigrant to find 'some points of identity with his previous life'. They compared different immigrant communities because they believed that the character of the immigrant community 'is the primary influence in determining the desire and capacity of the immigrant to participate in American life' (Park and Miller (1921) 1969: 120). They acknowledged, however, that the way in which non-hyphenated Americans treated the foreigners was also crucial in influencing the prospects of the immigrants (ibid.: 265).

On the one hand, Park and Thomas found that immigrant institutions and heritages which had the greatest affinity with the dominant American culture were most conducive to the acculturation and the integration of the newcomers. On the other hand, flourishing immigrant organizations, *regardless* of their character or objectives, and a rich communal life were considered by them to be invaluable aids to hasten participation in the wider community in five essential ways.

Immigrant institutions and practical needs

First, immigrant institutions were perceived as being 'devices to make life go on with some success and efficiency' by meeting the practical needs of the foreigners through rendering essential services not readily available outside the ethnic enclave. Boarding houses and restaurants, steamship agencies, labour contractors, real-estate agencies, mutual aid and benefit societies, and banks were tailored to the requirements of Poles, Bohemians, Italians, East European Jews, Japanese, and Mexicans in areas which, despite their ethnic heterogeneity, were known as 'Little Italy', 'Prague', 'Hamburg', 'Pilsen', and 'Polonia' (Park and Miller (1921) 1969: 119-44).

The extent to which insulation from the larger American society existed was revealed in documents such as the following: 'Until 1914 the Sicilian colony in Chicago was an absolutely foreign community .... Those who had been leaders in Sicily retained their power here ... and ... having greater force and intelligence, made contracts with local politicians, police officials, labour agents, and real estate dealers, and became the go-between for their colony and the outside-world labour agents.' The document continues,

> Women continued to live as they had in Sicily, never leaving their homes except to make ceremonial visits or to attend mass. The presence of several garment factories in the district made it possible for them to earn by doing finishing at home. In later years hundreds of women went into the garment factories to work, some taking the street cars out of the district; but they went to and from work in groups, their shawls carefully wrapped about them.
>
> In the entire district there was no food for sale that was not distinctly foreign; it was impossible to buy butter, American cheese, sweet potatoes, pumpkin, green corn, etc., but in season artichokes, cactus fruit (fichi d'India), pomegranates, cocozella, and various herbs and greens never sold in other parts of town were plentiful.
>
> (Marie Leavitt, *Report on the Sicilian Colony in Chicago*, manuscript, quoted in Park and Miller (1921) 1969: 151-2)

In New York City, Thomas and Park noted, 'There are immigrants on the lower East Side ... who have been here for twenty years and have never been up town' (Park and Miller (1921) 1969: 120).

For immigrants, 'foreign' contacts may first take place within the ethnic group between members of different villages, towns, regions, and, in the case of the Jews, different countries of origin. For example, a Galician Jew complained to a Yiddish newspaper that, 'God destined me to have a Russian (Jewish) wife and it is a misfortune for me – not because she feeds me with their Russian dishes, which are not bad, but the Russian company she brings up to our house is unbearable' (Letter to *Forward*, 6 December 1915, cited in Park and Miller (1921) 1969: 200).

Thomas and Park also described mutual aid and benefit societies as being indispensable to the immigrant, who, although 'strangely indifferent to death ... wants to die decently, ceremonially, and socially'. They go on to comment that,

> Since a man's death is usually the most conspicuous incident in his life, attracting the universal attention and interest of the group, since it is the occasion of judgements and speculations on the status of the family – whether they are rich – death and burial are not only the occasion of the natural idealisation of the dead, but a means of securing recognition. Immigrant families are notorious for lavish expenditure on funerals.
>
> (Park and Miller (1921) 1969: 125)

The immigrant press

The foreign-language press was particularly important as an instrument for disseminating information about life in America. 'Except for his paper', noted Park, the immigrant 'remains as provincial in the new country as he was in the old. Almost all that he knows about the larger political, social and industrial life about him, he gets indirectly, through the medium of his press' (Park (1922) 1970: 113).

Park believed that the 'natural history' of the foreign-language press would reflect the changes that occurred within immigrant communities, with respect to modification of both 'objective cultural elements' – their institutions – and 'subjective orientations' – the habits and attitudes of their members. Their press also expressed the struggle of immigrant groups to maintain their separate identities which, Park believed, facilitated the process of assimilation and 'Americanization'. 'It seems fairly clear that what the foreign press actually does, whether or not the editors desire it, is to facilitate the adjustment of the foreign born to the American environment, an adjustment that results in something that is not American, at least according to the standards of an earlier period, but that is not foreign either, according to existing European standards' (ibid.: 87-8).

Park's interest in the foreign newspaper also led him to speculate about the role of *language* in maintaining social solidarity. He noted that linguistic differences reinforce social distances and social hierarchies. For example, in tracing the consequences of maintaining a literary tradition which differs from the spoken or vernacular language, he observed that 'all the unrest which the economic and social changes of the nineteenth century had aroused among the "oppressed and dependent nationalities" of Europe has been gradually focused in the struggle to raise the folk languages, and the languages spoken by the peasants, to the dignity of a literary medium, the language of the schools and press' (ibid.: 48).[4]

Under the subtitle 'Literacy prevented', Park pointed out: 'The conquering races of Europe expected that the natives would adopt their culture when they suppressed all publications in the mother tongue and forbade its use in the schools.... This would simplify their governmental problems.' He went on to note that 'This policy was successful only with that small minority to whom intellectual development was of first importance. The exceptionally able secured education at the sacrifice of racial identity.' Ironically, Park concluded, 'Instead of giving their own culture to the conquered people, the conquerors cut them off from all culture transmitted by the written word' (ibid.: 28-9).

Park collected letters to the editor, editorials, human interest stories, anecdotes, announcements, and advertisements in order to 'get an intimate glimpse into the smaller world of the immigrant' and to demonstrate how 'the press reflects its group'. He used the contents of the press to derive a typology of immigrants. He compared the 'provincial' and 'cosmopolitan' foreign press (ibid.: 113-92). He also found it useful to include an excerpt from the Sixty-Sixth United States Senate Report on *Brewing and Liquor Interests and German and Bolshevik Propaganda*, (1918) so that he could discuss sources of revenue and control of foreign-language publications through national advertisers (ibid.: 377-411).

Park pointed out that even the advertisements in the foreign-language newspaper described the organization of the immigrant community. For example, he noted that 'Immigrant businesses flourish when immigration is recent or when there is segregation' so that 'The Syrian papers of New York, with their advertisements of lodging houses, groceries, restaurants, and clothing merchants, show that there are a large number of recent arrivals from Syria, all of whose life is spent among their countrymen on Washington Street'. On the other hand, 'the *Abendpost*, the big daily of the German colony long established in Chicago, has almost no advertisements of German business. The readers of the *Abendpost* patronise American merchants, and a single copy of the paper contains the advertisements of German professionals, doctors and lawyers, and of German organisations. During the winter, there are announcements of German plays' (ibid.: 113-14).

Park also observed that the 'Help Wanted' section figured prominently in the foreign-language press so that employers, especially those seeking factory labour and workers in steel mills and mines, could recruit among immigrants (ibid.: 137).

Park also used his material to determine the extent to which the immigrant press was controlled by un-American agencies and whether the United States government should impose controls upon foreign-language publications. Among the anti-American attitudes immigrants were suspected of harbouring were national-ism, meaning loyalty to country of origin, bolshevism, and anar-chism. Park discovered that, 'For a long time after the war began, in 1914, the cosmopolitan press was more concerned about it than was the American press. The war awakened old European antagonisms which the Americans did not share' (ibid.: 193). He cited the following excerpts from an editorial in a Hungarian newspaper and one response from its readership as examples of pro-American and anti-American sentiment among members of the same ethnic community. .

'What the Editor Wrote About America'

'(September 14, 1913): Registration is over. The Austro-Hungarians, too, have registered, not merely because it was

101

made their duty by law, but because they realized that if they help their adopted country – the United States – they also serve the land of their birth....The aim of the United States is the liberation of oppressed nations, and truly Hungary is one of the most oppressed.' (*Amerikai Magyar Nepszava* (Hungarian), New York City)

'What His Readers Wrote'

'My Dear Editor: It seems to us Bridgeport Magyars that they will have to send you to an insane asylum, but before you get there I would like to shoot you in the head like a dog, because you are nothing but a thief and a traitor....We are not going to subscribe to your paper because it is a paper that insults our kingdom and country.' (Letter received by the owner of the *Amerikai Magyar Nepszava* (Hungarian), New York City, 15 July 1918: ibid.: 209-10)

Park discussed the threat of subversion in a chapter on 'The class war' in which he observed that the object of the radical press is 'to make its readers class-conscious' (ibid.: 214). He complained that the radicals did not appreciate America and cited the following editorials and letters as characteristic: '"All over the United States the working class is doing the hardest labour. They made millions and millions of money, and at the same time they are treated as 'foreigners' ... 'who have not got any right' to express their mind about vital problems of this country" (*Radnicka Straza*, Croatian Socialist, Chicago).' And similarly, '"Today the courts of the American government are nothing else than the executors of the pleasure or orders of American trusts and capitalists" (*Obrana*, Bohemian-Socialist-Communist, New York)' (ibid.: 216-19).

Immigrant institutions and the 'apperception mass'

Park and Thomas cited a second way that participation within the ethnic enclave increased participation in the dominant society. Communal life organized around immigrant social institutions, they observed, formed a bridge between the immigrant's past experience, and the 'apperception mass' brought with him from his country of origin, and the immigrant's new environment. The immigrant's apperception mass consisted of 'all the meanings of past experience retained in the memory of the individual' and 'with which every new item of experience comes in contact, to which it is related, and in connection with which it gets its meaning' (Park and Miller (1921) 1969: 267).

Park and Thomas applauded immigrant communal life because they thought that, through participation in their own social institutions and in defence of their own heritage, immigrants would be able to find identities of meaning between their old experience and the new situations which they confronted and in this process they would begin to acquire a framework of interpretation in common with Americans of native stock. 'A wise policy of assimilation,' they noted, 'like a wise educational policy, does not seek to destroy the attitudes and memories that are there, but to build on them' (ibid.: 280).

Immigrant institutions, self-esteem, and social status

A third link between participation within the immigrant colony and full participation in the activities of the larger community was forged from Park's and Thomas's view of the relationship between the immigrant's desire for self-esteem and the status of the social group with which he was identified – whether voluntarily or involuntarily.

Park and Thomas argued that the immigrant experienced a lack of self-esteem and a 'diminished sense of personality' which stemmed from the 'loss of recognition of his role within the group' (Park and Miller (1921) 1969: 47). 'When the immigrant comes to America,' they noted, 'not only must he leave behind the community which was the basis of his personality and self-respect, but here the very signs of his personality (dress, language, and so forth), which in his own country were the signs of his self-respect, are regarded with contempt and made the occasions of his humiliation' (ibid.: 48).

Among the 'immigrant experiences' that they cited as evidence of this were an autobiographical description of the dismay with which an orthodox Jewish girl viewed her father clipping his beard, which in his home country had been a sign of piety, and the lamentations of a Syrian man, forced to abandon poetry and

103

contemplate peddling 'jewellry and notions' in 'the New World' so
that 'death lost its terror for me' (ibid.: 48-9, 54).

A loss of self-esteem was one source of immigrant 'demoralization'. A second source had its roots in the low social status of the
foreign nationality group to which the immigrant belonged. Park
and Thomas cited an interview with a woman of Italian descent
who remarked,

> I do not understand why Italians have been treated in this
> country as they have been. I go to a store and they say to me,
> 'are you French?' I say 'No'. They say 'Spanish?' 'No, I am
> Italian'. And then there is immediate coldness and con-
> tempt!
>
> (ibid.: 51)

The Americans' scornful attitude to foreigners was proclaimed
by a Polish intellectual to be astounding.

> I do not think most Americans realize how revolting to a
> more or less educated immigrant is their naive attitude of
> superiority, their astonishing self-satisfaction, their inability
> and unwillingness to look on anything foreign as worth being
> understood and assimilated ... and perhaps even more
> revolting ... is the current tendency of American society to
> interpret the relation between the immigrant and America as
> that of one-sided benefit and one-sided obligation.
>
> (Autobiography, cited in Park and Miller (1921) 1969:
> 110-11)

Park also used excerpts from the Japanese and Jewish papers to
explore ethnic consciousness. He cited the following documents
to illustrate 'the new race consciousness' among the Japanese.

> If the Japanese problem in America is to end, it will end only
> when the Japanese immigrants have all left the American
> shore, or when their place in this land has become too emin-
> ently prosperous to admit any hostile criticism. Until one of
> these two things happens, we will continue to be the object of
> discussion, and the victims of contempt and oppression.
>
> (*Tacoma Japanese Times*, Tacoma, Washington)

> There are some enlightened men in our Japanese group who
> are ashamed of teaching the Japanese alphabet to their

children, and refrain from the use of soy-bean soup, boiled rice, and bean sauce, this last named being offensive to the American nostrils. These people are doing everything they can to please Americans. How would they like it when they find, some day, a permanent yellow stratum in the American society as there is a black one already?

(*North American Herald*, Los Angeles, California: ibid.: 161-2)

As an example of 'the new nationalism' among Jews, Park cited the following document,

'From man to man' .... I do not like a Gentile who does not dislike a Jew, just as I have no love for the Jew who does not dislike a Gentile. An honest Gentile ... must be more or less of an anti-Semite, just as an upright Jew must be more or less of an anti-Gentile ... And when I walk through the woods with a Gentile who is a friend of the Jews .... I constantly keep my hand on the butt of my revolver.

(*Day*, New York City, 10 March 1917: ibid.: 166-8)

The social status of different immigrant groups and the self-esteem of its members were, like all other meanings, social products created within and between groups. A 'sense of group position' based upon conventions of dominance and subordination, exclusion, and inclusion was a feature of group identity and individual experience (Blumer 1958; 1965a).

Park and Thomas thought that new cultural contacts which sprang from migration and the interaction between formerly isolated groups formed one condition likely to upset a prevailing social order around which the social status of groups and individual self-conceptions had been organized. Other conditions conducive to challenging the prevailing distribution of status were periods of social unrest and far-reaching social change, as, for example, during rapid industrialization or political revolution.

Social conflict among immigrant groups and between these groups and America's native population was largely concerned with the distribution of status. With this in mind, Park and Thomas observed that foreigners

who begin by deserting their group end by attempting to improve the status of these groups ... seeking to make something with which a man may be proud to identify himself. The fact that the individual will not be respected unless his group is respected becomes thus, perhaps, the most sincere source of nationalist movements in America. *To this extent the nationalist movements represent an effort to increase participation in American life.*

(Park and Miller (1921) 1969: 143-4; my emphasis)

In this remarkable passage, as well as elsewhere, Park and Thomas contended that, while the celebration of old world heritages and the assertion of a separate group identity may be valued in and of themselves, they are also a strategy for improving the status of the immigrant group and the self-esteem of its members, *and as such* support the immigrants' claim to participate in the wider American community on something like their own terms. This interpretation was further supported by their observation that the leaders of different immigrant groups claimed social value precisely 'on account of their racial peculiarities' and that these leaders argued that each group was capable of contributing, in their own way, to American life (ibid.: 299).

Immigrant institutions and social control

There was yet another reason why Park and Thomas saw participation in separate institutions as a prerequisite for the immigrants' participation in the larger community and this has to do with an aspect of demoralization not previously touched upon, namely, the absence of mechanisms of social control in the urban areas to which the immigrants flocked. Park and Thomas argued that the immigrant, like rural folk generally, came from communities which had exercised total control over the lives of their members. In cities, such as Chicago, the traditional mechanisms of social control characteristic of immigrant communities were no longer effective, since the values which these represented were challenged by the 'American community, which lives by different and more individualistic standards, and shows ... a contempt for all the characteristics of the newcomers'. Under these conditions the habits of the immigrant, which are the individual's expression of the group's traditions, 'break down' and are no longer useful guides around which individual and collective action can be organized. In the 'crisis' which ensues, 'the individual tends either to reorganize his life positively, or to repudiate the old habits and their restraints without reorganizing his life ... which is demoralisation' (ibid.: 61).

Park and Thomas concluded that participation in the immigrant community facilitated participation in the larger community through reorganizing the immigrant's habits and providing him with new definitions of the situation which were appropriate to his changed circumstances. 'The organization of the immigrant community is necessary as a regulative mechanism', wrote Park and Thomas, who went on to observe that 'If you can induce a man to belong to something, to co-operate with any group whatever, where something is expected of him, where he has responsibility, dignity, recognition, economic security, you have at least regulated his life' (ibid.: 299-300). As already noted, in Park's schema, social disorganization, which is the collective manifestation of individual demoralization and lack of regulation, stands for the inability of the members of a group to act collectively.

Immigrant institutions as themselves adaptations

Finally, Park and Thomas believed that participation within the immigrant enclave facilitated acculturation and integration precisely because immigrant heritages and institutions, as these existed in cities such as Chicago, were themselves adaptive mechanisms. Thus, in anticipation of much of the current thinking about ethnicity, Park and Thomas noted that the elements of the immigrants' culture, although 'they reproduced to some extent the home society', were 'not, in fact, pure heritages', but rather 'the products of the immigrants' efforts to adapt their heritages to American conditions' (Park and Miller (1921) 1969: 120). Old world traits, once transplanted, reflected the changed circumstances in which these were forced to take root. It was because the church, the foreign-language press, and nationalist organizations were themselves adaptations, that they were effective ways of regulating and guiding the immigrant.

Park's and Thomas's view of immigrant heritages and institutions as adaptive mechanisms reflected the relativist perspective on culture which was being formulated by their contemporary, the anthropologist Franz Boas. Boas challenged the view that human groups could be classified in terms of their stage in the evolution of a single *culture*. Instead, he maintained that human groups created diverse *cultures*. In this way, he disengaged the normative connotation from the culture concept and replaced it with a sense of the variety of ways in which human groups adapt to the conditions of their lives (Boas (1911) 1938; Stocking 1968).

Boas saw culture as a process of intergenerational transmission of a changing body of knowledge and behaviour through learning. The unique cultures of human groups were 'the results of specific and complex historical processes' as well as being influences upon these processes (Stocking 1968: 211). Park reiterated Boas's distinction between culture and civilization, reserving for the last the evolutionary usage of a unique configuration existing to a greater or a lesser extent in all human groups.

By the 1920s, Park and Thomas had distanced themselves from the popular notion that culture was biologically transmitted through racial groups. Citing Boas's *The Mind of Primitive Man*, Park and Thomas concluded that it was unlikely that 'racial groups represented in immigration were specialised by heredity'. They went on to observe that 'It is easier to explain why the Jew is in the needle trades, is not a farmer, and is intelligent, on the ground of circumstances – that he has a racial history – than on the ground of inborn aptitudes' (Park and Miller (1921) 1969: 302).

Assimilation and cultural pluralism

Park and Thomas eschewed both popular jingoism and a 'melting pot' vision of American society and culture. The goal of assimilation, as they saw it, is not the repression or standardization of immigrant cultures, but the preservation of what is both worthwhile and unique within an embracing American context.

Citing 'the value of the principle of diversity', as having already been recognized in the scientific world and in specialized occupations, and 'individualization' of function, Park and Thomas argued for a model of intergroup relations which incorporates the basic features of cultural pluralism.

In the civilisation having the highest efficiency all are not in the same 'universe of discourse', but there tend to be smaller groups or circles who understand one another and cooperate. Although they are not understood by everybody, their products become useful to everybody. The physicists, for example, represent such a circle .... Now the representatives of different immigrant groups claim a similar social value that, on account of their racial peculiarities and the fact that they have developed by their past experiences different apperception masses, they are predisposed to individualised functions as groups, and that by permanently organising along the lines of their aptitudes they will not only express their peculiar genius, but contribute unique values to America.

(ibid.: 299-300)

However, although convinced of the benefits and committed to the preservation of minority group cultures, Park and Thomas were doubtful that the 'peculiar genius' characteristic of different ethnic groups would survive the homogenizing and leavening process of culture contact since what differentiates ethnic groups and race from one another is not due to 'inborn and ineradicable traits', but 'to a long train of common experiences' (ibid.: 301-3).

Park's vision of assimilation based upon co-operation rather than repression follows from his view, discussed in Chapter Two, that the hallmark of human society is collective, purposeful activity, founded upon a shared culture and, in particular, a shared language. Immigration poses a threat to democracy only if immigrants refuse to participate in corporate activity and, in particular, political life. 'We must make the immigrants a working part in our system of life, ideal and political, as well as economic, or lose the character of our culture', observed Park and Thomas. 'Self-preservation makes this necessary; the fact that they bring valuable additions makes it desirable' (ibid.: 264).

To summarize, in their study of immigrant life, Park and Thomas identified the 'ethnicity paradox': that participation in separate immigrant institutions and a commitment to a parochial minority group culture increased the effectiveness with which immigrant groups were able to compete for resources in the wider American community and ultimately to achieve fuller integration into its dominant institutions. It is this paradox which reconciles the perspectives of 'ethnicity as genuine culture' and 'ethnicity as a stratification phenomenon'.[5] The distinction between the perspectives of ethnicity as genuine culture (Sapir 1924) and ethnicity as a stratification phenomenon is meant to capture two prevalent attitudes which are found in both past and recent discussions describing ethnic relations.

Ethnicity as genuine culture and ethnicity as a stratification phenomenon

The perspective on ethnicity as genuine culture is based on the premise that ethnic traditions are influential in the organization of individual experience and group behaviour such that different ethnic groups support different cultural styles. This perspective favours a detailed ethnographic description of these different cultural styles, thought to be rooted in fundamental aspects of individual and group identity, such as similarities in physical appearance, a shared language, religion, and a sense of common origin and history (Isaacs 1977).

The view of ethnicity as genuine culture assumes that participation within the confines of the group is valued in and of itself, especially since the group is most likely to provide the context for vital or 'consummatory experience' (Sapir 1924). Furthermore, ethnic collectivities are depicted as being a resource 'for finding self-definition, social location and preferential role opposites' (Greeley 1974: 27). The ethnic group answers these individual needs because it is the social repository of what Clifford Geertz, following Edward Shils (Shils 1957), calls 'primordial attachments' and which, he asserts, has its origins in 'the assumed givens – of social existence'. Geertz goes on to observe that

> congruities of blood, speech, custom and so on, are seen to have ineffable, and at times, overpowering, coerciveness in and of themselves. One is bound to one's kinsmen, one's neighbour, one's fellow believer, *ipso facto*, as a result not merely of interest, or incurred obligation, but at least in great part by the virtue of some unaccountable absolute import attributed to the very tie itself. The general strength of such primordial bonds, and the types of them that are important,

differ from person to person, from society to society, and from time to time. But for virtually every person, in every society, at almost all times, some attachments seem to flow more from a sense of natural – some would say spiritual – affinity than from social interaction.

(Geertz 1973: 109-10)

On this view the individual's basic need to feel a sense of 'belonging' and to 'enjoy a respected and self-respecting status in society' is 'satisfied only in their most parochial groupings, and not satisfied well enough or at all in any broader, not to say brotherly, political systems or associations' (Isaacs 1977: 25).

From the perspective of ethnicity as genuine culture, elements of a group's cultural style may aid or impede members in attaining ends such as higher education, economic success, or political power. However, whether a cultural style aids or inhibits the attainment of such goals, it is thought that the framework of values that a person has acquired on the basis of a group affiliation is difficult to change and never completely disappears. It would seem, then, that at least some aspects of cultural styles are impervious to individual volition.

The premise underlying the perspective on ethnicity as a stratification phenomenon is that ethnic groups are interest groups. This view affirms that, despite variations in the cultural patterns between ethnic groups, all groups are more or less committed to increasing their share of scarce resources which are universally valued by the larger community, such as income, good jobs, good housing, good schooling, prestige, and political power. Therefore, the mobilization of ethnic groups and the pursuit of ethnic interests are a strategy for the achievement of goals or cultural values shared by everybody.[6]

Ethnic groups, however, are depicted as being one among many kinds of interest groups. According to the view of ethnicity as a stratification phenomenon, ethnic ties exist alongside other sorts of bonds between men, and ethnic solidarity is one of a number of competing sources of social integration (Higham 1974a).

The 'desocialization' of ethnic groups describes an increasing cultural similarity between ethnic groups as well as the persistence of individual attachment to them (Schneider, cited in Parsons 1975: 66-7). What is significant about American society, then, is the homogeneity between different ethnic groups. Rather than depicting ethnicity as the most important determinant of styles of life, those sharing the view of ethnicity as a stratification phenomenon also consider variations in life-styles which have been devised by groups differentiated from one another in terms of income, occupation, education, and age (Gordon 1964). The presumed inviolate quality sometimes ascribed to cultural legacies or patterns yields to the idea that the perception of their usefulness may explain the persistence, change, revival, or demise of both legacies and patterns. Therefore, the mystique of primordial attachments is considerably lessened (Steinberg 1982).

However, while ethnic identification may have an 'optional and voluntary aspect' to it, ethnic cultural patterns are not seen as being altogether matters of personal choice (Parsons 1975: 64).

Nathan Glazer and Daniel Patrick Moynihan are the primary advocates and pioneers of the approach to ethnicity as a stratification phenomenon (Glazer and Moynihan 1963; Glazer and Moynihan 1975; Glazer 1975). Ethnic groups, they argue, are most likely to be mobilized around class-related interests.

Thus, they observe that 'perhaps the single most important fact about ethnic groups in New York City' is that

> When one speaks of the Negroes and Puerto Ricans, one also means unorganised and unskilled workers, who hold poorly paying jobs in the laundries, hotels, restaurants, small factories or who are on relief. When one says Jews, one also means small shopkeepers, professionals, better-paid skilled workers in the garment industries. When one says Italians, one also means homeowners in Staten Island, the North Bronx, Brooklyn and Queens.
>
> (Glazer and Moynihan 1963: 17)

More recently, however, as they themselves note, ethnic groups have been organized to pursue foreign policy objectives, such as sending arms to Israel or supporting the IRA. In addition, affirmative action programmes in employment, housing, and in education, have stimulated the mobilization of ethnic groups in the interest of asserting collective rights or in the resistance to such claims (Glazer and Moynihan 1975; Glazer 1975).

'Ethnicity by consent' and 'compulsory ethnicity': the continuity of the ethnicity paradox

Ironically, neither Park nor Thomas anticipated that the very success of blacks in heightening their sense of race consciousness and wielding black culture as a mainstay in their ongoing struggle for social justice, racial equality and an opportunity to participate in all facets of American life, would precipitate a movement among many other American groups to use the idea of ethnicity as a basis for mobilization in pursuit of economic, political and social interests (Glazer and Moynihan 1975; Parsons 1975; Van den Berghe 1978; Smith 1982). Whether intended or not the very success of the black power movement and the transformation of American blacks into Afro-Americans, legitimized various existing covert collectivist practices. These were judicially and officially frowned upon as they ran counter to liberal individualism.

'Ethnicity by consent' refers to the creation of ethnic cultures and identities by people who are not related to one another by descent but who none the less lay claim to primordial sentiments and ties and who are committed to a special style of life and a set of conventions which they transmit to their children. The Black Jews of Harlem, the Hare Krishna movement, the Black Muslims, and the Rastafarians are examples of groups united around a shared ethnic identity by consent.

A second type of ethnicity by consent occurs when ethnic groups which have traditionally thought of themselves as distinct in terms of both culture and descent submerge their differences and assume a common identity. Thus, for example, Native Americans who have traditionally thought of themselves in terms of tribal affiliations are increasingly under pressure to assume the common ethnic identity in order to conform to the perceptions of the dominant society and, in particular, powerful government agencies whose objectives are to ensure rights and distribute resources to them (Petersen 1961; Wax 1971).

The ethnic by consent is in most respects the converse of what Park called 'the marginal man'. 'The marginal man', wrote Park, 'is a personality type that arises at a time and a place where, out of the conflict of races and cultures, new societies, new peoples and cultures are coming into existence' (Park (1937c) 1950: 375). While the ethnic by consent finds his identity and organizes his life around participation within a sectarian group, the marginal man either cannot or does not wish to immerse himself in such an association.

> The fate which condemns him to live, at the same time, in two worlds is the same which compels him to assume, in relation to the worlds in which he lives, the role of a cosmopolitan and a stranger. Inevitably, he becomes, relative to his cultural milieu, the individual with the wider horizon, the keener intelligence, the more detached and rational viewpoint. The marginal man is always relatively the more civilized human being.
>
> (ibid.: 375-6)

The 'mulatto' is one example of a marginal man. However, it is important to note that Park reversed the usual racist assumptions regarding the inferior nature of 'half-castes' and instead insisted that individuals of mixed race represented more sophisticated, if also more troubled, individuals.

It is misleading to depict ethnicity by consent as resulting in counterfeit cultures and bogus identities. Rather, it is useful to consider the proliferation of sectarian social movements as an expression of the unattached individual's efforts to gain self-esteem and to procure a satisfying personal identity through participation in a recognized social group.

The marginal man and the ethnic by consent are each a response to the dilemma of forging a personal identity in the rapidly changing urban environment. What neither Park nor Thomas anticipated was the more or less permanent attraction of 'real' or imagined ethnic group affiliation as a mode of partici-pation in a rapidly changing and uncertain urban milieu such that the marginal man, rather than serving as a prototype for the future, remains, as ever, marginal.

By 'compulsory ethnicity' is meant the institutionalization of ethnic identification as a basis for the assertion of collective claims concerning the distribution of scarce resources. While Park and Thomas were among the first to point out the importance of the maintenance of a sense of solidarity in the transition of socially isolated (and often also materially deprived) immigrant and racial minorities to a higher social status, they did not envision this particular pattern of social organization as a permanent basis of entitlement in democratic urban societies.

Compulsory ethnicity stems from two sources. First, from the intervention of the state in the allocation of scarce resources which were previously determined in a market. Thus, for example, affirmative action programmes which advocate preferential treatment in order to ensure a particular distributional outcome, rather than those which have as their objective equality of opportunity, interfere with market mechanisms in areas such as education and jobs. It has been persuasively argued that such affirmative action programmes have provided incentives for Americans to resurrect ethnic ties, along with other conventional bases for organizing pressure groups, in order to pursue interests which may or may not relate to the culture, as opposed to the economic or political interests, of a particular group (Glazer 1975; Bell 1975; Van den Berghe 1978).

In this context, it is also useful to consider William Yancey et al.'s observation that 'the conditions which generate ethnicity are not created only for immigrants or others with unique origins. They also exist for native-born Americans without a particular foreign heritage' (Yancey et al. 1976: 400). The authors argue that 'common occupational positions, residential stability and concentration, and dependence on common institutional services' which are the outcome of 'structural conditions which are intimately linked to the changing technology of industrial production and transportation' influence the emergence of ethnic identification and ethnically related behaviour (ibid.: 392).

As already pointed out, Glazer and Moynihan suggest that the motivation behind collective action on the part of ethnic groups is class-related interests. Yancey et al. add to this approach the idea that the changing ecology and economy of cities create opportunity structures which may inhibit or precipitate collective behaviour on the part of ethnic groups interested in maximizing their share of scarce resources. In particular, opportunities for widespread social mobility which challenge a prevailing structure of stratification may create or strengthen ethnic solidarity if the latter is perceived to be an effective means of securing resources or values, such as social status.

The concept of compulsory ethnicity raises questions concerning the extent to which ethnically oriented behaviour is voluntary

115

or is subject to structural inducements and constraints. The collective action of Native Americans provides an interesting example of the relationship between voluntarism and social structure as well as illustrating the links between ethnicity by consent and compulsory ethnicity. As already noted, tribes of Native Americans who had traditionally thought of themselves as distinct from one another, in terms of differences in both culture (e.g., language, religion, social organization) and descent, have assumed a common identity, in conformity to the perceptions of the United States federal government, in order to claim collective rights and resources. Thus, the opportunity structure created by the United States federal government through agencies such as the Bureau of Indian Affairs can also be credited with creating a 'generalised Indian' (Wax 1971: 192).

The second source of compulsory ethnicity is, ironically, the recent writings of social scientists intent upon convincing others that there is a movement, for instance in American society, 'to depolarise on social issues and to repolarise ethnically' (Isaacs 1972: 75). Social scientists have accorded various degrees of credibility to an alleged 'ethnic revival' (Smith 1981; Steinberg 1982). Compulsory ethnicity stemming from the intervention of the state in the allocation of market resources and the observation of ethnic polarization by social scientists might well result in a trend towards 'a compartmentalised society of groups' in which the equality of groups and the celebration of collective rights supersedes 'a unitary integrated community of individuals' in which the social equality of individuals and the assurance of individual rights is foremost (Isaacs 1977: 77). Under these conditions, it is to be expected that ethnic groups will continue to create cultures and reaffirm ethnic affiliations whenever this appears to be a reasonable strategy for pursuing their interests, and increasing their share of scarce resources.

'PAROCHIAL MINORITY GROUP CULTURES' AND 'CITY-WIDE SHARED CULTURE'[7]

In his essays on ethnicity and race relations, Park suggested two interrelated bulwarks against the disintegration of culture in urban civilization. On the one hand, he advocated supporting local 'parochial minority group cultures'. On the other hand, he also argued the case for a 'city-wide shared culture'.

In their study of immigrant life, Park and Thomas identified the 'ethnicity paradox'. In line with their discovery, Park considered parochial minority groups, which either preserve or facilitate the creation of particularistic cultures, to be of value to both the individual and the larger encompassing society in which such groups exist. Parochial minority groups are able to act collectively to achieve their specific goals. They are at one and the same time groups based upon culture, sentiment, and interest.

Parochial minority groups may be based upon race and ethnicity. However, such groups may also owe their existence to mystical or mythical connections of a newly created culture. The Hare Krishna devotees, the Moonies, the gay liberation movement, and emergent fundamentalist Christian sects are examples of parochial minority groups which have only recently created identities for their membership. These groups insist that the individual concern himself, in varying degree, with the welfare of the group as a whole. They impart meaning and occasion to an otherwise mundane world.

Parochial minority groups also act as mechanisms of social control and so benefit the society of which they are a part. The will to participate within the group, Park believed, required self-discipline and internalization of the idea of social obligation. He assumed that each member would desire to raise the status of his group within the community as a whole and that this would constrain members in desirable ways. Thus, for example, Park and Thomas noted that the Jewish 'Kehillah' in New York City undertakes, among other activities, '"to find ways and means of providing Jewish training for all the Jewish children of school age in this city"', '"to direct vocational training, to provide employment for the handicapped, as well as for the highly skilled, and to work out methods for the maintenance of peace in industries where Jews predominate"' (Park and Miller (1921) 1969: 236-7).

In addition to his argument for 'parochial minority group culture', Park put forward the case, seemingly contradictorily, for a 'city-wide shared culture'. Such an urban culture would promote communication and corporate activity between people who lived in 'physical propinquity' and 'social isolation' (Park (1926c) 1952). 'The stability and health of any society, tribe, nation or industrial group', warned Park, depend upon its ability to develop a tradition, a body of mores, and a code which represent at once the consensus and common understanding as well as the accumulated wisdom and common sense of the group. If changes are so rapid as to make it impossible to maintain and transmit this tradition, the social equilibrium and the *esprit de corps* which this tradition has supported will inevitably be dissipated and lost.

(Park (1934c) 1955: 298-9)

A city-wide shared culture would transcend the particularistic boundaries of parochial minority groups. It would foster empathy between groups and, in so doing, it would blunt social divisiveness.

Park's advocacy of a consciously created city-wide shared culture was a response to migration and to the increased physical mobility of people who used modern methods of transportation to move across oceans, and from the rural American hinterland, in order to reach the city. The automobile was the symbol of change brought about by such mobility. It facilitated relocation and encouraged movement outside the neighbourhood. Together with other forms of mass transportation, the automobile 'undermined what is in every society the primary source of control, namely, the vigilance of neighbours and the desire of every individual to retain the respect and esteem of his local community' (Park (1934c) 1955: 298). Here, as elsewhere, Park insisted that the basic source of self-control and social control is the restraining influence of others, in this case of neighbours, with whom one is integrated into groups and who confer (or withhold) status, self-esteem, and identity.

How then could a new kind of cultural consensus, more in keeping with the technology and social organization of cities, be encouraged? Park believed that communication – both personal and by way of the mass media – contributed to a city-wide cultural consensus. The school, workplace, trade union, settlement house, the church, the political club, and even boys' gangs were the localities likely to facilitate 'personal relations and personal friendships', which Park described as 'the great moral solvents'. These settings encouraged social interaction in which representatives of different groups 'discover in one another' 'sentiments, tastes, interests, and human qualities generally that

118

they can understand and respect' (Park (1926b) 1950: 253-4). Park believed, perhaps over-optimistically, that it is through participation in such groups and institutions that individuals develop commitments and allegiances. However, in cities, opportunities for face-to-face interaction over a long period of time are limited. Instead, 'casual contact', in which 'it is the offensive rather than the pleasing traits that impress us' is prevalent (Park (1913b) 1950: 209).

It is the press, and the mass media in general that Park believed to be crucial to the emergence of a city-wide shared culture. The city newspaper rendered diversity in the experiences of individual men intelligible. It was pivotal in 'making information about our common life accessible to everyone at less than the price of a telephone call' (Park (1923b) 1955: 91). Park went so far as to suggest that

> If public opinion is to continue to govern in the future as it has in the past, if we propose to maintain a democracy as Jefferson conceived it, the newspaper must continue to tell us about ourselves. We must somehow learn to know our community and its affairs in the same intimate way in which we knew them in the country villages.
>
> (ibid.: 93)

Park believed that the newspaper would develop the capacity of city dwellers to 'take the role of the other'. In this way he hoped that mutual understanding and social sentiments would develop between strangers who were also neighbours. He felt that even the most parochial newspapers integrated readers into the larger community by communicating the nature of the 'generalised other', and a common 'definition of the situation'.

Park acknowledged that the press was often biased and partisan, its language ambiguous, and its writers sometimes inclined to dramatize events. However, despite this, he also believed that the importance of the metropolitan newspaper was that it assured its readership that antagonistic class interests and differences in origin and experience were superficial when compared to the fundamental sameness of the human condition. This was most evident in the 'human interest story' 'that gives the reporter the character of a literary artist and the news story the character of literature' (Park (1940) 1955: 113).[8] The press encouraged

119

Americans to consider their sectarian interests within the context of a concern for the commonweal. Park would have agreed that 'The promise of an American identity held out to a mass audience made the American press itself a distinctly American phenomenon' of great social, political, and cultural significance (Barth 1980: 108).

The emerging discipline of sociology was itself a second source of mutual understanding and cultural consensus. The sociologist, like the newspaper reporter, was required by his vocation to observe city life and to communicate his findings to the public. Sociological studies of 'natural areas' of the city, such as Chicago's 'Gold Coast' (Zorbaugh 1929) or 'Hob-Bohemia' (Anderson (1923) 1961) and of social groups, such as hobos, Jews, Afro-Americans, taxi-dance hall denizens, real-estate agents, politicians, criminals, and juvenile delinquents, were intended to reveal empathetically the substance of people's lives. These investigations were also intended to aid such groups in their dealings with outsiders and members of the dominant society. Thus, for example, in his introduction to Pauline Young's study of the Molokan immigrants in California, Park observed that her research enabled members of this group to 'achieve a more adequate conception of themselves and of their peculiar problems in America than they would otherwise have done'. Her study also served 'to interpret these interesting folk both to their neighbours and to the American public in a way to make their intercourse less difficult and more fruitful than it has been in the past' (Park (1932) 1955:29).

One measure of the success with which sociologists have fulfilled the objective of furthering mutual understanding and thus contributing to a city-wide shared culture – if not a national culture – is indicated by the extent to which sociological research has restructured 'common-sense' assumptions about both human behaviour and the nature of American society. For example, the dissolution of the link between race and culture, which was helped along by Park and Thomas, is no longer an issue.

There is a distinction to be made between parochial minority group cultures on the one hand, and a city-wide shared culture on the other. However, contradictions between these are more apparent than real. It can be concluded, as Park did, that the first is actually a stimulus to the second.

The Janus-faced nature of cultures attributed to Park has been discussed more recently by the American sociologist, Robert Blauner, in his book *Racial Oppression in America* (Blauner 1972). Blauner argues that 'black culture' refers to a type of ethnic culture rather than the 'holistic' view of culture used by anthropologists to describe 'the integrated way of life, that system of customs, institutions, beliefs and values that fit together into some organic whole, perhaps dominated by a certain ethos ... developed from the study of primitive peoples'. Instead, he points out, 'Today when we characterise Jews, Italians, or Greeks as ethnic groups, we are referring implicitly to a different notion of culture. This is the idea that ethnic culture resides in a certain number of distinctive values, orientations to life and experience, and shared memories that co-exist within the framework of the general American life-style and allegiances' (Blauner 1972: 128-9).

Blauner contends that a 'culture building process' among Afro-Americans and the emergence of an ethnic group identity have been going on since slavery. However, development of this distinct ethnic culture and group consciousness 'has been paralleled by one of becoming more "American" in action and identity'. He argues, along lines similar to those set down by Park earlier, that 'The stronger that Negro ethnic culture becomes', the greater the possibility for individual and group mobility. 'For in American life', he concludes, 'ethnic culture is identity, there is no individual or group progress without a clear sense of who one is, where one came from, and where one is going.' He reiterates Park's conviction, discussed in Chapter Six, that white Americans 'will learn what Afro-American culture is from American blacks rather than from our own dogmas and fantasies' (ibid.: 146-55).

Contrary to Blauner's conclusion, the black novelist Ralph Ellison suggests that the term 'Negro culture' 'is so vague as to be meaningless'. He goes on to point out that 'due to the close links which Negro Americans have with the rest of the nation' the 'cultural expressions specific to them are constantly influencing the larger body of American culture and are in turn influenced by them'. Ellison concludes that the existence of a specifically 'Negro' idiom should not in any way 'be confused with the vague racist terms "white culture" or "black culture"; rather it is a matter of diversity within unity' (Ellison (1958) 1972: 262-3).

The historians August Meier and Elliot Rudwick have suggested

121

a different view of the relationship between 'black culture' and a distinctly American identity. They point out that

> Modern studies in social psychology have demonstrated that members of minority groups react in various ways to their subordinate status in society. They may hate and rebel against their oppressors, or they may accept the inferiority assigned to them by the dominant group. They may assert social pride and emphasize the value of their own collective action, or they may attempt to assimilate the dominant group's culture and strive for acceptance in it. They may escape into religious otherworldliness. Or individuals may exhibit a paradoxical and complex amalgam of these attitudes and reactions.
>
> (Meier and Rudwick 1970: 67)

In short, social scientists have come to a variety of conclusions about both the existence of a specifically 'black culture' and the positive or negative consequences of such a culture.

Park considered the revival of culture, whether it be a parochial minority group culture or a city-wide shared culture, to be an avenue for the collective mobility of immigrants and Afro-Americans. Culture-building was also his solution to mental instability and social unrest. 'Art, religion, and politics, are still the means through which we participate in the common life,' he noted, 'but they have ceased to be our chief concern.' In their absence, urbanites, in their frantic bid to 'escape reality', seek the adventure of 'dance halls and jazz parlours ... political revolution and social reform ... millennialism in religion' and other ways of 'hunting the bluebird of romance' (Park (1925b) 1952: 68).

The social historian Jean Quandt argues that Progressive intellectuals, among whom she includes Park, elevated the concept of culture to a position of dominance in 'an effort to deal with the problem of the division of labour, the specialisation of knowledge, and the fragmentation of social life'. She goes on to note that the culture concept was used to 'give the individual a sense of connection with the largely unseen and complex environment in which he played a part' and 'to foster a sense of solidarity which would mitigate conflict, selfishness and indifference to the common good' (Quandt 1970: 126). Quandt concludes that this framework dealt with social and economic issues as problems of culture and communication. They showed, she goes on to say, a 'disregard' among Progressives 'for questions of social structure, economic power and material reward' (ibid.: 130).

Quandt's conclusion reiterates complaints about Park's work in the area of race and ethnicity discussed earlier (see Chapter Three, pp. 59-68).

Chapter Six argues that the concepts of culture, communication, and social control were essential to Park's analysis of Afro-Americans and race relations as well as to his discussion of ethnicity and his general perspective (outlined in Chapter Two). Yet judgements concerning the balance between the advantages and the pitfalls of Park's elevation of these concepts to theoretical dominance must not rest upon the appraisals of his critics alone. Certainly, as will be shown, Park and his students never argued that discrimination, conflict, poverty, unemployment, illegitimacy, and other sources of misery and deprivation for ethnic and racial minorities were problems of culture and communication alone.

Moreover, Quandt's conclusion, valid as it is in some respects, overlooks an important dimension of the concept of culture developed in Park's work. This dimension sees culture as a mechanism of adaptation to a social environment as well as being a force that modifies this environment. In this sense, Park understood culture to be of a dual nature. On the one hand, culture has a historical referent. It can be understood only in the context of the events that give rise to experience. Traditions, customs, institutional arrangements, and art and literature are the residues of past events, the reflection of past solutions to collective problems (see Chapter Two).

On the other hand, cultures are a response to the present. They are adaptive mechanisms which enable groups to survive in changed circumstances. Individuals living in specifiable historical situations are the agents who modify their values, ideas, and behaviour, and in so doing, are the agents of cultural change. It is in this sense that black ghetto culture, according to one observer, can be regarded as 'the historical creation of persons who are disinherited by their society' (Rainwater 1970:7).[9]

Chapter Six

'BRIGHT LIGHTS, IMPENDING SHADOWS': AFRO-AMERICAN MIGRATION TO NORTHERN CITIES

Park's analysis of the migration of southern, rural blacks to cities, especially northern cities, although not analogous to his work on immigrant communities, was certainly influenced by it. He saw a similarity between immigrant cultures founded upon 'old world traits transplanted' and an emergent Afro-American urban, culture having its roots in slavery and racism in the United States: both of these minority group cultures met the needs of individuals for recognition and self-esteem and both contributed to the solidarity and mobility of minority groups.

Neither Park nor other members of the Chicago school were naive enough to believe that all ethnic neighbourhoods had once been ghettos, like the so-called 'Black Belt' of Chicago, or that blacks were 'just another ethnic group, whose segregation was largely voluntary and would prove to be temporary' (Philpott 1978: 139-40). Park was always aware that 'the chief obstacles to the assimilation of the Negro and the Oriental are not mental but physical traits' (Park (1913b) 1950: 208). Coloured Americans differed from white immigrants because they could not obliterate their racial uniform; skin colour was made the symbol of moral and cultural differences (Park (1926b) 1950: 252). Park did sometimes discuss the spontaneous character of segregation (Park (1913b) 1950: 214).[1] However, the dominant motif of his essays was that black Americans, unlike white immigrants, were violently excluded from the encompassing white society.

The first section of this chapter compares the relationship between blacks and whites before and after the emancipation of slaves at the conclusion of the Civil War in April 1865 (the actual Proclamation of Emancipation was in 1863). It also considers race relations in northern cities during the post-bellum period.

The second section considers Park's view that the spatial segregation of Afro-Americans in cities was favourable to the growth of separate social institutions and the emergence of an urban black culture – both of which contributed to race consciousness and race solidarity. This is followed by a discussion of his most useful and deservedly enduring insights. An analysis of the flawed aspects of his perspective and mention of a few of the ways in which his students modified his ideas about race relations in line with these weaknesses conclude this section.

DRAWING THE COLOUR LINE: RACE RELATIONS IN THE ANTE-BELLUM AND POST-BELLUM SOUTH AND NORTHERN CITIES

Park suggested that the relationship between blacks and whites is fundamentally dissimilar in the ante-bellum South, the South after the Civil War, and the urban North. In each of these contexts, blacks and whites see each other as different kinds of objects and act according to the meanings generated and sustained by particular social arrangements. He used his typology of processes of social interaction and the concepts of race prejudice, race 'antipathy', race consciousness, and social distance to clarify the nature of these differences.

Park concluded that race relations were problematical in the *post-bellum* rather than the *ante-bellum* South. Moreover, the antithesis of the social stability characteristic of the ante-bellum plantation, as he pictured it, is the ambiguous and shifting nature of race relations in northern cities.

The ante-bellum South

In the ante-bellum South race relations took the form of social accommodation in which master and slave saw themselves as members of immutable social categories, bound together in an intimacy born of 'everyday experience' and an acknowledged interdependence. Their 'friendly relations' 'which are so unintelligible to those who have looked upon slavery as if it were always and everywhere, something inhuman and monstrous' can be

125

explained, according to Park, by viewing the plantation situation in terms of the experience and subjective points of view of its participants. He suggested that 'there grew up, out of the daily experience of master and slave, the conception of the Negro, according to which he was predestined by God and Nature, to be forever a hewer of wood and a drawer of water, "a servant to his brethren".' Moreover, he went on to note,

> There is evidence to show that, on the whole, the black man accepted the position to which the white man assigned him. Negro servants spoke habitually in a proprietary sense of their masters' families as 'our white folks'. And, on the other hand, the masters' families thought of the slaves on their plantations as 'our Negroes'. In short, the plantation, in spite of differences of race and status, constituted what I have elsewhere described as a we-group.
>
> (Park (1928b) 1950: 234-5)

Park suggested that in slavery, as in any other type of institutional arrangement, consciousness enters into the construction of collective activity as well as being modified on the basis of this activity. Discrete acts taken together constitute experience for the individual and tradition for the group. Accordingly, slaves take on meaning as objects in terms of their work and their 'rightlessness' (Finlay 1968) compared with the style of life and privileges of whites.

Park's image of slavery corresponds to two different types of slave-holding enterprises. First, the smaller plantations or farms of the northern states of the Confederacy such as Virginia and North Carolina in which master and slave worked together raising tobacco, cereals, and vegetables for home consumption. Here 'owners were closer to their slaves than masters of large plantations' and 'a mutuality developed out of the social and physical closeness'. Planters, like their slaves, had neither very much education nor leisure (Harlan 1972: 7). In those instances in which both master and slaves actually laboured together, 'there was likely to be less brutality on the part of management and more work on the part of the labouring force than under other circumstances' (Franklin 1967: 193).

The second type of enterprise to which Park's notion of slavery corresponds is that of the domestic or house servants on the larger plantations. Paternalism and intimacy were the outcomes of the slaves' daily participation in the most personal aspects of family life, such as raising the master's children, preparing his food, and assisting in personal grooming. Slaves were encouraged to become Christians. Miscegenation sometimes provided the incentive for the bondsman's education and eventual emancipation (Stampp 1956: passim).

Slavery resulted in masters, slaves, and free whites each having a sense of group position, stable self-conceptions, and complementary understandings about the rights and obligations inherent in place and role. Whites were stratified on the basis of property and style of life, so that aristocratic 'Bourbons' of the larger planter class were differentiated from the uneducated rough-hewn 'red-necks' and other poor whites most of whom were not slave-owning. Blacks were ranked in terms of the extent to which they intermingled with whites and absorbed their masters' culture.[2]

Both of the above models of slave-holding enterprises provided opportunities for contact, communication, and participation in shared experience, and, in some senses, a common culture. Park implied that participation in a common enterprise under these relatively favourable conditions was of greater importance in determining attitude and degree of social solidarity than punishment and bondage. Thus, he argued, 'one learns that the plantation society, originally a mere *modus vivendi* to insure the co-operation of individuals of two divergent races, had achieved at the end of the era a social stability and a moral solidarity that enabled it to withstand the shock of a Civil War in which its very existence was involved' (Park (1928b) 1950: 234).

Ironically, participation in common life tended to break down the social distances upon which the slave system was based. Friendship and the recognition of a common humanity impressed themselves upon masters and slaves alike. For while

Men come together ordinarily because they are useful to one another ... human beings do not live for long, like plants, in relations that are merely symbiotic. *For men, unlike plants, communicate* ... a moral order grows up in which, under the happiest of circumstances, the individual feels himself

127

constrained only by those obligations which he freely accepts or imposes upon himself.

Park went on to observe that

It is characteristic of such a moral order that it is nonrational. That means that it is not devised to protect any special interest, to serve any policy, has no ulterior purposes of any sort. On the contrary, it arises in response to the *natural claims* which one individual makes upon another, as soon as he recognises that other individual is human like himself.

(Park (1937b) 1950: 180)

Etiquette and convention maintain 'social distances' undermined by contact, communication, and shared experience. In Park's words,

Social distance is a phenomenon of a society that is based on primary or face-to-face relationships ... at a given time and place, every individual may be said to occupy a position, defined in terms of his psychical distance or intimacy, with respect to every other....Thus it was quite possible, on the plantation, and particularly in the case of the house servants and the master's family, to maintain the most intimate relationships between master and slave provided the social ritual defining and maintaining the caste relationship was maintained in its integrity.

Park anticipated Gunnar Myrdal's idea of 'an American dilemma' when he wrote, 'The regime of slavery, constantly threatened from without was at the same time threatened from within; weakened by the claims of the slave on the one hand, and the conscience of the master on the other' (Park (1937b) 1950: 179-83).

Park emphasized etiquette as a mechanism of social control on the plantation. He made fewer references to the ways in which anti-black sentiment and violence among the white non-slaveholding population or of the implementation of state legislation such as 'Black Codes', proscribing marriage, education movement, and assembly, affected slaves.

Moreover, for the field-hands, especially on the large cotton plantations of the lower South during the nineteenth century, personal contact did not mitigate the worst abuses of chattel slavery. Between master and field-hand stood a white overseer, and sometimes a driver recruited from among the slaves. The overseer often had unlimited authority in the day-to-day administration of the plantation. Unlike the slave-owner, he had little interest in the slave as property with a long-term as well as a short-term commercial value. Naked and vicious exploitation rather than a benevolent paternalism characterized slave life. Physical mutilation and death, rape and forced sales were staple ingredients of the slaves' existence on many plantations, especially those in the Deep South.

The field hands greatly outnumbered domestic servants or slaves employed in crafts and other types of non-agricultural activities. However, it is precisely this group that Park fails to emphasize in his analysis of slavery in the ante-bellum South.[3]

It would be a mistake to conclude, however, that Park is a southern apologist or pro-slavery. Until relatively recently, studies of slavery were based on the narrative material of slave-owners, travellers, and historians who emphasized the paternalism of aristocratic planters and presented a favourable outlook on the ante-bellum South. Park undoubtedly had access to just such romanticized accounts, as his emphasis on the positive aspects of slavery in the ante-bellum South reflected such romanticized points-of-view. The standard book in this respect is Ulrich B. Phillips' *American Negro Slavery* published in 1918. Despite abolitionist literature, the image of slaves as 'docile, well-adapted to slavery and reasonably content with their lot' was popular among many scholars (Bauer and Bauer (1942) 1970; Genovese (1966) 1972).

Park was worried about the prospects for improved race relations offered by the 'New South' and the rapid uplift for the freedmen. As he pointed out, 'Slavery is dead, and no one now defends it. But caste remains, and is still so much a part of the natural and expected order that few people in the South either question its right to exist or discuss its function' (Park (1937b) 1950: 181). In his analysis the positive aspects of the ante-bellum South are highlighted by their absence from the post-bellum period.

The post-bellum South

According to Park, freedom in the 'New South' was a mixed blessing. For the freedmen, it meant first and foremost the right to move. Freedom also gave blacks the chance to improve their lives through education, hard work, thrift, sobriety, the acquisition of property, practice of a trade or profession, and a reasonable 'home life' (Park 1913(b) 1950). If it was the freedman's right, it was also his *duty* to succeed and to participate in the dominant middle-class culture: 'From the Yankee school-ma'ams, who came South after the war to complete in the schools the emancipation of the Freedmen, Negroes learned, among other things, that they, like other Americans, were destined and expected to rise' (Park (1935b) 1950: 174).

Booker Washington believed that for the bulk of the freedmen, emancipation was equated with withdrawal from manual labour and resulted in a general moral laxity subseqeunt to their release from the discipline slavery imposed (Harlan 1972: 28). In describing his education at Hampton Institute, Washington pointed out, 'At Hampton I not only learned that it was not a disgrace to labour, but learned to love labour, not alone for its financial value, but for labour's own sake and for the independence and self-reliance which the ability to do something which the world wants done brings' (Washington (1901) 1956: 51).

Park agreed with Washington that 'industrial education' was a practical strategy for attaining the habits and skills which would enable black men and women to assert themselves on the basis of their economic achievements – the kind of success Americans have always recognized. The anti-intellectual bias inherent in Washington's programme at Tuskegee, however, was absent from the plans of other educationalists, notably George Herbert Mead, who was himself interested in introducing industrial education in the Chicago public schools. Mead was concerned with the practical problem of keeping working-class children in school. He argued that industrial education provided youths with skills useful to the community, as well as enhancing their individual development. Mead took great pains to point out that vocational training would be initiated 'As an essential part of education – in no illiberal sense and with no intention of separating out a class of workingmen's children who are to receive trade training at the expense of academic training' (Mead (1912) cited in Rucker (1969) 1971: 96-7).

Washington, Mead, John Dewey, and Park all believed that the school must serve as an agency of socialization to prepare children (and adults) to participate in the larger community as both

130

economic producers and as citizens. Washington's programmes emphasized service to the community. For black people in the post-bellum South, service to the community meant learning trades such as brick-making, shoemaking, tinsmithing, black-smithing, printing, laundering, cooking, sewing, painting, broom-making, scientific farming, as well as accounting and merchand-izing. With the exception of the latter, these skills tended to be in short supply due to the reluctance of blacks to seek out employment in occupations which were associated with their former slave status or which meant remaining in the rural South.

Park's liberal view of the purposes of industrial education led him to modify the Tuskegee curriculum in favour of the development of non-vocational objectives. In a bibliography he prepared in 1910 entitled 'Fifty-one "Books Every Tuskegee Graduate Should Know"', Park included titles such as *Pilgrim's Progress, Tom Brown's School Days, Two Years Before the Mast, Pride and Prejudice, Silas Marner, Les Miserables* ('pronounced Lay Miseraabl'), Bacon's *Essays,* Shakespeare's *Merchant of Venice* and *Julius Caesar* ('the most popular of Shakespeare's tragedies and easiest to read'). He also cited books on slavery and Reconstruction. Included were *Uncle Tom's Cabin* ('the book that is said to have done more than anything else to free the slaves. It depicts slavery as it looked to one who knew about slavery from the stories of fugitive slaves'); *The Conjure Woman, and Other Stories* ('stories of Negro life by the only Negro novelist who has gained a national reputation'); *The Crisis, The Great Debate, Life of Lincoln and the Downfall of Slavery, Life and Times of Frederick Douglass, Abraham Lincoln, A Fool's Errand, Red Rock,* and *Up from Slavery* ('illustrating the ways in which the Negro masses are winning for themselves their moral independence in a kind of freedom, not granted by the Emancipation Proclamation' (Washington-Park Correspond-ence, Booker T. Washington Papers, 10 April 1910).

Under the heading 'Rules for Reading', Park advised,

Read Every Week .... Read Every Night .... Never Read a Book in which you are not interested. If you are not interested in the book you are reading, it is either because the book is not worth reading or because you do not understand it .... *Always Connect the Story* you are reading with what you know of the place and the people where the story takes place. Notice if the picture the story presents corresponds with your own previous ideas of the place and the people.... *Try to Learn Five New Words* every day. In looking them up, choose the smallest words and use the biggest dictionary .... *Never Think You Can Learn* the meaning of a word from the dictionary alone. Words represent ideas and only close and constant reading of the best authors will teach you to know them.

Nor did Park fail to mention, '*Every One Should Read Constantly* (a) Good daily newspapers, or, better still, a good weekly newspaper, like the *Independent* or *Outlook*; (b) Good magazines or books of general literature; (c) A book or magazine connected with some trade or profession; (d) The Bible or some other book of daily inspiration' (ibid.).

Park was sensitive to the requirements of Tuskegee students, who, he believed, had not known 'the companionship of books', or had come 'from regions into which few newspapers find their way' (Park-Washington Correspondence, Booker T. Washington Papers, n.d.). His bibliography included items and advice meant to introduce the reading habit to them as a way of overcoming the limitations of their actual experience through knowledge of the larger world, past and present. Park, like Dewey and Mead, took intelligence to be the practical activity of resolving problems through constant reorganization of experience in novel situations. Reading constituted a kind of vicarious experience and, as such, broadened the basis upon which students would be able to participate in the world of work and politics. Another aim of Park's bibliography was to give black students an idea of their history and their great race leaders.

Park thought that industrial education would eventually enable black people to define their own goals with regard to what they took to be their own welfare. This belief is expressed in a letter written by Park to Washington in 1905 urging him to attend the International Exposition in Belgium in order to point out the relevance of the methods adopted at Tuskegee to colonizing efforts in Africa.

The difference between your school and others, as I understand it, consists in this that it 'consults the negro in regard to his own welfare': it interests the negro in himself and his own welfare. Now I suspect from what I know of sociological

science abroad that very few of the people who attend this Congress have ever suspected that the aspirations, the *possibilities* of these people should be consulted as well as their present habits and tastes.
(Park-Washington Correspondence, Booker T. Washington Papers, 1905)

For Park, the question debated by many of his contemporaries of whether blacks can participate in the larger culture was less important than the discovery of the best techniques to enable them to 'catch up' with the modern world most rapidly. Similarly, the problem of ascertaining what of the white man's culture blacks would absorb was of less interest to him than what aspects of the dominant culture they would *choose* to make their own.

In the post-bellum period, the reality of geographical mobility and the promise of social mobility among the freedmen exacerbated the fears of southern whites about their future and reinforced their determination to maintain economic, social, and political advantages which had only been temporarily threatened during Reconstruction. Park argued that the proliferation of segregation statutes were the desperate attempts of whites to reassert the prerogatives of caste. Lynchings and race riots were more violent expressions of this same conservative effort. He went on to observe that 'Generally speaking, there was no such thing as a race problem before the Civil War and there was at that time very little of what we ordinarily call race prejudice, except in the case of the free Negro' (Park (1937b) 1950: 184-6).

Park shared the widely held conviction that 'the violent, often vituperative, and always tactless efforts of the New South' to preserve caste were largely the work of the poorer class of white people. In a letter to Washington, Park stated that he felt restrained from disseminating news of the business successes of blacks by his fear of 'the jealousy of the "cracker" element if they knew that coloured men were getting rich just like white men' (Park-Washington Correspondence, Booker T. Washington Papers).[4]

Park argued that for the freedmen, freedom meant the absence of the protection of a powerful slave-owning class. He agreed with Washington that the excesses of the ante-bellum planters were never equal to the racial hatred unleashed by that three-quarters of the white population who never owned slaves and 'who hated slavery with an intensity only equalled by their hatred of the Negro' (Park (1913b) 1950: 212). The New South threw up her own men of money and power, as well as legitimizing the claims of these formerly powerless, non-slaveholding, poorer whites.

The race problem in the post-bellum South, according to Park, was in some measure, a reflection of this breakdown of the ante-bellum stratification system *among whites*. In the New South, social equality did not refer to equality between men of similar accomplishments or property among members of both races, but to the apparent social equality between whites – regardless of these other attributes. The doctrine of white supremacy and racial solidarity – despite class differences among whites – brought about 'the emancipation of the poor white man. It gave him an equality with the planter aristocracy he had never had under the old regime. It made him an enthusiastic defender of the ritual of a caste system in which he had once occupied a distinctly inferior position' (Park (1937b) 1950: 185).

Economic exploitation and social segregation – for example, in public conveyances and schools – were the tangible expressions of 'a solid south' intent upon maintaining white supremacy. Voting, office-holding, jury duty, and the exercise of civil rights among blacks, put into place during Reconstruction, were attacked by the Redeemers ushering in the New South.

Park, like Washington, viewed the failure of Reconstruction politics as a mandate for blacks to substitute economic realism for political idealism as their first priority. Although sympathetic to old-style black politicians such as John Mercer Langston, Robert Brown Elliott, Blanch K. Bruce, and Hiram Revels, Park foresaw the emergence of a new type of race leader more suited to the times. These new men of power would base their claims on money, organization, and the votes of the black masses, a combination only possible in the cities of the North. For this 'new type of Negro', 'the personal touch which holds the races together in the South' was an irrelevance (Washington, quoted by Park (1913b) 1950: 212). The benefits of 'learning by example' in the South were to be dropped in favour of learning by doing in the North.[5]

134

NORTHERN CITIES

Park believed that improving race relations in northern cities required bridging social distances and establishing a moral basis of association between competitive groups. This could be accomplished through increased participation in common enterprises, and empathetic communication between members of different racial and ethnic groups. Park noted that

> The race problem turns out, then, in one of its aspects at least, to be a problem of communication. The barriers to communication are not differences of language and of culture merely, but more particularly of self-consciousness, race consciousness, and consciousness of kind; not physical distances merely, but social distances.

He concluded that 'Personal relations and personal friendships are the great moral solvents. Under their influence all distinctions of class, of caste, and even of race, are dissolved into the general flux which we sometimes call democracy' (Park (1926b) 1950: 253-4).

In northern cities, conflict and antagonism ensue as a result of competition between blacks and whites for jobs and housing. Neither inhibited nor protected by the proscriptions of caste as in the South, black migrants were now involved in intense rivalry for the rewards available.

Intense competition between previously isolated groups contributes to the incidence and ferocity of race conflict. Under these conditions, what Park conceived of as normal 'race prejudice', now interlaced with 'racial antipathy', is transformed into an assault on blacks. What, then, did Park mean by race prejudice and racial antipathy?

Race prejudice, Park thought, is a response to the existence of hierarchy. 'Where there are social classes', he noted, 'there will invariably be corresponding attitudes and sentiments. Racial distinctions, when they exist, will always be supported by racial prejudices' (Park (1928b) 1950: 234).

Race prejudice legitimizes prevailing stratification arrangements. Therefore, he concluded, 'Every effort of the Negro – to take the most striking example – to move, to rise and improve his *status*, rather than his *condition*, has invariably met with opposition,

135

arouses prejudice and stimulated racial animosities. Race prejudice, so conceived is merely an elementary expression of conserv-
atism' (emphasis is my own).

Race prejudice does not determine race conflict and antagonism. Rather, 'There is probably less racial prejudice in America
than elsewhere, but there is more racial conflict because there is
more change, more progress. The Negro is rising in America and
the measure of the antagonism he encounters is, in some very real
sense, the measure of his progress' (ibid.: 233–4).[6]

Park suggested that the initial historical contact between groups
determines the original social attitude which is the basis of a
continuing tradition. Prior to revolutions in communication and
transportation, migration and conquest were the events which
brought previously isolated groups into contact with one another,
precipitating new social arrangements and their accompanying
prejudices and ideologies.

However, race prejudice is no mere anachronism. It is a shared
attitude which defines the relative positions of social groups.
Membership influences the individual's self-conception and plays
an important role in the construction of both individual and
collective action. Race consciousness only arises when the legit-
imacy of institutional arrangements and attitudes defining the
status of one group in relation to others are challenged.

Put slightly differently, every racial group formulates its identity
around its opposition to other groups. The dimensions of this opposition are 'dominance' and 'subordination', and 'inclusion and
exclusion'. It is precisely because it has to do with feelings of dominance, privilege, and exclusiveness – or the relative lack of them –
that race prejudice is of such importance. Race prejudice serves as
an ideology to establish hegemony over desirable styles of life.

Prejudice is an outcome of membership of racial classes rather
than being either a unique individual experience or expressing a
disturbed personality.[7] Born into societies in which colour determines the basis of group affiliation, individuals are not free to
choose the group with which they will align themselves. (This
clarifies Park's belief that liberal whites have only a limited role to
play in the Afro-Americans' struggle to achieve racial justice (Park
(1923a) 1950: 300).)

As already noted, there is no stable set of social attitudes and
traditions defining the black southern migrants' 'place' with

136

respect to whites in the North. Blacks settling in cities such as Chicago rubbed shoulders with whites on public transport, in workplaces, and in residential areas as well as confronting whites as policemen, social workers, and school teachers.[8]

'Racial antipathy' is born of a lack of tradition and intimacy between races and the perception of Afro-Americans as 'strangers'. The added ingredient of 'racial antipathy', because it is based on an instinctive, irrational response to what is unfamiliar, transforms normal race prejudice into something 'more insidious'. Park, agreeing with Simmel, suggested that the 'sense of insecurity' 'which the presence of the stranger inspires, when not dispelled by more intimate acquaintance', fixes racial antipathy as a permanent feature of intergroup relations (Park (1913b) 1950; (1928b) 1950).

In cities the sense of confidence and trust contingent upon intimate association gives way to antipathy and insecurity. Secondary associations and the mass media become of increasing importance in influencing definitions of the situation. Moreover, in cities relationships are organized around commerce and tend to be symbiotic rather than social.

> In the city peoples of diverse races and cultures come together not to participate in and perpetuate a common life as is the case of a family, kinship group, or religious sect, but as individuals who have discovered that they are useful to one another. Society and the moral order indubitably have had their origin in the family, but civilisation has grown up around the market place and has expanded with the expansion of the market.
>
> (Park (1939a) 1950: 86-90)[9]

The lack of familiarity between black and white urbanites blots out the perception of differences in personality and temperament between individual members of the same race. By virtue of his colour the Afro-American is denied both homogeneity within the white world and diversity within the black one. A white skin, observed Park,

> so far as it makes each individual look like every other – no matter how different under the skin ... removes the social taboo. In obliterating the external signs, which in secondary

137

groups seem to be the sole basis of caste and class distinctions, it realises, for the individual, the principle of *laissez-faire, laissez-aller*. Its ultimate economic effect is to substitute personal for racial competition, and to give free play to forces that tend to relegate every individual, irrespective of race or status, to the position he or she is best fitted to fulfil.

(Park (1913b) 1950: 203)

The obliteration of the coloured American's individuality behind his 'racial uniform' constitutes a violation of his democratic right to be treated on his 'merits, as an individual' rather than as a representative of his race (Park (1923c) 1950: 160). The substitution of group characteristics for individual attributes in the determination of life chances is contradictory to the principles of democratic societies. Yet, in reality, while 'democracy abhors social distinction' it none the less maintains them (Park (1924a) 1950: 258-9).

Thus, the black migrant from the South once settled in a northern city, like the Japanese-American, may experience, 'A profound transfiguration in sentiment and attitude, but he cannot change his physical characteristics ... he cannot, much as he may sometimes like to do so, cast aside his racial mask' (Park (1926b) 1950: 252). White immigrants and their children can pass into the dominant society despite ethnic prejudice because, once in possession of the language and culture of the dominant group, they cannot be easily identified as 'foreign'. Non-white Americans, regardless of their acculturation to the requirements of city life, remain visible and therefore their claims to full participation in American life continue to be effectively resisted. 'The trouble is not with the Japanese mind but with the Japanese skin', remarked Park. 'The "Jap" is not the right colour' (Park (1913b) 1950: 208).

Non-white Americans cannot erase visible marks of identification which are symbols of *moral* and *cultural* differences and which locate them in a subordinate position within the prevailing stratification system regardless of individual attributes and accomplishments. Race consciousness is organized around the symbolic meanings and moral evaluations that colour takes on in the context of existing racial hierarchies. As Park put it, race relations

are the relations existing between peoples distinguished by

138

marks of racial descent, particularly when these racial differences enter into the consciousness of the individuals and groups so distinguished, and by so doing determine in each case the individual's conception of himself as well as his status in the community....*Race relations, in this sense, are not so much the relations that exist between individuals of different races as between individuals conscious of these differences.*

(Park (1939a) 1950: 81; emphasis is mine)[10]

Park's accomplishment, then, as Fred Matthews points out, is to 'shift scholarly attention away from the description of racial traits' and to redefine 'the ideas of "race" and "racial differences" as themselves subjective and problematic' (Matthews 1977: 157).

NO RACIAL JUSTICE WITHOUT RACIAL CONFLICT: BLACK CULTURE AND COLLECTIVE ACTION

The 'great migration of Negroes from the plantation and small towns of the South to the manufacturing cities and metropolitan centres of the North', observed Park in 1935, 'has brought about, for good and for all, a great change in the condition and in the outlook of the Negro people in America' (Park (1935b) 1950: 167-8). The magnitude of this population movement can be gleaned from the following statistics.

In 1900, 62.3 per cent (47,379,699) of all Americans lived in the North, while 32.3 per cent (24,523,527) resided in the South and the remaining 5.4 per cent (4,091,349) in the West. Among Afro-Americans, 10 per cent (880,771) lived in the North, 89.7 per cent (7,922,969) in the South, and 0.3 per cent (30,254) in the West. Thirty years later, 59.5 per cent (73,021,191) of the entire population and 20.3 per cent (2,409,219) of blacks lived in the North. Thus, while the percentage of the entire population living in the North decreased slightly, the percentage of blacks in this region doubled (Katznelson 1976: 30-3).

Labour demands created by the First World War increased 'the steady though inconspicuous, exodus from the southern to the northern states that has been in progress since 1860, or, in fact since the "underground railway"'. In addition to the 150,000 blacks who had migrated to the North between 1900 and 1915, approximately half a million more moved there between 1916 and

1918 (Chicago Commission on Race Relations (1922) 1968: 79).

In the city of Chicago in 1900 blacks numbered 1.8 per cent (30,150) of the city's population while immigrants and their children constituted about 80 per cent (2,701,150) of a total population of 3,376,438 (Philpott 1978: 116-17). Between 1910 and 1920 Chicago's black population increased by 148 per cent (from 44,103 to 109,594) 'with a corresponding increase in the white population of 21 per cent, including foreign immigration'. The increase due to migration, as opposed to natural increase during this period, was estimated to be 51 per cent (Chicago Commission on Race Relations (1922) 1968: 79). By 1930, the percentage of blacks in Chicago had risen to 6.9 per cent (223, 803) (Philpott 1978: 116).

Like the foreign-born with whom they competed for jobs and living space, southern blacks were mainly rural 'folk' drawn to the city in pursuit of economic opportunity and education for themselves and their children. In the South, without capital or suitable means of obtaining credit to purchase land, blacks 'continued to engage in the various forms of tenancy and sharecropping which had evolved during the period following the abolition of slavery'. Ironically, in cities in the South, competition for jobs from newly arrived immigrants lessened economic opportunity for blacks in manufacturing and mining as well as in those occupations concerned with rendering personal services, such as cooking, catering, and barbering, that they had previously monopolized. 'Everywhere there was sentiment against hiring Negroes in jobs that had even the semblance of respectability. Negroes living in cities in the South discovered that urban life could be almost as frustrating as rural life' (Franklin 1967: 398-401).

In 1914 in the South, wages varied from 75 cents per day for farm work, in which most blacks were employed, to $1.75 for doing other sorts of jobs. In 1916 and 1917, blacks in Chicago were receiving between $3.00 to $8.00 per day for working shorter hours and doing a variety of jobs (Chicago Commission on Race Relations (1922) 1968: 84, 357-435).

The testimony of Negroes who at some time had lived in the South was mainly that they were obliged to work harder for what they got North. They also declared that they were unable to save as much as they hoped or expected, because of high prices. But in the great majority of cases satisfaction was expressed over their economic situation.

(ibid.: 168-9)

In addition to improved economic prospects, blacks came North to escape from the burdens of the 'reconstructed' South where they were deprived of political rights, such as the vote, and were routinely denied access to public and private schools, restaurants, and parks. More than one recent arrival from the South luxuriated in not having 'to give up the sidewalk for white people as in my former home' or being 'compelled to say "yes ma'am" or "yes sir" to white people whether you desired or not'. They also went North to escape mob violence, segregated transportation facilities, and 'injustices in the courts' (ibid.: 79-105).

The majority of southern blacks coming to Chicago were young people, unmarried, and generally unskilled. They were the children of freedmen and they left the South without having known the reality of slavery (Spear 1967: 11-27).

Southern blacks were old stock Americans in terms of language, religion, and shared history. Yet, it soon became apparent to prescient onlookers, such as Park, that the stigma of colour was to render the lot of America's black native offspring more onerous than that of the immigrant. In the areas of housing and employment, by convention if not by statute, Chicago's newly arrived black population suffered the indignities of prejudice and of discrimination even at the hands of foreigners (Philpott 1978: 113-203).

Chicago's 'dark' ghetto developed as blacks were systematically excluded from white residential areas and became more and more concentrated in the south and west sides of the city. As Park observed,

the migration of the Negroes to northern cities took place at a time when urban residents were abandoning their homes in the centre of the city for the more spacious suburbs. As these suburbs multiplied the abandoned and so-called 'blighted' area surrounding the central business core steadily expanded. These areas are now largely occupied by immigrants and Negroes. The result has been that by a singular turn of fortune the southern Negro, lately from the 'sticks' – the man politically farthest down – now finds himself living in the centre of a great metropolitan city.

(Park (1935b) 1950: 173)

The emergence of the physical ghetto was an indication of the deteriorating status of the Afro-American in Chicago.

The concentration of large numbers of blacks employed *outside* the 'Black Belt' but living *within* the ghetto provided ambitious and talented black entrepreneurs and professionals with customers and clients denied to them in other areas of the city. Prior to the turn of the century, among the blacks who made their way to northern cities, some were able to establish manufacture and retail businesses, craft and service enterprises, dependent upon white patronage. Between 1890 and 1920 such patronage declined and Afro-American entrepreneurs and professions turned to the growing black urban masses, whose requirements became the basis of a proliferation of small businesses such as barbers, tailors, cleaners, restaurateurs, and grocers as well as cemetery associations, insurance companies, real-estate agencies, banks, and building and loan associations (Meier 1964: 139-71). In 1920 there were 1,500 commercial and industrial enterprises conducted by Afro-Americans in Chicago, the most numerous of which were barber shops (211), groceries and delicatessens (110), hairdressing parlours (108), and restaurants (87), serving, almost exclusively, the black community (Chicago Commission on Race Relations (1922) 1968: 140-1).

The First World War resulted in the extension of invitations to blacks to fill the ranks of semi-skilled and skilled labour in industries which had previously been closed to them. A combination of increased production, a shortage of white labour due to recruitment into the army (for which black men were also eligible), the return of some aliens to their mother countries, and a halt in immigration, resulted in an increase in the employment of blacks in industry. The Chicago Commission on Race Relations estimated that in 1910, out of a black population of 44,103, only 27,000 were engaged in industry while in 1920, out of a population of 109,594, about 70,000 were so engaged (ibid.: 358-9).

After the War, the widespread policy of 'last hired, first fired' forced the bulk of black labour to revert to pre-war employment expectations, except for a fortunate number of men who had secured a hold in the meat-packing and steel industries and women working in the manufacture of clothing (Drake and Cayton (1945) 1962: 228).

Although 1924-28 were prosperous years for residents of the Black Belt, continued industrial growth and economic prosperity in Chicago did not bring with it a dispersal of Afro-Americans throughout the occupational pyramid proportionate to that achieved by white newcomers to the city (ibid.: 218-23). Discrimination against black workers by employers and trade unions resulted in constraints on mobility which did not apply to other members of the labour force.[11] Among the unions which excluded blacks from membership, either in conformity with the laws of their national unions or in exercise of a 'local option' (such as that allowed by the American Federation of Labour which in its national constitution set down a policy of no racial discrimination), were the Machinists' International Alliance, Amalgamated Sheet Metal Workers' International Alliance, International Brotherhood of Electrical Workers of America, and United Association of Plumbers and Steamfitters of the United States and Canada. On the other hand, unions such as the International Ladies Garment Workers' Union made special efforts to organize black workers (Chicago Commission on Race Relations (1922) 1968: 463-5).

Organized labour's unfriendly attitude towards Afro-Americans was exacerbated by the latter's periodic use by employers as strikebreakers. Blacks had to wait until the mid-1930s, when the Congress of Industrial Organizations organized the steel, meat-packing, and stockyards industries, before they could be assured that unions would work for them rather than against them (Drake and Cayton (1945) 1962: 312).

By 1915, Afro-Americans had

emerged as a special group in the social structure of pre-war Chicago. The systematic proscriptions they suffered in housing and jobs, the discrimination they often – although not always – experienced in public accommodations and even municipal services, the violence of which they were frequently victims, set them apart from the mainstream of

143

Chicago life in significant ways. They were *forced* to work out their destiny within the context of an increasingly biracial society.

(Spear 1967: 49)

The growth of specifically black institutions, like the development of immigrant institutions, facilitated the transition of black migrants from rural to urban life. Like the immigrants, black migrants to northern cities such as Chicago benefited from the services, as well as from the recognition and regulation that participation in black institutions provided. Political machines, mutual aid and benefit societies, black churches, and a black press were essential resources for the survival of blacks in the face of both spontaneous and organized resistance to their claims for jobs, housing, municipal services, and political office. Moreover, these black institutions greatly contributed to the emergence of Afro-Americans as a national minority, a process that had its origin in the post-Civil War South.

In addition to building urban social institutions, America's black migrants, like its immigrants, confronted the task of how best to appropriate the culture of cities for their own use. In order to create a specifically Afro-American culture, which would promote self-esteem and enhance group status, black Americans had to shed their rural 'folk' culture built upon the experience of slavery and its racialist aftermath. A specifically Afro-American urban culture required reinterpreting southern history and communicating a different view of the role and destiny of black Americans (Park (1923a) 1950; (1943a) 1950).

Initially, Park agreed with Booker T. Washington, that the growth of a self-conscious, unified black community was taking place in the South (Park (1913b) 1950). By the 1920s, however, he reversed this opinion. He offered various reasons, in addition to that of migration itself, to explain the growth of an organized, black national minority in northern cities.

First of all, Park noted that black Americans experienced two kinds of isolation: physical and cultural. Physical or spatial isolation resulted in ghettos where blacks, although differentiated by occupation, class, education, and place of birth, were forced to live together in the same area and to recognize their shared predicament. Cultural isolation, on the other hand, resulted in the

144

exclusion of Afro-Americans from education and 'the techniques of communication and organization of the white man' (Park (1913b) 1950: 214-15).

Furthermore, Park suggested that the physical isolation of blacks from whites in cities in the North differed fundamentally from the more debilitating cultural isolation of blacks in rural areas of the South. Rural, southern blacks constituted 'a folk' whose 'habit' was 'fixed', whose culture was 'local', whose political influence was negligible, and whose intellectual horizon was circumscribed by 'the shadow of the plantation', outside which 'the only centres of Negro life are the rural churches and rural schools' (Park (1934b) 1950; Johnson 1934). The strength of Park's conviction of the deleterious effects of such exclusion is expressed in his observation that 'isolation from participation in the cultural life of the larger community' brings about an 'inevitable deterioration' (Park (1931b) 1950: 391).

Blacks in northern urban ghettos were brought into close contact with each other and were presented with new opportunities for education, intellectual endeavour, business enterprise, religious organization, politics, a black press, and – in all these areas – the emergence of black leadership (Park (1935b) 1950: 166-7). Moreover, the ability to read, whether poetry or newspapers, 'which was regarded as a luxury in the rural community, becomes a necessity to the city' (Park (1923a) 1950: 297).

Second, Park believed that the absence of the southern caste system, inhibiting the entrance of blacks into a range of occupations, and the existence of a class system, encouraged the growth of a 'robust and vigorous middle class' in the urban North. He envisioned 'pioneers' on a 'racial frontier' who would provide leadership for the black world within the white world (Park (1935b) 1950: 176). Like Washington, Park thought that individual economic success and occupational mobility were essential conditions for the collective mobility of blacks (Washington (1901) 1956). He also assumed that racial justice was possible within a class system and that racism – whether through a caste system or benign paternalism that sets apart Afro-Americans from others – impeded the free market's distribution of rewards on the basis of effort and skill (Park (1943a) 1950). Comparing Washington's self-help programme for blacks with the federal government's paternalistic policies for Native Americans, Park noted that 'the race which advances under special burdens and restraints is doing better than that which needs the special care and protection of the Government in order to maintain itself' (Park to Emmett J. Scott, Park-Washington Correspondence, Booker T. Washington Papers, n.d.).

Park believed that 'bi-racial organization', which he thought contributed to the emergence of a black middle class, was the 'unique' outcome of racial conflict in the United States. Bi-racial organization meant that blacks would not be relegated strictly to menial occupations, but would work at jobs in trades, businesses, and the professions, which, although not integrated, were the same as those in which whites worked. Park wrote:

> The most profound changes in race relations, if not in racial ideology, have come about with the rise of a hierarchy of occupational classes within the limits of the Negro race, so that Negroes can and do rise to some sort of occupational and professional equality with other races and peoples who have not been handicapped by the degradations and institutions of a caste system....At present, at least in the northern cities, to which Negroes in recent years have migrated in such large numbers, the status of the Negro population is no longer that of a caste. It is rather that of a racial and cultural minority.
>
> (Park (1943a) 1950: 311)

Bi-racial organization actually helped to transform racial attitudes. Although the 'distinctions' and the 'distances which separate the races are maintained', what changes is that '[t]he races no longer look up and down; they look across' (Park (1928b) 1950: 243). This arrangement challenged stereotypes and encouraged changing the social imagery of blacks.

Moreover, bi-racial organization supports a sense of shared identity and a shared culture, and the positive evaluation of both of these. Park believed that in societies organized along 'horizontal lines', 'loyalty attaches to individuals, particularly to the upper class, who furnish, in their persons and in their lives, the models for the masses of the people below them'. As with the nationalistic movements in Europe, Park thought that Afro-Americans, once emancipated from the constraints of caste, would create 'models based on their own racial individuality and

146

embodying sentiments and ideals which spring naturally from their own lives' rather than embrace the attitudes and behaviour of the dominant white world (Park (1913b) 1950: 219).

Park propounded the idea that racial groups which comprise all social classes are 'intractable minorities engaged in a ruthless struggle for political privilege or economic advantage'. He maintained that they are 'cultural groups' as well, struggling to preserve an identity, a heritage, and differences in life-style (ibid.: 218). Moreover, foreshadowing contemporary debates about the obligations of the state in a multi-ethnic society, Park observed that a racial group that is also a national minority may 'retain its loyalty to the state of which it is a part, but only insofar as that state incorporates, as an integral part of its organization, the practical interests, the aspirations and the ideals of that nationality' (ibid.: 220).

Park's analysis of bi-racial organization demonstrates his sensitivity to the importance of group identity and 'culture' in maintaining or undermining a given racial order. He placed a strong emphasis in his perspective on culture building in transforming race relations.[12]

In general, culture building requires that members of a minority reinterpret the group's past and positively identify with its ethos and its life-style as these exist in all of their present complexity. Culture building activities include the creation and transmission of social meanings such as those of self and group and their implicit or explicit evaluations, together with all the definitions of the situation which arise out of and underlie social interaction in objective social settings. Social meanings and definitions of the situation are created and disseminated by a variety of groups within the community, such as its intellectuals, politicians, musicians, clergy, teachers, and people in the media (Blumer and Duster 1980). Culture-building also includes creating and modifying institutions such as the family and the church.

Institutions are a facet of a group's culture. They are relatively permanent patterns of social interaction (e.g., roles, offices) organized to achieve shared or complementary goals, and include subjective factors such as shared meanings and shared values. As Everett Hughes noted,

> institutions are just those social forms which grow up where men collectively face problems which are never completely

settled. In various times and places, men have voluntarily met to solve problems. It seems likely that, when they do so, and continue to do so for long enough, they produce relation-ships and ideas which succeeding generations accept some-what involuntarily.

(Hughes (1931) 1979: preface)[13]

What are of interest here are Park's ideas about the subjective aspects of culture and, in particular, his view of the function of black literature and black history in altering race relations. In the 'stimulating environment' of northern cities, Park wrote, 'the Negro has developed an intellectual life and produced a literature which otherwise and elsewhere there would have been neither the occasion nor the opportunity' (Park (1935b) 1950: 168). An important function of such literature was 'to state the case of the Negro to Negroes' and, thus, to heighten race consciousness, to sustain race conflict, and to present a positive evaluation of the Afro-American community (Park (1943a) 1950: 308-9). 'Literature and art', wrote Park,

when they are employed to give expression to racial sentiment and form to racial ideals, serve, along with other agencies, to mobilise the group and put the masses *en rapport* with their leaders and with each other. In such cases literature and art are like silent drummers which summon to action the latent instincts and energies of the race.

(Park (1913b) 1950: 216-17)

While spirituals were the 'literature of slavery', black poetry was 'a transcript of Negro life' in the present. Unlike spirituals, which emphasized life in the next world and urged 'patience, humility and resignation in this life', the poetry of writers such as Claude McKay and James Weldon Johnson, Park noted, exhorted blacks to aspire to the best that life had to offer on this earth now (Park (1923a) 1950: 290-3). The 'poetry of the Negro renaissance', wrote Park, 'is distinctly of this world. It is characteristically the poetry of rebellion and self-assertion' (ibid.: 294).

Park's study of contemporary black poetry led him to observe that rather than intending to 'prove to himself and the white world that he was a man like other men; that he could think the white

148

man's thoughts and practice the white man's arts', black poets were 'more concerned ... in defining their own conception of their mission and destiny as a race' (ibid.: 290, 293). In this sense, poets such as McKay, Johnson, and Paul Laurence Dunbar were akin to the black politicians who had risen in ward politics and who, while they 'have very few illusions ... in regard to the people they seek to represent... make no apologies for them either' (Park (1935b) 1950: 171). Journals such as *The Crisis, Opportunity*, and *The Messenger* dealt with political issues as well as publishing stories and listing cultural activities of interest to blacks. These similarities in attitude between black poets and writers and black political leaders in cities were further evidence of the connections between culture and politics.[14]

In his analysis of race consciousness, Park himself turned to a metaphor used by Dunbar in his poem 'We wear the mask' (Park (1923a) 1950: 291).[15] As already noted above, Park suggested that the mask of colour hides the Afro-American's sentiments and his individuality from whites. To the average white American, all blacks, like all Chinese and all Japanese, look alike. Once the individual man is concealed behind the racial type, blacks become the objects of white imaginations (Park (1926a) 1950).

Park also emphasized the role of black history in forging a positive image of blacks for blacks in the face of conventional stereotypes. Early in his affiliation with Washington at Tuskegee Institute, Park volunteered to write a history of American blacks in the form of a 'self-help reader' to be distributed throughout the southern school system, particularly in schools for 'coloured boys and girls'. He intended the reader to modify the self-imagery of blacks in much the same way as his journalistic efforts for Washington were intended to modify the white's image of blacks. This project was to be an integral part of 'that work at Tuskegee which interests me most ... I refer to attempts to build up a "race consciousness"' (Park to Emmett Scott, Park-Washington Correspondence, Booker T. Washington Papers, March 1905). In this letter to Emmett J. Scott, Washington's secretary at Tuskegee, Park expressed the opinion that this proposed 'anecdotal history of the Negro' would suggest that '[n]othing short of the history of Italy in the period of the Renaissance or France during the Revolution seems to me equal to the story of this people – if you

149

consider it as the story of a *people*, a race and not a history of a political controversy, as it usually is considered' (ibid).

The self-help reader was also aimed at mitigating the problem of educating black children in the rural South, whose experience was fundamentally different from that of their teachers and textbook writers. 'When knowledge which the school is seeking to impart is remote from the experience of the pupil, the task of translating it into the language that the student understands is a difficult one' (Park (1937d) 1950: 55). In the jargon of the 1960s, Park proposed to make education 'relevant' to black students.

It must be emphasized that Park did not think that institutional arrangements and the nascent culture of black Americans were African in nature. After describing the slave trade and the policies adopted to destroy the slaves' ties to kin and tribe, he concluded that '[t]he fact that the Negro has brought with him from Africa so little tradition which he was able to transmit and perpetuate on American soil makes that race unique among all people of our cosmopolitan population' (Park (1918) 1950: 269).

Park's dismissal of the idea (or the value) of an indigenous African culture taking root and flourishing among black Americans is revealed in an address to Tuskegee students in 1906, in which he compared the heritage of the Japanese with that of Afro-Americans. Park pointed out that the Japanese, unlike Afro-Americans, 'had acquired great technical skill in manual labour and had attained such habits of thrift and industry that no labourers in the world could or can now compete with them except the Chinese. The negro has these two things yet to learn.' Moreover, 'Before the Japanese became acquainted with western culture, Japan had acquired a very complete civilisation of her own.' 'The negro', he continued, 'is of course not in that condition. He has nothing in particular to throw overboard except his religious superstitions – the fetishism that he brought from Africa and which still survives to some extent I am told.'

However, Park assumed that black people could participate as equals in all spheres of American life. He concluded his address by cautioning that

Least of all should you or any of your race be discouraged by any facts in regard to your people that investigation and

150

science makes known to you ... As soon as the negro finds out where he is supposed to be racially inferior he will rouse himself and prove that he is not. that [sic] is human nature. Knowledge is power and when he realises his weaknesses knowledge will give him the means to overcome them.
(Park-Washington Correspondence, Booker T. Washington Papers, February 1906)

In conclusion, the aim of black Americans was, therefore, not to adapt 'old world traits' to an urban environment. Rather, theirs was the task of reinterpreting for themselves the dominant white culture and Afro-American history of which the experience of slavery and its racist aftermath is so much a part.

Thus, Park suggested that, for Afro-Americans, the process of forging a minority identity and culture differed from the pattern found among immigrant groups. However, for both immigrants and blacks, separate cultures, identities, and social institutions are adaptive mechanisms that should contribute to the survival and collective mobility of the group, and to its eventual full participation in American life as socially equal on terms that are negotiated and not merely imposed.

Trouble in Paradise

What, then, are the strengths of Park's innovative analysis of the factors affecting Afro-Americans in cities?

First of all, Park correctly claimed that black Americans would achieve racial justice and the opportunity to participate fully in American life only as an outcome of racial conflict. Race conflict, he thought, was an indication of the greater aspiration to social betterment among Afro-Americans and the ongoing resistance to their claims by whites (Park (1928b) 1950; (1923a) 1950).

In anticipation of Gunnar Myrdal, Park expressed the hope that white America's commitment to democratic principles would eventually undermine racial discrimination (Myrdal (1944) 1962). 'The difference between democracy and other forms of society is that it refuses to make class or race, i.e., group distinctions. Distinctions and distances must be of a purely individual and personal nature' (Park (1928b) 1950: 230-43). However, by the

1920s, Park was commenting upon the similarities in attitude among all white Americans. In both the North and the South, racial antagonism was sustained by the privileges conferred by patterns of segregation and discrimination favouring whites whether native or foreign-born. Moreover, among white Americans, belief in black inferiority and the insoluble link between race and culture persisted in spite of the influential studies of the anthropologist Franz Boas, which sought to discredit this conceptual confusion (Stocking 1968; Matthews 1977: 157-62).

Eventually Park concluded that it has become a 'necessity that Negroes should cooperate to win for themselves a place and the respect in the white man's world that the Constitution could not give them' (Park (1923a) 1950: 294). Blacks themselves would have to provide leadership in the conflict ahead.

Second, Park anticipated that racial conflict would take place in cities rather than in the rural American South. The anonymity of city life along with the heterogeneity of the urban population tended to blur distinctions between people. The city offered greater opportunities for minorities to escape from the constraints of a prescribed status and its hallowed conventions.

Migration from the rural South to the urbanizing North resulted in black competition for scarce resources. As Park predicted, in cities there were increasingly frequent incidents of interracial conflict, ranging from personal intimidation to public rioting, as blacks pressed for equal access to jobs, housing, transportation, schooling, and political office (Waskow 1967; Polenberg 1980). In cities where blacks experienced occupational mobility and increasing civil rights, interracial tensions were greatest. 'From the black perspective the lowering of some barriers made those remaining seem more intolerable. To many whites, however, the remaining barriers seemed even more desirable than before' (Polenberg 1980: 78). The Second World War accelerated changes in the relationship between black and white Americans that were already evident at the turn of the century (Osofsky 1966; Spear 1967). By 1964, despite the successful agitation to ensure greater civil liberties for Afro-Americans in the South, ghetto riots became a more usual way of expressing interracial tensions in northern cities. Rioting in New York, Chicago, and Los Angeles, and the limitations imposed by blacks upon white participation in

152

civil rights organizations bore out Park's prediction, although not in ways of which he would necessarily have approved, that racial struggle would more and more depend upon black leadership. Writing about race riots between 1964 and 1972, the American historian Richard Polenberg points out that 'The typical rioter was not a deviant member of the community, not the most economically disadvantaged, and poorly educated, but rather a "new ghetto man", more intensely sensitive to his deprivation relative to other blacks and more keenly conscious of his racial identity' (Polenberg, citing Caplan (1970) 1980: 235).

Park celebrated the creation of an urban, black culture, believing that race consciousness, identity, and solidarity were advantageous to the collective mobility and political mobilization of Afro-Americans. Intelligence and accomplishment, he believed, 'are incidents of action, and it is only the sense of participation in the great action that gives individuals and races the courage and the élan that is necessary to rise from a lower to that higher level of intellectual life which is standard in the modern world' (Park (1931c) 1950: 392).

Third, Park was among the first to recognize the qualities of minority group cultures in general, and of Afro-American culture in particular. As already noted, settlement house workers had pointed out that foreign cultures benefited immigrants in their adjustment to urban life in America (Higham 1984: 217-18). However, the advantages of a similar development among black southern migrants often went unnoticed.

Park's enthusiastic endorsement of black culture as an aid to the collective mobility of Afro-Americans suggests that he was increasingly willing to accommodate strategies which focused upon 'class actions', as opposed to policies which fostered individual effort and achievement alone, as a route to overcoming racial disadvantage. In this sense, he departed from the position that both he and Booker Washington advocated during the early part of the century. Moreover, Park's change in emphasis presages the dilemma faced by liberals today confronted with social policies, such as those of affirmative action, which argue that class actions are the only effective way of achieving racial justice (Glazer 1975; Duster 1978; 1987).

Fourth, Park played a major role in bringing about a transition from biological to cultural explanations of supposed racial differences.[16] His formulation of the relationship between black culture and the environment that Afro-Americans confronted in northern cities contradicted the popular view that culture, like physical appearance, was an aspect of a racial inheritance and, hence, unalterable. He joined forces with Boas and other anthropologists at Columbia University in New York City, by demonstrating that, among Afro-Americans, changes in social institutions and an emergent urban culture were adaptations to an environment which required and rewarded certain types of behaviour and which provided opportunities, however limited, for achieving the goals of material well-being, social honour, and political power, all of which were believed to be accessible to deserving citizens.

Park rejected Social Darwinism, all its implications regarding the biological basis of cultural differences, and its belief that racial stratification reflected a 'natural order' of selection and fitness. He agreed with Albion Small's contention that 'the biological bias creates an erroneous notion of social phenomena' and stimulates 'fruitless lines of investigation' in sociology (Small cited in Hofstadter (1944) 1964: 158).

The conclusion that Park was among the first to differentiate between race and culture contradicts those misleading interpretations of his work which emphasize his description of Afro-Americans as 'the lady among races' and argue that he furthered the view that biology is destiny (Park (1918) 1950: 269). Actually, Park's discussion of 'racial temperament' is of little consequence. This theme is mentioned in very few of his publications. The essay in which he dealt with this topic most extensively, 'Education in its relation to the conflict and fusion of cultures', was written in 1918, fairly early in his career as a sociologist. Park believed that blacks *could* compete effectively in economic life and that they must participate as equals in social and political activities. Moreover, at a time when it was almost always assumed that Afro-Americans were innately of inferior intelligence compared with whites, Park asserted in this same essay that with regard to intellectual capacity 'racial as compared with individual differences were small and relatively unimportant' (ibid.: 264). His emphasis upon race relations, rather than the alleged hereditary attributes of different races, also suggests that the influence he accorded to racial temperament was very limited.

Park's characterization of Afro-American temperament now sounds pejorative and patronizing. However his depiction does suggest an appreciation of qualities absent from native, white, middle-class Americans, not unlike those mentioned by his contemporary, the sociologist, journalist, and founding member of the National Association for the Advancement of Colored People, W. E. B. Du Bois. 'We black men seem the sole oasis of simple faith and reverence in a dusty desert of dollars and smartness', noted Du Bois, who went on to ask, 'Will America be poorer if she replaces her brutal dyspeptic blundering with light-hearted but determined Negro humility? Or her coarse and cruel wit with loving jovial good-humor?' (Du Bois (1903) 1961: 22). Park's evaluation of the Afro-American racial temperament emphasized those traits that would impede the attainment of goals he himself thought important, such as occupational success. Du Bois, on the other hand, argued that the materialism which springs from the excesses of capitalism has to be rejected as surely as racism itself. However, while Park and Du Bois were both in favour of heightening race consciousness among blacks through the exploration of black history and black culture, they disagreed about the objectives this strategy should serve.

Clearly, Park's insights into race relations in cities and his influence upon research in this area are of continuing importance. However, having pointed out the strengths of Park's analysis, it is also necessary to consider the flawed aspects of his thinking. These were just as effectively revealed in the subsequent research of his students as they were in the comments of his less sympathetic critics.

To begin with, Park underestimated the degree to which the progress of black Americans would depend upon the goodwill of white Americans rather than the efforts of blacks alone. Thus, he exaggerated the extent to which heightened race consciousness and racial solidarity could mitigate discrimination.

One of the reasons why Park did not anticipate the ways in which the white-dominated society would affect how blacks live is because he confronted a world in which the ravages of economic depression, white racism, demands for an increasingly skilled and educated labour force, and the exclusionary policies of many labour unions had not yet conspired to dry up aspirations and opportunities among blacks for both individual and group advancement. Thus Stanley Lieberson points out that between Reconstruction and the 1930s, when the economic prospects for Afro-Americans declined both absolutely and relative to white groups, blacks demonstrated the same desire for literacy and education as immigrants (Lieberson 1980: 123-252). It was Park's students who were compelled to address the question of how the economic and political institutions of the dominant white society determined the organization of black life and the development of Afro-American personality.

With regard to Park's belief in the efficacy of self-help, for example, his students St Clair Drake, Horace Cayton, and E. Franklin Frazier each pointed out that the fate of the black community was overwhelmingly determined by decisions made by whites and upon events occurring outside the black ghetto. 'The fate of Black Metropolis', wrote Drake and Cayton in 1945, 'is dependent on the fate of Midwest Metropolis, of the country, and of the world. Forces which are in no sense local will in the final analysis determine the movement of this drama of human relations toward hope or tragedy' (Drake and Cayton (1945) 1962: 767).

The same observation is relevant to Park's discussion of bi-racial organization, which he had hoped would improve interracial communication, for, as his student E. Franklin Frazier pointed out, the parallel emergence of 'the coloured world within' depended on the resources available and the extent to which the interests of powerful whites permitted such development (Frazier (1949) 1968). Moreover, Frazier noted that 'occupations in the Negro group do not have the same connotations and so do not give the same social status as similar occupations in the white community. The standard of living and the modes of behaviour are derived from their relative position in the Negro community' (Frazier (1931) 1968: 215).

Subsequent historical events vindicated the appraisal of Park's students that, by-and-large, white Americans determined outcomes for black Americans. The refusal or willingness of the federal government to enforce existing civil rights legislation or to frame new legislation promoting equal opportunities for blacks, the policies of white-dominated labour unions and businesses, the restricted covenants entered into by real-estate agents combined to influence the experience of blacks after the Second World War as they had before.

A second shortcoming in Park's approach is his relative indifference to those features of the black urban community that contributed to social fragmentation and disorganization. Foremost among these is the temptation for emergent middle-class business and political leaders to use their economic and political power to further self-interest at the expense of working-class blacks. Park preferred to stratify populations in terms of occupations rather than social classes. He tended to over-emphasize the homogeneity of goals and outlooks among blacks. Subsequently, Frazier, Drake, Cayton, and another of Park's students, Charles Spurgeon Johnson, revealed the sources of divisiveness within America's 'dark ghettos'.

Frazier's study of the black bourgeoisie, for example, uncovered types of race consciousness and cultural activities that were based on economic success and not on education or intellectual accomplishments. These activities, founded upon consumption and attempts to imitate the white world, fragmented the black community rather than providing it with group leadership (Frazier 1957). Park had applauded black poets and anticipated their contributions to a redefinition of black identity. In 1955, Frazier wrote bitterly of the failure of the Negro Renaissance of the 1920s. 'The short stories, novels, and poems which expressed this new evaluation of the Negro and his history in America by artists and intellectuals', he said, 'were unread and ignored by the new middle class that was eager to gain a few dollars' rather than a 'new conception of themselves' (Frazier (1955) 1968: 262).

Third, the thrust of Park's analysis of race prejudice and race consciousness is to emphasize status as a value which influences the self-esteem of the individual and the conduct of groups. Yet, status and group position are what economists call 'positional goods'. Therefore, the collective mobility of one group relative to others would not resolve racial antagonisms but merely change the relative positions of groups and engender efforts to challenge whatever pattern of racial stratification exists at a particular point in time.

A fourth problematic aspect of Park's approach has to do with the overwhelmingly positive outcomes that he attributes to minority group cultures. Park's use of the culture concept begs the question of whether cultures which perpetuate a set of beliefs and values which are self-destructive, and a style of life which inhibits success as this is measured by the dominant culture, should be judged 'inferior' or 'less adaptive to a particular set of circumstances' (Sowell 1981: 285; Flew 1985). Frazier prefigured the 'culture of poverty' debate stirred by Oscar Lewis (Frazier 1934; (1939) 1966; Lewis 1959, 1961, 1966; Valentine 1968).

There are hazards attendant on seeing discrimination, race prejudice, poverty, unemployment, illegitimacy, and other sources of misery and deprivation for black Americans as problems of culture and communications *alone*. However, this observation should not lead to the conclusion that the concepts of culture and communication are superfluous to the analysis of race and ethnicity. Rather, sociologists should continue to ask how a wide range of factors, including culture and communication, influence minority relations.

Park's own students and other scholars working within the Chicago school tradition have, in fact, included social class and social structure, the dilemmas of status and reference group to the battery of concepts used in their analysis of race relations. For example, Drake and Cayton argued that material and emotional impoverishment for blacks in the 'underclass' of the Black Metropolis could be understood only when related to both social stratification in the encompassing city of Chicago and the historical context of national unemployment and underemployment (Drake and Cayton (1945) 1962).

The appearance of such terms as 'social structure' and 'social class' represented a shift in the sociological thinking of this later generation of scholars working within the Chicago tradition. This transformation did not signify a 'scientific revolution' (Kuhn 1964), as one might be tempted to argue with respect to the emergence of the 'caste and class school' or social systems theories. Nor does it support the view that both 'the idiom' and 'the Negro subject matter' of the Chicago school were eclipsed between 1940 and 1960 because 'this tradition' lacked 'an authoritative theoretical formulation capable of demanding explicit incorporation into a new analytical scheme developing at Harvard' (Shils 1970: 808). Rather, the work of Frazier, Drake and

Cayton, Johnson, Hughes, Blumer, Killian, and others represents developments *within* the shared approach originating with Park at Chicago which placed the concepts of culture and communication, and the methods of ethnography, at the head of the sociological agenda.

The fundamental difference between Park and these scholars was less a matter of perspective than of their prognosis for the future. Park's students were more pessimistic than he was about the future of race relations and the achievement of racial justice for blacks. Drake and Cayton, for example, saw no reason to suppose that the contradiction between democratic values and the policies of segregation and discrimination would be resolved as Park himself hoped. They showed that the 'contradictory principles' of 'free competition' and 'fixed status' continued to govern race relations in Chicago and that 'it is conceivable that the Negro question – given the moral flabbiness of America – is incapable of solution' (Drake and Cayton (1945) 1962: 757-66). Park himself would have applauded these later efforts to explore the condition of Afro-Americans in cities and to provide a more realistic assessment of the prospects of racial justice in America.

Chapter Seven

GETTING IT TOGETHER: A SCHEME OF INTERPRETATION

What then are the elements of Park's approach and that of the Chicago school tradition which may be usefully combined with contemporary theorizing and methods of social research to suggest a fruitful scheme of interpretation of race and ethnic relations? The centrality of the concepts of culture and communication to Park's perspective and his insistence that sociology concern itself with the subjective aspects of human experience and the symbolic nature of collective life argue for the inclusion of ethnography and the collection of human documents as staple ingredients of sociological investigation.

Park saw culture as an adaptation to an environment. Cultures set out appropriate courses of action in line with the norms and values of a group, in the circumstances they confront. However, Park tended to overlook the ways in which cultures (and sentimental groups) sometimes inhibit the efforts of the individual to change his way of living or to achieve goals deemed to be unimportant by members of his group but highly regarded by others outside the group. As Glazer and Moynihan point out years later, ethnic group affiliation influences both style of life and the chances for individual survival and triumph, not least through the distribution of norms that have more or less utility in the spheres of education and work. The authors thus forge a link between ethnic cultures and stratification (Glazer and Moynihan 1963; 1975). Frazier had already provided an example of this in his (questionable) observation that family life renders the middle-class black college student 'unfitted for life in a world of competition' and instead inclines black youth to 'preparing themselves for such salaried positions as teaching or social work where in either case incomes may be derived from the community or philanthropy' (Frazier (1939) 1966: 317-33).

Moreover, as argued throughout this book, Park's equation of culture with internal mechanisms of social control and his emphasis upon the roles of volition and co-operation led him to overlook the constraints inherent in the context in which choices are made. Not surprisingly, subsequent critical responses to Park's work, especially among his students and those generally sympathetic to his approach, suggested that any scheme of interpretation must locate subjective accounts, that record motive, meaning, and definition of the situation, with respect to the 'objective' conditions in which experience takes place and choices get made and the historical run of events which gives rise to particular opportunity structures. This is implicit in C. Wright Mills's requirement that the sociological imagination locate 'private worries' in the context of 'public issues' such that individual biography is viewed with respect to prevailing social structure and historical circumstance (Mills 1959).

Thus, *The Negro in Chicago, The Negro Family in Chicago, Shadow of the Plantation, Negro Politicians*, and *Black Metropolis* show how the scope for black initiative in shaping a style of life for self and family was constrained by the opposition of white people intent upon maintaining their privileges and their sense of propriety in a culture in which blacks were by tradition and convention subordinate, excluded and, often, abused (The Chicago Commission of Race Relations (1922) 1968; Frazier 1932; Johnson 1934; Gosnell (1935) 1967; Drake and Cayton (1945) 1962). These studies suggest that emergence, persistence, and change in cultural styles, personality types, world-views, and the orientations of racial groups, towards themselves and towards one another, be looked at in the context of fairly specific factors, such as the rate of unemployment for Afro-Americans and patterns of residential segregation in Chicago, or more general factors, such as a legacy of slavery and the process of black migration from the rural South to northern cities.

More recently, ethnographic monographs which aim to reveal the subjective outlook of the actor and the symbolic nature of group life have paid more attention to those factors in the actor's environment that constrain choice and nullify the putative right to achieve aspirations valued by members of a dominant group

161

(Rainwater 1971; di Leonardo 1984). Park himself acknowledged this to be a requirement of sound social research. However, as already suggested, his overriding interest in self-help, communication, group consciousness, informal mechanisms of social control, status, and the role of culture in general in mitigating individual demoralization and social disorganization, especially with regard to immigrants and Afro-Americans, led to a relative neglect of institutional arrangements which limit action. Such omissions endanger accurate sociological analysis.

The following discussion of how the areas of special theoretical importance in Park's approach to race and ethnicity have been taken up and elaborated upon by others working within the Chicago tradition indicates the ways in which this criticism has been, and might in future be, successfully met.

AREAS OF SPECIAL THEORETICAL IMPORTANCE

'Race prejudice as a sense of group position' and 'the process of collective definitions'

Park suggested that race prejudice is not an attribute of individuals but a property of the shifting relationship between racial groups. He argued that race prejudice is aroused when there is a real or an imaginary threat to an existing pattern of dominance and subordination, inclusion and exclusion.

As already noted, Park thought that cities were most often the place in which 'race problems' emerge because it is here that groups which were previously either isolated or enjoyed (or suffered) a fixed 'place' meet as competitors for jobs and housing and as antagonists in the fight to preserve or to change their group's status. In cities, new situations require that groups fit their lines of action together in new ways. Moreover, like Simmel, Park believed that a money economy offered new possibilities for a subordinate group to improve its status and widen its sphere of influence.

In his essay 'Race prejudice as a sense of group position', first published in 1958, Herbert Blumer confirmed Park's view that race prejudice is 'fundamentally a matter of the relationship

162

between racial groups' rather than individuals and he reiterated the conditions that Park suggested give rise to or intensify race prejudice (Blumer 1958). Blumer extended Park's ideas in several important ways. First, he explicitly set out the types of feelings that are present in the dominant group. (In a later essay, he and Troy Duster deal with the feelings of the subordinate group (Blumer and Duster 1980).) These are 'a feeling of superiority', 'a feeling that the subordinate group are intrinsically different and alien', 'a proprietary claim to certain areas of privilege and advantage', and 'a fear and suspicion that the subordinate race harbours designs on the prerogatives of the dominant race'. The two conditions that are essential to race prejudice and that differentiate this orientation from others are the sense of proprietary claim to certain areas of group life and the fear of social change through the 'encroachment' of the subordinate group. In a later essay Blumer included, alongside what he calls a 'domination-subordination' axis of the relationship between racial groups, an 'inclusion-exclusion' axis (Blumer 1965a).

Second, Blumer shifts the focus of social change from the realm of personal experience and 'equal status contacts' within a 'bi-racially' organized society as suggested by Park to the realm of the public and the intervention of politically powerful leaders of the dominant group. Political leaders may initiate social change by changing the objective conditions under which racial groups co-exist or by changing the imagery of these groups, for example, in speeches or statements appearing in the mass media, and hence changing the 'collective definitions' which he and Troy Duster claim to be the fulcrum of race relations (Blumer and Duster 1980).

The third contribution that Blumer and Duster make to race relations theory, which both builds upon and transcends the previous work of Park, is to focus upon the process of 'collective definition'. What they mean by 'collective definition' is

the basic process by which racial groups come to see each other and themselves and poise themselves to act towards each other; the process is one in which the racial groups are defining or interpreting their experiences and the events that bring these experiences about. The outcome of this process of definition is the aligning and realigning of

relations and the development and re-formulation of pros-
pective lines of action towards one another.

(ibid.: 222)

They go on to note that the process is collective 'in that judgements and interpretations are presented to others and are subject
to their evaluation; and, in turn, the views of these others enter
back into the circle of consideration' (ibid.: 230). Their concern
with 'the kinds of objects racial groups form of one another', the
process of interpretation and judgement concerning self and
other, and the patterns of behaviour seen as 'appropriate or
necessary in their associations with one another' which arise out of
these definitions and judgements, clearly puts their perspective
within Park's theoretical brief.

Blumer and Duster contend that scholars should study the
whole range of situations in which racial groups experience one
another, including social interaction in the home and workplace
and through media such as the press and television. Like Park,
they advocate that the investigator study such a range of behaviour
in its natural setting. As they put it, 'one cannot gainsay the
presence and occurrence of an ongoing process of "experiencing"
among racial groups in association with one another .... A scholar
who is removed from this body of experience or who ignores it is
cut off from the elementary ingredients of race relations' (ibid.:
230).

In addition to noting that racial groups interact in a variety of
situations, Blumer and Duster point out that there are 'variable
interpretations' of human experience and that 'It is the variable
interpretation of these human experiences that is the starting
point of social theory' (ibid.: 218).

The interplay between subjective accounts based upon participant observation and the analysis of human documents and
accounts of the objective conditions and historical events in which
human experience and its interpretation are generated, is implicit
in the discussion of 'the process of collective definitions'. To begin
with, Blumer and Duster themselves resolve the tension between
'the collective', or the general and constraining aspects of social
interaction, and the 'particular' by arguing that 'race relations,
certainly in their problematic form, do operate inside of an
essentially common and constant framework. Thus, while the

variability that is suggested by the process of definition may, and indeed does take place, *it is held within the framework and takes place along the line that is set by the framework'* (ibid.: 232) and, later, 'the defining process is relentlessly brought inside a common framework, a framework which forces the definitions to deal with the basic orientations of racial groups' (ibid.: 236). This framework is the existing, constraining pattern of racial stratification and Blumer and Duster's discussion of what they term 'dualisms' further indicates how context, and in particular opportunity structures, directs social choice and the construction of collective action.

The problem of dualisms refers to subordinate groups vacillating between an insistence upon their own 'specialness', and thus reinforcing solidarity among group members, and emulating the behaviour of a dominant group in an effort to improve the status of individuals or the group as a whole. 'The conflict for groups (and individuals inside these groups) at the base of the social, economic and political structure, most simply put, is whether to celebrate and retain their "likeness" (which some may come to feel consigns them to the base), or whether to emulate and assimilate' (ibid.: 225). These two contradictory attitudes may be held by different members of the group at the same time.

Blumer and Duster suggest that a trend towards emulation usually occurs under favourable economic conditions when the subordinate group might reasonably hope to improve their lives and their status by economic activity which results in increased rewards. On the other hand, an insistence upon 'specialness' usually occurs when economic mobility is not likely and the group instead opts for an improvement of their lives through political action. They later talk about this dualism as 'two major divergent directions of effort' which they call the 'assimilationist' orientation and the 'separatist' orientation.

Blumer and Duster see the duality of emulation/ assimilation and specialness, solidarity/separateness as a useful way of describing the internal discussions within the subordinate group, which, in turn, contribute to stability or to shifts in collective definitions. As such, duality is an important part of their theory of collective definition. For example, they use this conception of dualism to explain changes in the outlook of American blacks between 1920 and 1980 (ibid.: 226, 238).

It is also, however, an attempt to incorporate structural constraints into Park's original scheme of interpretation by insisting that the analysis of choice be located with respect to the objective conditions in which decisions are made.

The opposing orientations that Blumer and Duster depict as dualisms have also been discussed by the historians August Meier and Allan Spear. In his study, *Negro Thought in America, 1880-1915* (1964), Meier documents the vacillation among black leaders between ideologies of 'accommodation' and those of 'integration' between 1880 and 1915. The former wanted separate black institutions and supported the growth of race consciousness, and race solidarity among Afro-Americans. The integrationists argued for the abolition of segregation in all aspects of society and for the development of multi-racial institutions. Meier contends that ideologies of accommodation and the growth of separate black institutions (which through the passage of time took on their own characteristics and therefore emerged as specifically 'black' institutions) were a reflection of policies and the actual conditions of segregation imposed by the dominant white community. That is to say that separatist ideas and institutions were a response to the antagonism of white Americans to black aspirations – aspirations which did not differ much from those of the prevailing 'white' culture – as well as objective situational constraints. An ideology of accommodation, separate black institutions, race consciousness, and race solidarity were a strategy for survival. However, once they were articulated and established, Afro-Americans discovered the benefits of a separatist ideology and organizational life in advancing group interests (Meier 1964: 13).

Similarly, Spear's study suggests that the growth of Chicago's physical black ghetto hastened the growth of the institutional ghetto, that is to say, the development of black churches, hospitals, newspapers, and self-help organizations. Both the physical ghetto and the institutional ghetto contributed to the emergence of race leaders and racial ideologies which supported the ideas of race consciousness, pride, solidarity, and the special destiny of black Americans. However, Spear agrees with Meier that only after black people's actual exclusion from jobs, housing, educational facilities, and other aspects of white institutional life did black leaders opt for separatist policies which represented a strategy for survival (Spear 1967).

As already pointed out above, both the concept of an 'ethnicity paradox' and that of 'culture building' exhibit a duality similar to that noted by Blumer and Duster. However, what the 'ethnicity paradox' suggests is that rather than only being a response to a specific state of the economy, as Blumer and Duster suggest, dualisms, and, in particular, an insistence upon specialness, solidarity/separateness, might on occasion function as a more general strategic device to facilitate an improvement in the collective status of the group as a whole and their obtaining a larger share of scarce values.

Group status and self-esteem

According to Park, the individual's self-esteem and his evaluation of his group in relation to others of which he was a member influenced both personal activity (for example, with respect to educational and economic success) and collective activity.

As already noted, the ethnicity paradox suggests that membership in a parochial minority group is a prophylactic against individual demoralization and social disorganization. Park believed that personal malaise and social disorders were alternatives to the sense of well-being that he associated with heightened race or ethnic consciousness which encouraged and was fortified by struggle. 'Cultural conflicts', he noted, 'when they do not provoke mass movements, are likely to manifest themselves in family disorganisation, in delinquency, and in functional derangement of the individual psyche' (Park (1931d) 1950: 369).

In American society, membership in a racial group is of greatest importance in conferring or denying status and self-esteem. However, race relations research has yet to adequately explore the relationship between the status of a group and self-esteem on the one hand, and achievement and mobility on the other. Studies by Lee Rainwater, Geoffrey Driver, and Heidi Mirza are examples of what might fruitfully be done in this area of research (Rainwater 1971; Driver 1979; Mirza, forthcoming). However, much more needs to be known about why a strongly adhered to culture and a sense of identity are assets for members of minority groups. How does participation in separate racial and ethnic institutions contribute to greater participation in the dominant institutions of

167

a society? In what ways do the status of a group and the self-esteem of individuals work towards individual and collective mobility?

Also of importance, is the analysis of how ideas about a shared identity and a shared fate held by minority group members not only influence their activities, but, because these ideas are taken into account by others, also affect the attitudes and the behaviour of culturally dominant groups (Killian and Grigg 1967).

'The urban community as a spatial pattern and a moral order': physical spaces, social distances, and culture building

Park summarized his view of the relationship between human ecology and sociology in the essay 'The urban community as a spatial pattern and a moral order', published in 1925. Here he noted that

> It is because communication is fundamental to the existence of society that geography and all the other factors that limit or facilitate communication may be said to enter into its structure and organization at all. Under these circumstances the concept of position, of distance, and of mobility have come to have a new significance. Mobility is important as a sociological concept only in so far as it insures new social contact, and physical distance is significant for social relations only when it is possible to interpret it in terms of social distance.

> (Park (1926c) 1952: 174-5)

Recently, the contributions of the Chicago sociologists to human ecology have been taken up by social geographers and others interested in 'spatial sociology'. Collections of essays such as *Social Interaction and Ethnic Segregation* (Jackson and Smith 1981) suggest how patterns of settlement are related to patterns of communication and social relations between heterogeneous groups in cities (Rex and Moore 1967; Jackson and Smith 1981; Peach *et al.* 1981; Wallman 1984). Social geographers seek 'to understand and explain the role of ethnicity as a pervasive and persistent social basis for spatial segregation' as well as the 'roles of choice and constraint' underlying patterns of segregation and dispersal and 'its meaning for the groups involved' (Peach *et al.* 1981).

Here it is worth noting that the recent concern with 'ethnic boundaries' among anthropologists has been picked up by those social geographers exploring physical boundaries between segregated areas.

The foregoing is an indication of some of the areas of future research into race relation suggested by Park's work. This chapter concludes by identifying other innovations in recent research into race and ethnicity which, while not directly attributable to Park, are based upon concerns, concepts, and directives for social investigation which reiterate much of the wisdom that comes from the Chicago school and which should remain as characteristics of any emergent scheme of interpretation.

What, then, are these features of contemporary social research which should be integrated into any new perspective on race and ethnic relations building upon Park's legacy? First, seeing race and ethnic relations in terms of social processes, most important of which is the transformation of cultures.

During the early part of this century Thomas and Znaniecki investigated changes in rural Polish culture in cities in the United States at the level of both the individual and the group (Thomas and Znaniecki 1918-20). Their study, *The Polish Peasant in Europe and America*, was based upon the currently fashionable insight that 'it is impossible to gain a true picture of immigration as a process without investigating the people and their families on both sides' (Watson 1977: 2; Khan 1979: 1-11).

The idea of 'the transformation of traditional cultures' was also discussed by Park and Thomas who agreed with the anthropologist Boas, and the philosophical pragmatists Mead and Dewey, that cultures are constantly recreated by groups in their attempts to better adapt themselves to their environment. In this respect the suggestion that 'ethnic boundaries' are important both as a mode of adjustment to an 'encompassing society' and as a mechanism for preserving the autonomy of minority groups bears some resemblance to what Park thought to be the functions of bi-racial organizations (Barth 1981; Wallman 1978).

Second, any emergent perspective should concern itself with the subjective, symbolic aspects of race and ethnic relations and the complexity of social life. Ethnographic studies must anchor social interaction, including the meanings which people bring to

169

bear in the construction of their activities, in the specific context in which these occur. The logic of Park's perspective is to argue that the meanings of objects, including categories of people such as racial groups, are influenced by the nature of the specific situation in which interaction occurs. In this sense, while not disputing the importance of history and social heritage, a new scheme of interpretation should accommodate Sandra Wallman's observation that 'ethnicity is not always relevant to social relationships in which people of different "race" or culture interact; and when it does count it does not always count in the same way' (Wallman 1979: 6).

However, studies which explicitly seek to anchor activity in specific situations face the dilemma of finding patterns or constructing generalizations about race and ethnic relations while at the same time respecting the nature of any single instance of empirical life, a dilemma which, as already noted, has often been attributed to work within the Chicago school tradition (see Chapter Four).

Finally, new studies in urban race and ethnicity take for granted the need to locate social groups in a present which has a historical past and, like Park and the Chicago sociologists, these seek to understand human experience and social institutions taking into account the play of historical events (Killian (1970) 1985; di Leonardo 1984; Wallman 1984).

NOTES

INTRODUCTION

1. The term 'ethnicity paradox' is my own.

CHAPTER ONE

1. This phrase 'the romance of culture in an urban civilization' is my own.
2. A provocative analysis of the place of Protestant theology in the development of American sociology is contained in a recent study by Vidich and Lyman (1985).
3. The date of Park's arrival to teach at the University of Chicago is given variously between 1913 (Matthews 1977: 1) and 1916 (Faris (1967) 1970: 26). The evidence suggests that Park began teaching part-time in 1913 and full-time in 1914. He was promoted to full professor in 1923 (Matthews 1977: 85-6).
4. Park married Clara Cahill in 1894. His variegated career as a reporter, editor, graduate student, public relations agent, and, finally, university professor resulted in Clara moving about with Park some of the time and being left behind with a young family to look after at other times.
   Clara Park was both an accomplished artist and an effective social reformer, successfully lobbying for mothers' pensions in the state of Massachusetts. She was a source of emotional and at times financial support to Park (Raushenbush 1979: 61-2).
5. Gosnell was a graduate student in political science at Chicago before joining its faculty. Park wrote the introduction to his study, *Negro Politicians* (Park (1935b) 1950: 166-76).
6. More detailed discussion of Park's life, as well as the period in which he lived, can be found in Fred Matthews's excellent intellectual biography of Park (Matthews 1977: passim). This is nicely complemented by Winifred Raushenbush's very lively personal account of Park's life (Raushenbush 1979: passim).

171

More recently, Martin Bulmer has published a detailed study of Park's role in the Department of Sociology at Chicago between 1915 and 1935 (Bulmer 1984: 89-150). In addition, Stein (1960), Robert Faris ((1967) 1970), Ernest Burgess and Donald Bogue (1967), Stephen Diner (1975; 1980), Norbert Wiley (1979; 1986), Lewis and Smith (1980), Fred Wacker (1985), Stow Persons (1987), Fisher and Strauss (1979) and Dennis Smith (1988) also present useful essays on the development of sociology at Chicago between 1913 and 1944.

CHAPTER TWO

1. 'I follow Sapir in the assumption that the essence of culture is under-standing' (Park (1938) 1950: 39; Sapir 1924). Edward Sapir was an emi-nent anthropologist and a colleague of Park's at the University of Chicago.
2. Park sometimes referred to the 'cultural order' as a 'moral order'. The two terms are interchangeable because cultures always have a moral dimension to them.
3. This is also the conclusion of the sociologist Arnold Rose, who noted that 'The term "Chicago School" in sociology is ... sometimes used to refer to approaches in the fields of human ecology and urban sociology developed by Robert Park and Ernest Burgess. Actually the Chicago sociologists always regarded ecology as a minor sub-field of sociology' (Rose (1962) 1971: viii).
4. 'From the point of view of sociology, social evolution might profitably be studied in its relation to the development and perfection of the means and techniques of communication' (Park and Burgess (1921) 1969: 131-3). Also see Thompson (1975).
5. As Mead pointed out, 'Man's behaviour is such in his social group that he is able to become an object to himself, a fact that constitutes him a more advanced product of evolutionary development than are the lower animals' (Mead (1934) 1962).
6. Park concluded his essay on etiquette by noting 'one small but significant change in the ritual of race relations' and that is the adoption of 'the term "Negro" as a racial designation in preference to another more logical but less familiar expression like "Afro-American", which however, they insist upon spelling with a capital N' (Park (1937a) 1950: 188). This casts an interesting light upon recent efforts to designate 'Negroes' as 'Afro-Americans' or 'blacks' sometimes spelled with a capital B.
7. For an alternative definition of social disorganization and an analysis of the role it played in the sociological perspective developed at Chicago, see Carey 1975.

CHAPTER THREE

1. Recently Nathan Glazer has considered this point in the context of the

social sciences generally (Glazer 1985).

2. Park departed from this position in his use of concepts such as 'social forces', 'vicious cycles', and 'natural histories'. These notions discuss collective action as if it transcends the purposes and activities of individual men and women.

3. The term 'sentimental groups' is my own and not Park's.

4. Park included a 'normal' dislike of sudden change among such constraints. He failed to note, however, that this is not always the case. Thus, for example, as he himself pointed out, in the American South, the period of Reconstruction following the Civil War resulted in blacks leaving plantations, enrolling in Freedman Bureau schools, and engaging in other activities that contradicted the conclusion that human nature is inimical to sudden change, especially when change results in desired benefits.

5. On the other hand, in one of his later essays Park did predict that, in modern industrial society, social divisions based upon race and ethnic origins would eventually disappear and result in the increasing importance of social classes based upon a diversity of occupations and their complementary life-styles (Park (1939a) 1950). Second, in his very early essay on the German army discussed by Vidich and Lyman, and in his articles on the Belgian Congo, Park did use the concepts of class conflict in his discussion (Park 1900; 1906a; 1906b; 1907; Vidich and Lyman 1985: 198-202).

6. Two recent studies which disagree with this conclusion are those of Vidich and Lyman (1985) and Smith (1988).

CHAPTER FOUR

1. Recent studies of the hostility between ethnic groups living in the same neighbourhoods also illustrate the necessity of examining 'collective definitions' (National Advisory Commission on Civil Disorders 1968; Hannerz 1971; Scarman 1981; Gifford 1986).

2. Therefore, while critics such as Alvin Gouldner have condemned field-work as a way of exploiting 'underdog' informants, it is likely to have had its origin in a democratic 'impulse' (Gouldner 1968).

3. One has only to compare *Black Metropolis* to later studies, such as *Negroes in Cities*, to appreciate the difference in perspective, method, and interest between earlier and later sociologists, and, in particular, the consequences of excluding the subjective point of view of the actor from such study in favour of other kinds of data (Tauber and Tauber 1965).

4. For further discussion see Chapter Seven. Wallman claims, for example, that the theory of ethnic boundary processes 'may be adapted to different research settings and objectives' (Wallman 1986: 230)

5. The theory of ethnic boundary processes also includes a concern with 'generative' social structure (as opposed to the static typological

concept of social structure used by most sociologists), social organization, and social system. The inclusion of these concepts differentiates this perspective from that of the Chicago school. However, the way in which these concepts are used within the perspective on boundary processes offers interesting clues as to the potentially creative synthesis between the perspective and method developed by Park, Thomas, and other sociologists working within the Chicago tradition and the recent work of these anthropologists. It is pertinent to recall here that the earlier work of the Chicago scholars benefited from close working arrangements with anthropologists in what was, until 1929, a joint department of sociology and anthropology.

6. The sociologist Edward Shils has suggested that collaborative field-work between staff and students, as this was first practised at Chicago, could develop only within American society in the absence of the non-democratic hierarchical offices within and outside the university characteristic of European society (Shils 1970).

CHAPTER FIVE

1. Park cited William Graham Sumner's statement that 'what is custom in the group is habit in the individual' (Sumner (1906) 1959).
2. The term 'ethnicity paradox' is my own.
3. The concepts 'ethnicity by consent' and 'compulsory ethnicity' are my own.
4. Park's observations about the significance of language for individual and group identity and the role of language in facilitating collective action, including political conflict, follow from the general views on language and communication held by the philosophical pragmatists and their sociological counterparts. Given *current* interest in socio-linguistics, particularly in linguistic variations on the bases of colour and class within a single society, Park's insights seem timely. For example, his discussion of the effects of a discrepancy between a vernacular spoken language and a written literary language which corresponds to status differences between groups seems relevant to current investigations of 'black English' and 'restricted codes' and how these influence educational achievement among blacks and working-class whites (Labov (1969) 1973; Bernstein 1961; 1966).
5. The terms 'ethnicity as genuine culture' and 'ethnicity as a stratification phenomenon' are my own.
6. A contemporary example of this paradox is in the creation of a Congressional Black Caucus. The Black Caucus which utilizes the putative separateness and distinctiveness of Afro-Americans as a basis for organization is a means of exercising greater influence for blacks in many important areas of American political life, which are of similar concern to black and white Americans.
7. The terms 'parochial minority group culture' and 'city wide shared

culture' are my own.

8. 'Thus', jibed Park, 'while the *New York Times* has sought to preserve data for history, Mr Hearst's contributions have been in the field of literature and sociology' (Park (1940) 1955: 113).

9. Rainwater's statement continues by noting that Afro-Americans have

> adapted to the twin realities of disinheritance and limited functional autonomy for their group by developing existential perspectives on social reality (including the norms and practices of the larger society) that allow them to stay alive and not lose their minds, that allow them some modicum of hope about a reasonably gratifying life, and that preserve for many the slim hope that somehow they may be able to find admittance for themselves or their children to the larger society. In line with these existential perspectives, the ghetto culture has developed as the repository of a set of survival techniques for functioning in the world of the disinherited.
>
> (Rainwater 1970: 7)

CHAPTER SIX

1. Nathan Kantrowitz's suggestion that Park believed that assimilation 'requires residential desegregation' and that 'Park introduced the idea that segregation is "bad", within a Social Darwinist mode of thought' is an over-simplified and misleading summary of Park's views (Kantrowitz 1981: 47).

2. Park observed that after emancipation, stratification within the black community corresponded to stratification within the slave population during the ante-bellum period (Park 1913a).

3. John Hope Franklin points out that

> It is estimated that only 400,000 slaves lived in towns and cities in 1850. This left approximately 2,800,000 to do the work on farms and plantations. The great bulk of them, 1,800,000, were to be found on cotton plantations, while the remainder were primarily engaged in the cultivation of tobacco, rice, and sugar cane. The cotton plantation was, therefore, the typical locale of the Negro slave .... What may be termed the productive work was done in the fields by a force that constituted the principal group of slaves.
>
> (Franklin 1967: 190-1)

Park himself noted that

> The assimilation of the Negro field hand, where the contact of the slave with his master and his master's family was less intimate, was naturally less complete. On the large plantations,

175

where an overseer stood between the master and the majority of
his slaves, ... and where the master and his family were likely to
be merely winter visitors, this distance between master and slave
was greatly increased.

(Park (1913b) 1950: 210)

4. On the other hand, according to Park's contemporary, the journalist
   Ray Stannard Baker, 'White men of the employing class will do almost
   anything to keep the Negro on the land and his wife in the kitchen –
   so long as they are obedient and unambitious workers' (Baker (1908)
   1964: 87).
5. 'Learning by example' was used by Washington as an argument
   against segregation in the South and as an argument against blacks
   going North where 'separate but equal' was more likely to prevail.
6. The sociologist André Bétielle puts the matter in a more general
   perspective in his observation that

   Inequalities of condition have existed in all historically known
   societies but the attitudes towards them have differed greatly.
   There are those societies in which inequalities have not only
   existed in fact but have also been accepted as legitimate; these I
   would describe as harmonic systems. In other societies
   inequalities in the conditions of existence co-exist with a
   normative order committed to equality; these I would call
   disharmonic systems.

   (Béteille 1971)

   Race relations in the ante-bellum South were an example of an
   harmonic system, while those in the North represented disharmonic
   systems.
   The nature of a 'disharmonic system' is a theme elaborated on in
   Gunnar Myrdal's *An American Dilemma* ((1944) 1962).
7. For examples of 'psychologistic' and 'individualistic' explanations of
   race prejudice, see Adorno *et al.* 1950; Ackerman and Jahoda 1950;
   Bettelheim and Janowitz 1950.
8. Park noted that when irritating superficial contacts are not offset by
   other kinds of experiences, race conflict is exacerbated (Park (1913b)
   1950).
9. Park, as well as Simmel in Germany, and Cooley and Mead in America,
   thought that

   The conditions under which men buy and sell, have
   undoubtedly had a profound influence on human relations and
   upon human nature ... Men go to market and women too, not as
   they go to church, namely, to revive a sense of their social
   solidarity and of their participation in a common destiny. One
   meets at the market place, not friends merely, but strangers,
   possibly enemies. They have all, each motivated by interests

176

presumably personal to himself, come together because they need one another and because, by an exchange of goods and services, they hope not only to satisfy their own needs but also profit by the needs of others.

(Park (1939a) 1950: 89-90; Simmel (1950) 1964; 1971)

10. For a more recent statement of this view see Banton 1971; 1988.
11. In 1920, employers in commercial and industrial enterprises, asked to account for the increase in the number of Afro-American employees, gave as their primary reason inability to obtain competent white labour (Chicago Commission on Race Relations (1922) 1968: 362).
12. Peter Kolchin's comparison of black slaves in the USA and Russian serfs supports Park's view that 'cultural autonomy and heightened group consciousness contribute to the ability of a subordinate group to engage in collective protest in order to change their condition' (Kolchin 1988, reviewed by R.S. Dunn, *Times Literary Supplement* 1988: 668).
13. For a discussion of the difficulties in differentiating between institutions, social structure, and culture, see Blau 1976.
14. The Harlem Renaissance provides a useful case study of the alliance between literature and the arts generally and politics (Osofsky 1966; Anderson 1981). Also suggestive of the relationship between politics and art are Keil (1966), Cruse (1967), Barker 1981 and Blauner (1972).
15. Dunbar's poem goes as follows:

> We wear the mask that grins and lies,
> It hides our cheeks and shades our eyes –
> This debt we pay to human guile,
> With torn and bleeding hearts we smile
> And mouth with myriad subtleties.

(Dunbar, cited in Park (1923a) 1950: 291)

16. This conclusion is independently arrived at, but for different reasons, by Matthews in his excellent intellectual biography of Park (Matthews 1977: 157).

BIBLIOGRAPHY

Ackerman, N.W. and Jahoda, M. (1950) *Anti-Semitism and Emotional Disorder*, New York: Harper & Brothers.

Addams, J. (1965) *The Social Thought of Jane Addams,* ed. C. Lasch, Indianapolis, Ia: Bobbs-Merrill.

Adorno, T.W., Frenkel-Brunswik, E., Levinson, D.J., and Sanford, R.N. (1950) *The Authoritarian Personality*, New York: Harper & Brothers.

Amersfoort, H. van (1982) *Immigration and the Formation of Minority Groups: The Dutch Experience 1945-1975*, Cambridge: Cambridge University Press.

Anderson, J. (1981) *This Was Harlem, 1900-1950*, New York: Straus Giroux.

Anderson, N. ((1923) 1961) *The Hobo: The Sociology of the Homeless Man*, Chicago: University of Chicago Press.

Baker, P.J. (1973) 'Life histories of William I. Thomas and Robert E. Park', *American Journal of Sociology* 79 (September): 243-60.

Baker, R.S. ((1908) 1964) *Following the Color Line: American Negro Citizenship in the Progressive Era*, New York: Harper & Row.

Banton, M. (1971) *Racial Minorities*, London: Fontana/Collins.

Banton, M. (1988) *Racial Consciousness*, London & New York: Longman.

Barker, M. (1981) *The New Racism, Conservatives and the Ideology of the Tribe*, London: Junction Books.

Barth, F. (1981) 'Ethnic groups and boundaries', in F. Barth *Process and Forms in Social Life: Selected Essays*, London: Routledge & Kegan Paul.

Barth, G. (1980) *City People: The Rise of Modern City Culture in Nineteenth-Century America*, New York and Oxford: Oxford University Press.

Bauer, R.A. and Bauer, A.H. ((1942) 1970) 'Day to day resistance to slavery', *Journal of Negro History* XXVII (October 1942); reprinted in P.I. Rose (ed.) *Americans From Africa*, Vol. II, *Old Memories, New Moods*, New York: Atherton Press.

Becker, H.S. ((1963) 1966) *Outsiders: Studies in the Sociology of Deviance,*

London: Collier-Macmillan.

Becker, H.S. (1964) *The Other Side: Perspectives on Deviance*, New York: The Free Press of Glencoe.

Becker, H.S. (1971) *Sociological Work: Method and Substance*, London: Allen Lane.

Becker, H.S. and Geer, B. (1957) 'Participant observation and interviewing', *Human Organisation* 16: 28-32.

Bell, D. (1975) 'Ethnicity and social change', in N. Glazer and D.P. Moynihan (eds) *Ethnicity, Theory and Experience*, Cambridge, Mass.: Harvard University Press, pp. 141-74.

Bennett, J. (1981) *Oral History and Delinquency*, Chicago: University of Chicago Press.

Berger, B. and Berger, P. (1976) *Sociology: A Biographical Approach*, London: Penguin.

Berger, P.L. and Luckmann, T. (1966) *The Social Construction of Reality: A Treatise in the Sociology of Knowledge*, Garden City, New York: Doubleday.

Bernstein, B. (1961) 'Social class and linguistic development', in A.H. Halsey, J. Floud, and C.A. Anderson (eds) *Education, Economy and Society*, Glencoe, Ill.: Free Press.

Bernstein, B. (1966) 'Elaborated and restricted codes: their social origins and some consequences', in A.G. Smith (ed.) *Communication and Culture*, New York: Holt & Winston.

Béteille, A. (1971) 'The politics of "non-antagonistic" strata', in *Contributions to Indian Sociology*, New Delhi: Vikas.

Bettelheim, B. and Janowitz, M. (1950) *Dynamics of Prejudice*, New York: Harper & Brothers.

Blau, P. (ed.) (1976) *Approaches to the Study of Social Structure*, London: Open Books.

Blauner, R. (1972) 'Black culture', in *Racial Oppression in America*, New York: Harper & Row, pp. 124-61.

Blumer, H. (1939) *Critiques of Research in the Social Sciences: I, An Appraisal of Thomas and Znaniecki's 'The Polish Peasant in Europe and America'*, New York: Social Science Research Council, *Bulletin 44*.

Blumer, H. (1955) 'Reflections on theory of race relations', in A. Lind (ed.) *Race Relations in World Perspective*, Honolulu: University of Hawaii Press.

Blumer, H. ((1956) 1969) 'Sociological analysis and the "Variable"', in H. Blumer *Symbolic Interactionism, Perspective and Method*, Englewood Cliffs, NJ: Prentice-Hall, pp. 127-39.

Blumer, H. (1958) 'Race prejudice as a sense of group position', *Pacific Sociological Review* I (1) (spring): 3-8.

Blumer, H. (1965a) 'The future of the color line', in J.C. McKinney and E.T. Thompson (eds) *The South in Continuity and Change*, Durham,

NC: Duke University Press, pp. 322-36.

Blumer, H. (1965b) 'Industrialism and race relations', in G. Hunter (ed.) *Industrialisation and Race Relations*, London: Oxford University Press, pp. 220-53.

Blumer, H. (1969) *Symbolic Interactionism, Perspective and Method*, Englewood Cliffs, NJ: Prentice-Hall.

Blumer, H. (1978) 'Social unrest and collective protest', in N.K. Denzin (ed.) *Studies in Symbolic Interaction*, Vol. I, Greenwich, Conn.: JAI Press Inc., pp. 1-54.

Blumer, H. Personal conversation, Berkeley, California, 6 August 1979.

Blumer, H. and Duster, T. (1980) 'Theories of race and social action', in *Sociological Theories: Race and Colonialism*, Paris, UNESCO: pp. 211-38.

Boas, F. ((1911) 1938) *The Mind of Primitive Man*, New York: Macmillan.

du Bois, W.E.B. ((1903) 1961) *The Souls of Black Folk*, Greenwich, Conn.: Fawcett Publications.

Bowker, G. and Carrier, J. (1976) *Race and Ethnic Relations*, London: Hutchinson.

Bramson, L. (1961) *The Political Context of Sociology*, Princeton, NJ: Princeton University Press.

Brittan, A. (1973) *Meanings and Situations*, London and Boston: Routledge & Kegan Paul.

Broadwater Farm Inquiry *see* Gifford (1986).

Brotz, H. (1964) *The Black Jews of Harlem*, New York: Schocken Books.

Bulmer, M. (ed.) (1977) *Sociological Research Methods: An Introduction* London: Macmillan.

Bulmer, M. (1984) *The Chicago School of Sociology: Institutionalization, Diversity, and the Rise of Sociological Research*, Chicago and London: University of Chicago Press.

Burgess, E.W. ((1924) 1967) 'The growth of the city: an introduction to a research project', *Publications of the American Sociological Society*, 18 (Annual): 85-97, reprinted in E. Park, E. Burgess, and R. McKenzie, *The City*, (1925) 1967, Chicago: University of Chicago Press: 47-62.

Burgess, E.W. and Bogue, D.J. (1967) 'Research in urban society: a long view', in E.W. Burgess and D.J. Bogue (eds) *Urban Sociology*, Chicago and London: University of Chicago Press (Phoenix Books).

Caplan, N. (1970) 'The new ghetto man: a review of recent empirical studies', *Journal of Social Issues* (winter): 53-79.

Carey, J.T. (1975) *Sociology and Public Affairs: The Chicago School*, London: Sage Publications.

Carmichael, S. and Hamilton, C. (1967) *Black Power: The Politics of Liberation in America*, New York: Random House.

Castells, M. (1977) *The Urban Question: A Marxist Approach*, Cambridge, Ma.: MIT Press.

Castles, S. and Kosack, G. (1973) *Immigrant Workers and Class Structure in Western Europe*, London: Oxford University Press.

Cayton, H. (1965) *Long, Old, Road*, New York: Trident Press.

Chicago Commission on Race Relations ((1922) 1968) *The Negro in Chicago: A Study of Race Relations and a Race Riot*, New York: Arno Press and the *New York Times*.

Cicourel, A. (1964) *Method and Measurement in Sociology*, New York: Free Press; London: Collier-Macmillan.

Cicourel, A. (1973) 'Interpretive procedures and normative rules in the negotiation of status and role', in *Cognitive Sociology, Language and Meaning in Social Interaction*, London: Penguin, pp. 11-41.

Colfax, J.D. and Roach, J.L. (eds) (1971) *Radical Sociology*, New York: Basic Books.

Collins, R. and Makowsky, M. (1972) *The Discovery of Society*, New York: Random House.

Conzen, K.N. (1979) 'Immigrants, immigrant neighborhoods and ethnic identity, historical issues', *Journal of American History* 66, 3: 603-15.

Cooley, C.H. ((1902) 1964) 'The looking glass self', *Human Nature and the Social Order*, New York: Charles Scribner's Sons.

Cooley, C.H. ((1909) 1962) *Social Organization: A Study of the Larger Mind*, New York: Schocken Books.

Cox, O.C. ((1948) 1970) *Caste, Class and Race*, London: Modern Reader Paperbacks.

Cruse, H. (1967) *The Crisis of the Negro Intellectual*, New York: Morrow.

Cruse, H. (1987) *Plural but Equal, A Critical Study of Blacks and Minorities and America's Plural Society*, New York: William Morrow.

Davidson, D. (1973) 'The furious passage of the black graduate student', in J. Ladner (ed.) *The Death of White Sociology*, New York: Random House (vintage), pp. 23-51.

Denzin, N. (1978) *The Research Act: A Theoretical Introduction to Sociological Methods*, New York: McGraw-Hill.

Dewey, J. (1927) *The Public and Its Problems*, Chicago: Swallow Press.

Dewey, J. (1958) *Experience and Nature*, New York: Dover Publications.

Diner, H. (1977) *In the Almost Promised Land: American Jews and Blacks, 1915-1935*, Westport, Conn.: Greenwood Press.

Diner, S. (1970) 'Chicago social workers and blacks in the progressive era', *Social Service Review* 44 (December): 393-410.

Diner, S.J. (1975) 'Department and discipline: the Department of Sociology at the University of Chicago, 1892-1920', *Minerva* 13 (winter): 514-53.

Diner, S.J. (1977) 'Scholarship in the quest for social welfare: a fifty year history of the *Social Service Review*', *Social Service Review* 51 (March): 1-66.

181

BIBLIOGRAPHY

Diner, S.J. (1980) *A City and Its Universities: Public Policy in Chicago, 1892-1919*, Chapel Hill, NC: University of North Carolina Press.

Dinnerstein, L., Nichols, R.L., and Reimers, D.M. (1979) *Native and Strangers: Ethnic Groups and the Building of America*, New York: Oxford University Press.

Douglas, J. (ed.) ((1971) 1970) *Understanding Everyday Life: Toward the Reconstruction of Sociological Knowledge*, London: Routledge & Kegan Paul.

Doyle, B.W. ((1937) 1971) *The Etiquette of Race Relations in the South*, Chicago: University of Chicago Press.

Drake, St Clair and Cayton, H.R. ((1945) 1962) *Black Metropolis: A Study of Negro Life In A Northern City*, 2 vols, New York: Harcourt, Brace.

Driver, G. (1979) 'Classroom stress and school achievement: West Indian adolescents and their teachers', in K. Verity (ed.) *Minority Families, Support and Stress*, London: Macmillan, pp. 131-44.

Du Bois, W.E.B. ((1903) 1961) *The Souls of Black Folk*, Greenwich, Conn.: Fawcett Publications.

Dumont, L. (1970) *Homo Hierarchicus: the Caste System and Its Implications*, London: Weidenfeld & Nicolson.

Dunn, R.S. (1988) 'Of human bondage', review of Peter Kolchin's *Unfree Labour: American Slavery and Russian Serfdom* (1988), Cambridge, Ma: Harvard University Press, in *Times Literary Supplement*, no. 4446, June 17-23, 1988: 667-8.

Duster, T. (1978) 'Review of Nathan Glazer's "Affirmative Discrimination"', *American Journal of Sociology* 84 (1): 252-6.

Duster, T. (1987) 'Purpose and bias', *Society* (January/February): 8-12.

Ellison, R. ((1944) 1972) 'An American dilemma: a review', in R. Ellison *Shadow and Act*, unpublished, written in 1944 for *The Antioch Review*, New York: Random House, pp. 303-17.

Ellison, R. ((1958) 1972) 'Some questions and some answers', *Preuves*, May; reprinted in R. Ellison *Shadow and Act*, New York: Random House, (1972), pp. 261-72.

Faris, R.E.L. ((1967) 1970) *Chicago Sociology, 1920-1932*, Chicago: University of Chicago.

Filmer, P., Phillipson, M., Silverman, D., and Walsh, D. (1972) *New Directions in Sociological Theory*, London: Collier-Macmillan.

Finlay, M.I. (1968) 'Slavery', in D.L. Sills (ed.) *International Encyclopedia of the Social Sciences* 14, London: Crowell, Collier & Macmillan: 307-13.

Fisher, B.M. and Strauss, A. (1979) 'Interactionism', in T. Bottomore and R. Nisbet (eds) *A History of Sociological Analysis*, London: Heinemann, pp. 457-98.

Flew, A. (1985) *Thinking About Social Thinking*, Oxford: Blackwell.

Franklin, J.H. (1967) *From Slavery to Freedom: A History of Negro Americans*, New York: Alfred A. Knopf.

Frazier, E.F. ((1931) 1968) 'Certain aspects of conflict in the Negro family', *Social Forces* 10 (October 1931): 76-84; *E. Franklin Frazier on Race Relations*, Chicago: University of Chicago Press (1968); pp. 210-24.

Frazier, E.F. (1932) *The Negro Family in Chicago*, Chicago: University of Chicago Press.

Frazier, E.F. (1934) 'Tradition and patterns of Negro family life in the United States', in E.B. Reuter (ed.) *Race and Culture Contacts*, New York: McGraw-Hill.

Frazier, E.F. ((1939) 1966) *The Negro Family in the United States*, Chicago: University of Chicago Press.

Frazier, E.F. ((1949) 1968) 'Race contacts and the social structure', *American Sociological Review* 14 (1) (February 1949): 1-11; reprinted in *E. Franklin Frazier on Race Relations*, Chicago: University of Chicago Press (1968), pp. 43-61.

Frazier, E.F. ((1955) 1968) 'The new Negro middle class', in *The New Negro Thirty Years Afterward*, Washington DC: Howard University Press (1955), pp. 25-32; reprinted in *E. Franklin Frazier on Race Relations*, Chicago: University of Chicago Press (1968), pp. 256-64.

Frazier, E.F. (1957) *Black Bourgeoisie*, New York: Free Press.

Frazier, E.F. ((1963) 1974) 'The Negro Church in America', in E.F. Frazier and C.E. Lincoln *The Negro Church in America, The Black Church Since Frazier*, New York: Schocken Books, pp. 9-98.

Frazier, E.F. (1968) *E. Franklin Frazier on Race Relations, Selected Papers*, edited and with an introduction by G. Franklin Edwards, Chicago: University of Chicago Press.

Fredrickson, G. (1971) *The Black Image in the White Mind: the Debate on Afro-American Character and Destiny, 1827-1914*, New York: Harper & Row.

Friedrichs, R.W. (1970) *A Sociology of Sociology*, New York: Free Press.

Furner, M.O. (1975) *Advocacy and Objectivity*, Lexington, Ky: University of Kentucky Press.

Garfinkel, H. (1967) *Studies in Ethnomethodology*, Englewood Cliffs, NJ: Prentice-Hall.

Geertz, C. (1973) 'The integrative revolution: primordial sentiments and civil politics in new states', in *The Interpretation of Cultures*, New York: Basic Books, pp. 255-310.

Genovese, E.D. ((1966) 1972) 'Rebelliousness and docility in the Negro slave: a critique of the Elkins thesis', originally published in *Civil War History*, 13 December 1966: 293-314; reprinted in E.D. Genovese (ed.) in *Red and Black: Marxian Explorations in Southern and Afro-American History*, New York: Random House, (1972), pp. 73-101.

Genovese, E.D. (1972) *Red and Black: Marxian Explorations in*

Southern and Afro-American History, New York: Random House, Vintage Books.

Gifford, Lord (1986) *Report of the Independent Inquiry into Disturbances of October 1985 at the Broadwater Farm Estate, Tottenham*, London: Broadwater Farm Inquiry.

Glaser, B. and Strauss, A. (1967) *The Discovery of Grounded Theory*, Chicago: Aldine.

Glazer, N. (1975) *Affirmative Discrimination: Ethnic Inequality and Public Policy*, New York: Basic Books.

Glazer, N. (1983) *Ethnic Dilemmas, 1964-1982*, Cambridge, Ma.: Harvard University Press.

Glazer, N. (1985) 'Interests and passions', *The Public Interest* (Fall): 17-30.

Glazer, N. (1988) *The Limits of Social Policy*, Cambridge, Ma. and London: Harvard University Press.

Glazer, N. and Moynihan, D.P. (1963) *Beyond the Melting Pot: The Negroes, Puerto Ricans, Jews, Italians, and Irish of New York City*, Cambridge, Ma.: MIT Press.

Glazer, N. and Moynihan, D.P. (1975) *Ethnicity, Theory and Experience*, Cambridge, Ma.: Harvard University Press.

Glazer, N. and Young, K. (1983) *Ethnic Pluralism and Public Policy: Achieving Equality in the United States and Britain*, London: Gower.

Goffman, E. ((1956) 1969) *The Presentation of Self in Everyday Life*, London: Penguin.

Goffman, E. ((1961) 1968) *Asylums: Essays in the Social Situation of Mental Patients and Other Inmates*, London: Pelican.

Goffman, E. (1963) *Stigma: Notes on the Management of Spoiled Identity*, Englewood Cliffs, NJ: Prentice-Hall.

Gordon, M.M. (1958) *Social Class in American Sociology*, Durham, NC: Duke University Press.

Gordon, M.M. (1964) *Assimilation in American Life: The Role of Race, Religion and National Origins*, New York: Oxford University Press.

Gosnell, H.F. ((1935) 1967) *Negro Politicians: The Rise of Negro Politics in Chicago*, Chicago: University of Chicago Press.

Gossett, T.F. (1965) *Race: The History of An Idea in America*, New York: Schocken Books.

Gouldner, A.W. (1968) 'The sociologist as partisan: sociology and the welfare state', *American Sociologist* 3: 103-16.

Gouldner, A.W. (1971) *The Coming Crisis of Western Sociology*, London: Heinemann.

Greeley, A.M. (1971) *Why Can't They Be Like Us? America's White Ethnic Groups*, New York: E.P. Dutton.

Greeley, A.M. (1974) *Ethnicity in the United States: A Preliminary Reconnaissance*, New York: John Wiley & Sons.

Hannerz, U. (1971) *Soulside: Inquiries into Ghetto Culture and Community*, New York and London: Columbia University Press.

Harlan, L.R. (1972) *Booker T. Washington: The Making of a Black Leader, 1856-1901*, New York: Oxford University Press.

Harlan, L.R. (1983) *Booker T. Washington: The Wizard of Tuskegee, 1901-1915*, New York: Oxford University Press.

Henretta, J.A. (1983) 'Ethnography, drama and historical method', *Past and Present* 101 (November): 158-61.

Higham, J. ((1955) 1988) *Strangers in the Land, Patterns of American Nativism 1860-1925*, 2nd ed., New Brunswick and London: Rutgers University Press.

Higham, J. (1974a) 'Hanging together: divergent unities in American history', *Journal of American History* 61: 5-28.

Higham, J. ((1974b) 1984) 'Another American dilemma', *The Center Magazine* VII (July/August 1974): 67-73; reprinted in J. Higham *Send These to Me: Jews and other Immigrants in Urban America*, Baltimore, MA.: The Johns Hopkins University Press (1984), pp. 233-48.

Higham, J. (1984) *Send These to Me: Jews and Other Immigrants in Urban America*, Baltimore, Ma.: The Johns Hopkins University Press.

Hinkle, R.C. (1963) 'Antecedents of the action orientation in American sociology before 1936', *American Sociological Review* XXVIII (October): 705-15.

Hofstadter, R. ((1944) 1964) *Social Darwinism in American Thought*, Boston: Beacon Press.

Hofstadter, R. (1955) *The Age of Reform*, New York: Random House.

Hollinger, D.A. (1980) 'The problem of pragmatism in American history', *Journal of American History* 67 (1) (June) 88-107.

Hughes, E.C. ((1931) 1979) *The Chicago Real Estate Board*, New York: Atheneum.

Hughes, E.C. ((1943) 1963) *French Canada in Transition*, Chicago: University of Chicago Press.

Hughes, E.C. ((1945) 1971) 'Dilemmas and contradictions of status', *American Journal of Sociology* (March 1945); reprinted in *The Sociological Eye*, Chicago: Aldine-Atherton (1971), pp. 141-50.

Hughes, E.C. ((1962) 1971) 'Going concerns: the study of American institutions', reprinted in *The Sociological Eye*, Chicago: Aldine-Atherton (1971), pp. 52-64.

Hughes, E.C. ((1964) 1971) 'The sociological point of view: the challenge of the deep South to research in the social sciences', in R.B. Highsaw, *The Deep South in Transformation*, reprinted E.C. Hughes, *The Sociological Eye*, Chicago and New York: Aldine-Atherton (1971), pp. 159–66.

Hughes, E.C. (1971) *The Sociological Eye: Selected Papers*, Chicago and New York: Aldine-Atherton.

Hughes, E.C. Interview with author, 18 April 1973.

Isaacs, H.R. (1972) 'The new pluralists', *Commentary* (March): 75-9.

Isaacs, H.R. (1977) *Idols of the Tribe: Group Identity and Political Change*, New York: Harper & Row.

Jackson, P. and Smith, S. (eds) (1981) *Social Interaction and Ethnic Segregation*, London: Academic Press.

James, W. ((1928) 1970) 'The social self', *Psychology*, New York: Henry Holt and Co., pp. 189–226, reprinted in G. Stone and H. Farberman (eds) *Social Psychology Through Symbolic Interaction*, Waltham, Ma: Xerox College Publishing (1970).

James, W. ((1899) 1958) 'A certain blindness in human beings', *Talks to Teachers on Psychology; and to Students on Some of Life's Ideals*, New York: W.W. Norton & Co.

James, W. ((1902) 1961) *The Varieties of Religious Experience*, Gifford Lectures, New York: Collier; London: Collier-Macmillan.

Janowitz, M. (1966) 'Introduction', in *W.I. Thomas on Social Organisation and Social Personality*, Chicago: University of Chicago Press, pp. vii-lviii.

Janowitz, M. (1980) *The Last Half Century*, Chicago: University of Chicago Press.

Johnson, C.S. (1934) *Shadow of the Plantation*, Chicago: University of Chicago Press.

Kantrowitz, N. (1981) 'Ethnic segregation: social reality and academic myth', in C. Peach, V. Robinson, and S. Smith (eds) *Ethnic Segregation in Cities*, London: Croom Helm.

Katznelson, I. (1976) *Black Men, White Cities: Race, Politics, and Migration in the United States 1900-30, and Britain, 1948-68*, Chicago and London: University of Chicago Press (Phoenix).

Keil, C. (1966) *Urban Blues*, Chicago and London: University of Chicago Press.

Khan, V.S. (1979) 'Introduction', in V.S. Khan (ed.) *Minority Families: Support and Stress*, London: Macmillan.

Killian, L. (1970) 'Herbert Blumer's contributions to race relations', in T. Shibutani (ed.) *Human Nature and Collective Behavior*, Englewood Cliffs, NJ: Prentice-Hall, pp. 179-90.

Killian, L. ((1970) 1985) *White Southerners*, Amherst, Mass.: University of Massachusetts Press.

Killian, L. and Grigg, C. (1967) *Racial Crisis in America*, Englewood Cliffs, NJ: Prentice-Hall (Spectrum).

Kramer, D. (1966) *Chicago Renaissance, The Literary Life in the Midwest 1900-1938*, New York: Appleton Century.

Kuhn, T. (1964) *The Structure of Scientific Revolutions*, Chicago: University of Chicago Press.

Kurtz, L.R (1982) 'Robert E. Park's "Notes on the Origin of the Society for Social Research"', *Journal of the History of the Behavioral Sciences* 18 (October): 332-40.

Kurtz, L.R. (1984) *Evaluating Chicago Sociology*, Chicago and London: University of Chicago Press (Heritage of Sociology).

Labov, W. ((1969) 1973) 'The logic of non-standard English', *Georgetown Monographs on Language and Linguistics* 22 (1969): 1-31, reprinted in N. Keddie (ed.) *Tinker, Tailor: The Myth of Cultural Deprivation*, London: Penguin, pp. 21-66.

Ladner, J. (ed.) (1973) *The Death of White Sociology*, New York: Random House, pp. xix-xxix.

Lal, B.B. (1982) 'So near and yet so far: the "Chicago School" of symbolic interactionism and its relationship to developments in the sociology of sociology and ethnomethodology', in N. Denzin (ed.) *Studies in Symbolic Interaction* 4, Greenwich, Conn. and London: JAI Press, Inc.

Lal, B.B. (1983) 'Perspectives on ethnicity: old wine in new bottles', *Ethnic and Racial Studies* 6 (2) (April): 154-73.

Lal, B.B. (1986) 'The "Chicago School" of American sociology, symbolic interactionism, and race relations theory', in J. Rex and D. Mason (eds) *Theories of Race and Ethnic Relations*, Cambridge: Cambridge University Press, pp. 280-98.

Lee, A.M. (1973) *Toward Humanist Sociology*, Englewood Cliffs, NJ: Prentice-Hall.

Lengermann, P.M. (1979) 'The founding of the ARS: the anatomy of a rebellion', *American Sociological Review* 44 (April): 185-98.

di Leonardo, M. (1984) *The Varieties of Ethnic Experience: Kinship, Class and Gender Among California Italian-Americans*, Ithaca, NY: Cornell University Press.

Levine, D.N. (1972) 'Note on the crowd and the public', in R.E. Park ((1904) 1972) *The Crowd and The Public and Other Essays*, Chicago: The University of Chicago, pp. xxvii-xxxii.

Lewis, J.D. and Smith, R.L. (1980) *American Sociology and Pragmatism: Mead, Chicago Sociology and Symbolic Interaction*, Chicago and London: University of Chicago Press.

Lewis, O. (1959) *Five Families*, New York: Basic Books.

Lewis, O. (1961) *The Children of Sanchez*, New York: Random House.

Lewis, O. (1966) *La Vida*, New York: Random House.

Lieberson, S. (1980) *A Piece of the Pie, Blacks & White Immigrants Since 1880*, Berkeley, Ca: University of California Press.

Liebow, C. (1967) *Tally's Corner, Washington DC: A Study of Negro Street Corner Men*, London: Routledge & Kegan Paul.

Light, I.H. (1972) *Ethnic Enterprise*, Berkeley, Los Angeles, and London:

187

University of California Press.

Light, I. (1984) 'Immigrant and ethnic enterprise in North America', *Ethnic and Racial Studies* 7 (2) (April).

Light, I. and Bonacich, E. (1988) *Immigrant Entrepreneurs: Koreans in Los Angeles*, Berkeley, CA: University of California Press.

Lipset, S.M. (1950) 'Changing social status and prejudice: the race theories of a pioneering sociologist', *Commentary* 9: 475-9.

Lipset, S.M. (1976) 'Social structure and social change', in P. Blau (ed.) *Approaches to the Study of Social Structure*, London: Open Books, pp. 176-209.

Lofland, J. (1970) 'Interactionist imagery and analytic interruptus', in T. Shibutani (ed.) *Human Nature and Collective Behavior*, Englewood Cliffs, NJ: Prentice-Hall.

Lofland, L. (1980) 'Reminiscences of Classic Chicago: the Blumer-Hughes talk', *Urban Life* 9 (3) (October): 251-81.

Lofland, L.H. (1983) 'Understanding urban life, the Chicago legacy', *Urban Life* 11 (4) (January): 491-511.

Lubove, R. (1962) *The Progressives and the Slums: Tenement House Reform in New York City, 1890-1917*, Pittsburgh, Penn.: University of Pittsburgh Press.

Lyman, S. (1973) *The Black American in Sociological Thought: A Failure of Perspective*, New York: Capricorn Books.

Mann, A. (ed.) (1975) *The Progressive Era*, New York: Holt, Rinehart & Winston, pp. 1-10.

Mannheim, K. ((1932) 1953) 'American sociology', *American Journal of Sociology* 38 (2) (September): 273-82; reprinted in *Essays on Sociology and Social Psychology*, London: Routledge & Kegan Paul (1953), pp. 185-94.

Masuoka, J. and Valien, P. (ed.) (1961) *Race Relations: Problems and Theory, Essays in Honour of Robert E. Park*, Chapel Hill, NC: University of North Carolina Press.

Matthews, F.H. (1970) 'The revolt against Americanism: culture pluralism and cultural relativism as an ideology of liberation', *Canadian Review of American Studies* I (spring): 4-31.

Matthews, F.H. (1977) *Quest for an American Sociology: Robert E. Park and the Chicago School*, Montreal and London: McGill-Queen's University Press.

Matthews, F.H. (1984) 'Cultural pluralism in context: external history, philosophic premise, and theories of ethnicity in North America', *Journal of Ethnic Studies* 12 (2) (summer): 63-78.

Mead, G.H. ((1924-5) 1964) 'The genesis of the self and social control', *International Journal of Ethics* 35: 251-77; reprinted in A.J. Reck (ed.) *Selected Writings, George Herbert Mead*, Indianapolis, NY: Bobbs Merrill: 267-93.

Mead, G.H. ((1934) 1962) *Mind, Self and Society*, Chicago: University of Chicago Press.

Meier, A. (1964) *Negro Thought in America, 1880-1915: Race Ideologies in the Age of Booker T. Washington*, Ann Arbor, Mich.: University of Michigan Press.

Meier, A. and Rudwick, E. (1970) *From Plantation to Ghetto*, London: Constable, revised edition.

Meltzer, B.N. and Petras, J.W. (1970) 'The Chicago and Iowa schools of symbolic interactionism', in T. Shibutani (ed.) *Human Nature and Collective Behavior: Papers in Honor of Herbert Blumer*, Englewood Cliffs, NJ: Prentice-Hall, pp. 3-17.

Meltzer, B.N., Petras, J.W., and Reynolds, L.T. (1975) *Symbolic Interactionism: Genesis, Varieties and Criticism*, London: Routledge & Kegan Paul.

Merton, R. (1957) *Social Theory and Social Structure*, New York: Free Press.

Miles, R. (1984) 'Marxism versus the sociology of "race relations"', *Ethnic and Racial Studies* 7 (1): 217-37.

Mills, C.W. ((1941) 1963) 'The professional ideology of social pathologists', in *Power, Politics and People: The Collected Essays of C. Wright Mills*, New York: Oxford University Press, pp. 423-38.

Mills, C.W. (1959) *The Sociological Imagination*, New York: Oxford University Press.

Mills, C.W. (1966) *Sociology and Pragmatism: The Higher Learning in America*, New York: Oxford University Press.

Modood, T. (1988) '" Black", racial equality and Asian identity', *New Community* XIV (spring): 397-404.

Myrdal, G. ((1944) 1962) *An American Dilemma: The Negro Problem and Modern Democracy*, New York: Harper & Row.

National Advisory Commission on Civil Disorders, United States (1968) *Report*, Washington, DC: Government Printing Office.

Novak, M. (1971) *The Rise of the Unmeltable Ethics*, New York: Macmillan.

Oberschall, A. (1972) 'The institutionalization of American sociology', in A. Oberschall (ed.) *The Establishment of Empirical Sociology: Studies in Continuity, Discontinuity and Institutionalization*, New York: Harper & Row, pp. 225-32.

Osofsky, G. (1966) *Harlem: The Making of a Ghetto*, New York: Harper & Row.

Osofsky, G. (ed.) (1969) *Puttin' on Ole Massa*, New York: Harper & Row.

Ovington, M.W. ((1947) 1970) *The Walls Came Tumbling Down*, New York: Schocken Books.

Park, R.E. (1900) 'German Army', *Munsey's Magazine* 24 (December): 386-405.

Park, R.E. ((1904) 1972) *The Crowd and The Public and Other Essays*, H. Elsner Jr (ed.), Chicago: University of Chicago.

Park, R.E. (1906a) 'A king in business', *Everybody's* 15 (November): 624-33.

Park, R.E. (1906b) 'The terrible story of the Congo', *Everybody's* 15 (December): 763-72.

Park, R.E. (1907) 'Blood-money of the Congo', *Everybody's* 16 (January): 60-78.

Park, R.E. (1913a) 'Negro home life and standards of living', *Annals of the American Academy of Political and Social Science* 49 (September): 147-63.

Park, R.E. ((1913b) 1950) 'Racial assimilation in secondary groups with particular reference to the Negro', *American Sociological Society* VIII: 66-83; reprinted in E.C. Hughes *et al.* (eds) *Collected Writings of Robert E. Park*, Vol. I, *Race and Culture*, Chicago: Free Press (1950), 204-20.

Park, R.E. ((1915) 1952) 'The city: suggestions for the investigation of human behaviour in the urban environment', *American Journal of Sociology* XX (March 1915): 577-612; reprinted in E.C. Hughes *et al.* (eds) *Collected Writings of Robert E. Park*, Vol. II, *Human Communities, the City, Human Ecology*, Glencoe, Ill.: Free Press (1952), pp. 13-51, and in R.E. Park, E.W. Burgess, and R. McKenzie ((1925) 1967) *The City*, Chicago: University of Chicago Press, pp. 1-46.

Park, R.E. ((1917) 1950) 'Race prejudice and Japanese-American relations', Introduction to J.F. Steiner *The Japanese Invasion*, Chicago: A. S. McClurg, pp. vii-xvii; reprinted in *Race and Culture* (1950), pp. 223-229.

Park, R.E. ((1918) 1950) 'Education in its relation to the conflict and fusion of cultures, with special reference to the problems of the immigrant, the negro, and missions', *Publication of the American Sociological Society* XIII (1918): 38-63; reprinted in *Race and Culture* (1950), pp. 261-83.

Park, R.E. ((1920-21) (1921-22) 1955) 'Sociology and the social sciences', *American Journal of Sociology* 26 (1920-21) January 1921: 401-24; 27 July 1921: 1-21; September 1921:169-83; reprinted in E.C. Hughes *et al.* (eds) *Society, Collective Behavior, News and Opinion, Sociology and Modern Society*, Glencoe, Ill.: Free Press (1955), pp. 187-242.

Park, R.E. ((1922) 1970) *The Immigrant Press and Its Control*, Westport, Conn.: Greenwood Press.

Park, R.E. ((1923a) 1950) 'Negro race consciousness as reflected in race literature', *American Review* 1 (September-October 1923): 505-16; reprinted in *Race and Culture*, pp. 284-300.

Park, R.E. ((1923b) 1955) 'Natural history of the newspaper', *American Journal of Sociology* XXIX (3) (November 1923): 80-98; reprinted in R.E. Park, E.W. Burgess, and R.D. McKenzie *The City*, Chicago:

University of Chicago Press (1925); reprinted in *Society* (1955), pp. 89-104.

Park, R.E. ((1923c) 1950) 'A race relations survey: suggestions for a study of the Oriental population of the Pacific Coast', *Journal of Applied Sociology* VIII (1923): 195-205; reprinted in *Race and Culture* (1950), pp. 158-65.

Park, R.E. ((1924a) 1950) 'The concept of social distance: as applied to the study of racial attitudes and racial relations', *Journal of Applied Sociology* 9 (July 1924): 339-344; reprinted in *Race and Culture* (1950), pp. 256-60.

Park, R.E. ((1924b) 1950) 'Experience and race relations, opinions, attitudes, and experience as types of human behavior', *Journal of Applied Sociology* IX (September 1924): 18-24; reprinted in *Race and Culture* (1950), pp. 152-7.

Park, R.E. ((1925a) 1950) 'Culture and cultural trends', publications of the *American Sociological Society* XIX (December 1925): 24-36; reprinted in *Race and Culture* (1950), pp. 24-35.

Park, R.E. ((1925b) 1952) 'Community organization and the romantic temper', *Social Forces* (May 1925): 675-7; reprinted in R.E. Park, E.W. Burgess, and R.D. McKenzie *The City*, Chicago: University of Chicago Press (1925), pp. 113-21; reprinted in *Human Communities* (1952): 64-72.

Park, R.E. ((1926a) 1950) 'Our racial frontier on the Pacific', *Survey Graphic* IX (May 1926): 192-6; reprinted in *Race and Culture* (1950), pp. 138-51.

Park, R.E. ((1926b) 1950) 'Behind our masks', *Survey Graphic* LVI (May 1926): 135-9; reprinted in *Race and Culture* (1950), pp. 244-55.

Park, R.E. ((1926c) 1952) 'The urban community as a spatial pattern and a moral order', Presidential Address to the American Sociological Society (1925); published under the title 'The concept of position in sociology', *Publications of the American Sociological Society* XX (1925): 1-14; E.W. Burgess (ed.) *The Urban Community*, Chicago: Chicago University Press (1926), pp. 3-18; reprinted under original title in *Human Communities* (1952), pp. 165-77.

Park, R.E. ((1927) 1955) 'Human nature and collective behavior', *American Journal of Sociology* XXXII (5) (March 1927): 695-703; reprinted in *Society* (1955), pp. 13-21; first appeared in *Zeitschrift für Völkerpsychologie* II, Heft 3 (September 1926): 209-23.

Park, R.E. ((1928a) 1950) 'Human migration and the marginal man', *American Journal of Sociology* XXXIII (6) (May 1928): 881-93; reprinted in *Race and Culture* (1950), pp. 345-56.

Park, R.E. ((1928b) 1950) 'The bases of race prejudice', *Annals of the American Academy of Political and Social Science* CXL (November 1928): 11-20; reprinted in *Race and Culture* (1950), pp. 230-43.

Park, R.E. ((1929a) 1952) 'Sociology, community and society', in W.
Gee (ed.) *Research in the Social Sciences*, New York: Macmillan Co
(1929), pp. 3-49; reprinted in *Human Communities* (1952), pp.
178-209.

Park, R.E. ((1929b) 1952) 'The city as a social laboratory', in T.V.
Smith and L.D. White (eds) *Chicago: An Experiment in Social Science
Research*, Chicago: University of Chicago Press (1929), pp. 1-19;
reprinted in *Human Communities* (1952), pp. 73-87.

Park, R.E. ((1931a) 1955) 'The sociological methods of William
Graham Sumner, and of William I. Thomas and Florian Znaniecki',
in S.A. Rice (ed.) *Methods in Social Science: A Casebook*, Chicago:
University of Chicago Press (1931); reprinted in *Society* (1955), pp.
243-66.

Park, R.E. ((1931b) 1955) 'Human nature, attitudes and mores', in K.
Young (ed.) *Social Attitudes*, New York: Henry Holt & Co (1931), pp.
17-45; reprinted in *Society* (1955), pp. 267-92.

Park, R.E. ((1931c) 1950) 'Mentality of racial hybrids', Address
delivered to the Fourth Pacific Science Congress, Batavia-Bandoeng,
Java, 16-25 May 1929, *American Journal of Sociology* XXXVI (January
1931): 534-51; reprinted in *Race and Culture* (1950), pp. 377-92.

Park, R.E. ((1931d) 1950) 'Personality and cultural conflict',
Publications of the American Sociological Society XXV (May 1931):
95-110; reprinted in *Race and Culture* (1950), pp. 357-71.

Park, R.E. ((1932) 1955) 'Introduction', in P. Young *The Pilgrims of
Russian Town*, Chicago: University of Chicago Press (1932), pp. xi-xx;
reprinted in *Society* (1955), pp. 22-9.

Park, R.E. ((1934a) 1950) 'Race relations and certain frontiers' in E.B.
Reuter (ed.) *Race and Culture Contacts*, New York: McGraw-Hill
(1934), pp. 57-85; reprinted in *Race and Culture* (1950), pp. 117-37.

Park, R.E. ((1934b) 1950) 'The Negro and his plantation heritage',
'Introduction', in C.S. Johnson *Shadow of the Plantation*, Chicago:
University of Chicago Press (1934), pp. xi-xxiv; reprinted in *Race and
Culture* (1950), pp. 66-78.

Park, R.E. ((1934c) 1955) 'Industrial fatigue and group morale',
American Journal of Sociology 40 (November 1934): 349-56; reprinted
in *Society* (1955), pp. 293-300.

Park, R.E. (1935a) 'Assimilation, social', *Encyclopedia of the Social Sciences*
11, pp. 281-3.

Park, R.E. ((1935b) 1950) 'Politics and the man farthest down',
'Introduction', in H.F. Gosnell *Negro Politicians*, Chicago: University
of Chicago Press (1935); reprinted in *Race and Culture* (1950), pp.
166-76.

Park, R.E. ((1937a) 1950) 'The race relations cycle in Hawaii',
'Introduction', in R. Adams *Interracial Marriage in Hawaii*, New York:

Macmillan (1937); reprinted in *Race and Culture* (1950), pp. 189-95.

Park, R.E. ((1937b) 1950) 'Introduction', in B.W. Doyle *The Etiquette of Race Relations in the South*, Chicago: University of Chicago Press (1937), pp. xi-xxiv; reprinted in *Race and Culture* (1950), pp. 177-88.

Park, R.E. ((1937c) 1950) 'Cultural conflict and the marginal man', 'Introduction', in E.V. Stonequist *The Marginal Man*, New York: Charles Scribner (1937), pp. xiii-xviii; reprinted in *Race and Culture* (1950), pp. 372-6.

Park, R.E. ((1937d) 1950), 'A memorandum of rote learning', *American Journal of Sociology* XLIII (July 1937): 23-36; reprinted in *Race and Culture* (1950), pp. 53-65.

Park, R.E. ((1938) 1950), 'Reflections on communication and culture', *American Journal of Sociology* XLIV (September 1938): 187-205; reprinted in *Race and Culture* (1950) pp. 36-52.

Park, R.E. ((1939a) 1950) 'The nature of race relations' in E. Thompson (ed.) *Race Relations and the Race Problem*, Durham, NC: Duke University Press (1939), pp. 3-45; reprinted in *Race and Culture* (1950), pp. 81-116.

Park, R.E. ((1939b) 1952) 'Symbiosis and socialization: a frame of reference for the study of society', *American Journal of Sociology* XLV July (1939): 1-25; reprinted in *Human Communities* (1952), pp. 240-62.

Park, R.E. ((1939c) 1982) 'Notes on the origin of the Society for Social Research', *Bulletin of the Society for Social Research* (August 1939): 3-5; reprinted in L.R. Kurtz, in *Journal of the History of the Behavioral Sciences* (October 1982): 332-40.

Park, R.E. ((1940) 1955) 'News and the human interest story', in H.M. Hughes *News and the Human Interest Story*, Chicago: University of Chicago Press (1940), pp. xi-xxiii; reprinted in *Society* (1955), pp. 105-14.

Park, R.E. ((1941a) 1955) 'The social function of war: observations and notes', *American Journal of Sociology* XLVI (4) (January 1941): 551-70; reprinted in *Society* (1955), pp. 50-68.

Park, R.E. (1941b) 'Methods of teaching: impressions and a verdict', *Social Forces* 20 (October): 36-46.

Park, R.E. ((1943a) 1950) 'Race ideologies', in F.W. Ogburn (ed.) *American Society in Wartime*, Chicago: University of Chicago Press, pp. 165-83; reprinted in *Race and Culture* (1950), pp. 301-15.

Park, R.E. ((1943b) 1950) 'Education and the cultural crisis', *American Journal of Sociology* XLVIII (May 1943): 728-36; reprinted in *Race and Culture* (1950), pp. 316-30.

Park, R.E. (1950a) 'An autobiographical note', in *Race and Culture*, pp. v-ix.

Park, R.E. (1950b) 'Culture and civilization', in *Race and Culture*, pp. 15-23.

Park, R.E. (1950c), *Race and Culture*, vol. I, The Collected Papers of
  Robert Ezra Park, ed. E.C. Hughes *et al.*, Glencoe, Ill.: Free Press.
Park, R.E. (1952a) 'The city as a natural phenomenon', in *Human
  Communities*, pp. 118-27.
Park, R.E. (1952b), *Human Communities, the City, Human Ecology*, vol. II,
  The Collected Papers of Robert Ezra Park, ed. E. C. Hughes *et al.*,
  Glencoe, Ill.: Free Press.
Park, R.E. (1955) *Society, Collective Behavior, News and Opinion, Sociology
  and Modern Society*, vol III, The Collected Papers of Robert Ezra Park,
  ed. E.C. Hughes *et al.*, Glencoe, Ill.: Free Press.
Park, R.E. and Burgess, E.W. ((1921) 1969) *An Introduction to the Science
  of Sociology*, Chicago: University of Chicago Press.
Park, R.E. and Miller, H.A. ((1921) 1969) *Old World Traits Transplanted*,
  New York: Arno Press and the *New York Times*, 1969.
Park, R.E. and Washington, B.T. (1922) 'Documents, letters collected
  by R.E. Park and Booker T. Washington', *Journal of Negro History* 7
  (1922): 206-22.
Park, R.E., Burgess, E.W., and McKenzie, R. ((1925) 1967) *The City*,
  Chicago: University of Chicago Press (Heritage of Sociology).
Parsons, T. (1951) *The Social System*, New York: Free Press.
Parsons, T. (1975) 'Some theoretical considerations on the nature and
  trends of change of ethnicity', in N. Glazer and D.P. Moynihan (eds)
  Ethnicity, Theory and Experience, Cambridge, Mass.: Harvard University
  Press, pp. 53-83.
Patterson, O. (1975) 'Context and choice in ethnic allegiance: a
  theoretical framework and Caribbean case study', in N. Glazer and
  D.P. Moynihan (eds) *Ethnicity, Theory and Experience*, Cambridge,
  Mass.: Harvard University Press, pp. 305-49.
Peach, C. (ed.) (1975) *Urban Social Segregation*, London: Longman.
Peach, C., Robinson, V., and Smith, S. (eds) (1981) *Ethnic Segregation in
  Cities*, London: Croom Helm.
Persons, S. (1987) *Ethnic Studies at Chicago 1905-45*, Urbana and
  Chicago, Ill.: University of Illinois Press.
Petersen, W. (1961) *Population*, New York: Macmillan.
Phillips, U.B. ((1918) 1967) *American Negro Slavery: A Survey of the Supply,
  Employment and Control of Negro Labour as Determined by the Plantation
  Regime*, Baton Rouge, LA: Louisiana State University Press.
Phillipson, M. (1971) *Sociological Aspects of Crime and Delinquency*,
  London: Routledge & Kegan Paul.
Philpott, T.L. (1978) *The Slum and the Ghetto: Neighborhood Deterioration
  and Middle-Class Reform, Chicago, 1880-1930*, New York: Oxford
  University Press.
Phizacklea, A. and Miles, R. (1980) *Labour and Racism*, London:
  Routledge & Kegan Paul.

Pickvance, C.G. (ed.) (1976) *Urban Sociology: Critical Essays*, London: Tavistock.

Pierson, D. ((1942) 1967) *Negroes in Brazil: A Study of Race Contact at Bahia*, Chicago: University of Chicago Press (1942); reprinted Carbondale, Ill.: Southern Illinois University Press (1967).

Plummer, K. (1983) *Documents of Life*, London: Allen & Unwin.

Polenberg, R. (1980) *One Nation Divisible: Class, Race and Ethnicity in the United States since 1938*, New York: Pelican.

Popper, K. (1957) *The Poverty of Historicism*, London: Routledge & Kegan Paul.

Quandt, J.B. (1970) *From the Small Town to the Great Community: The Social Thought of Progressive Intellectuals*, New Brunswick, NJ: Rutgers University Press.

Rainwater, L. (ed.) (1970) 'Introduction', *Soul*, Chicago: Trans-Action Book, Aldine Press.

Rainwater, L. (1971) *Behind Ghetto Walls: Black Families in a Federal Slum*, London: Allen Lane.

Raushenbush, W. (1979) *Robert E. Park: Biography of a Sociologist*, Durham, NC: Duke University Press.

Reeves, F. (1983) *British Racial Discourse*, Cambridge: Cambridge University Press.

Rex, J. and Moore, R. (1967) *Race, Community and Conflict*, London: Oxford University Press.

Reynolds, L. and Henslin, J.M. (eds) (1974) *American Society: A Critical Analysis*, New York: David McKay.

Reynolds, L.T. and Reynolds, J.M. (eds) (1970) *The Sociology of Sociology*, New York: David McKay.

Rock, P. (1979) *The Making of Symbolic Interactionism*, London: Macmillan; New York: Rowman & Littlefield.

Rose, A. ((1962) 1971) 'Introduction', *Human Behavior and Social Processes: An Internationalist Approach*, London: Routledge & Kegan Paul, pp. vii-xii.

Rucker, D. ((1969) 1971) *The Chicago Pragmatists*, Madras, India: Higginbothams.

Sapir, E. (1924) 'Culture: Genuine and spurious', *American Journal of Sociology* 29: 420-9.

Scarman, The Rt Hon Lord (1981) *The Brixton Disorders: Report of an Inquiry*, London: HMSO, Cmnd. 8427.

Schneider, D.M. (1968) *American Kinship: A Cultural Account*, Englewood Cliffs, NJ: Prentice-Hall.

Schneider, D.M. (1969) 'Kinship, religion and nationality', in V. Turner (ed.) *Forms of Symbolic Action, Proceedings of the 1969 Spring Meeting of the American Ethnological Society*, Seattle: University of Washington Press.

Schwendinger, J. and Schwendinger, H. (1974) *The Socioligists of the Chair: A Radical Analysis of the Formative Years of North American Sociology (1883-1922)*, New York: Basic Books.

Scott, M.B. (1970) 'Functional analysis: a statement of problems', in G. Stone and H.A. Farberman (eds) *Social Psychology Through Symbolic Interaction*, Waltham, Ma: Xerox Publishing: pp. 21-8.

Sherman, H.J. and Wood, J.L. (1979) *Sociology, Traditional and Radical Perspectives*, New York and London: Harper & Row.

Shibutani, T. (1961) *Society and Personality: An Interactionist Approach to Social Psychology*, Englewood Cliffs, NJ: Prentice-Hall.

Shils, E. (1957) 'Primordial, personal, sacred and civil ties', *British Journal of Sociology* (June): 130-45.

Shils, E. (1970) 'Tradition, ecology and institution in the history of sociology', *Daedalus* 99: 760-825.

Shipman, M. (1988) *The Limitations of Social Research*, London and New York: Longman.

Simmel, G. ((1950) 1964) *The Sociology of Georg Simmel*, ed. K. Wolff, Glencoe, Ill.: Free Press.

Simmel, G. (1971) *Georg Simmel on Individuality and Social Forms*, ed. and intro. by D.N. Levine, Chicago: University of Chicago Press (Heritage of Sociology).

Smith, A.D. (1981) *The Ethnic Revival in the Modern World*, Cambridge: Cambridge University Press.

Smith, D. (1988) *The Chicago School: A Liberal Critique of Capitalism*, London: Macmillan Education.

Smith, M.G. (1982) 'Ethnicity and ethnic groups in America: the view from Harvard', *Ethnic and Racial Studies* 5 (January): 1-22.

Sowell, T. (1981) *Ethnic America: A History*, New York: Basic Books.

Spear, A. (1967) *Black Chicago: The Making of a Negro Ghetto, 1890-1920*, Chicago: University of Chicago Press.

Stack, C. (1975) *All Our Kin: Strategies for Survival in a Black Community*, New York and London: Harper & Row (Harper Colophon Books).

Stampp, K. (1956) *The Peculiar Institutions: Slavery in the Antebellum South*, New York: Vintage Books.

Stein, M.(1960) *The Eclipse of Community*, Princeton, NJ: Princeton University Press.

Steinberg, S. (1982) *The Ethnic Myth*, Boston: Beacon Press.

Stocking, G.W. Jr. (1968) 'Franz Boas and the culture concept in historical perspective', in *Race, Evolution and Culture*, New York: Free Press, pp. 195-233.

Stone, J. (1985) *Racial Conflict in Contemporary Society*, London: Fontana Press/Collins.

Stone, G. and Farberman, H.A. (1970) *Social Psychology Through Symbolic Interaction*, Waltham, Mass.: Xerox College Publishing.

196

Stonequist, E.V. ((1937) 1961) *The Marginal Man: A Study in Personality and Culture Conflict*, New York: Russell & Russell.

Strickland, A.E. (1966) *History of the Chicago Urban League*, Chicago: University of Chicago Press.

Sumner, W.G. ((1906) 1959) *Folkways*, Boston: Dover Publications.

Tauber, K.E. and Tauber, A.F. (1965) *Negroes in Cities*, Chicago: Aldine Publishing Co.

Thomas, J. (1982) 'New ethnographies', reviews of *Praxis and Method: A Sociological Dialogue*, and *Lukacs and Gramsci and the Early Frankfurt School* by Richard Rilmister, in *Urban Life* 1 (April 1982): 129-32.

Thomas, J. (1983) 'Towards a critical ethnography: a re-examination of the Chicago legacy', *Urban Life* 11 (4) (January): 473-84.

Thomas, W.I. (1909) *Source Book for Social Origins: Ethnological Material, Psychological Standpoint, Classified and Annotated Bibliographies for the Interpretation of Savage Society*, Chicago: University of Chicago Press.

Thomas, W.I. ((1917) 1981) *Social Behavior*, ed. E. Volkart, Greenwood, Conn.: Greenwood Press.

Thomas, W.I. ((1923) 1969) *The Unadjusted Girl: With Cases and Standpoint for Behavior Analysis*, Boston: Little, Brown & Co.

Thomas, W.I. and Thomas, D.S. ((1928) 1966) *The Child in America*, New York: Alfred Knopf; cited in M. Janowitz (1966) 'Introduction' in *W.I. Thomas on Social Organization and Social Personality*, Chicago: University of Chicago Press, pp. vii-lviii.

Thomas, W.I. (1966) *W.I. Thomas on Social Organization and Social Personality*, *selected papers* M. Janowitz (ed.), Chicago: University of Chicago Press.

Thomas, W.I. and Znaniecki, F. (1918-20) *The Polish Peasant in Europe and America*, 5 vols, Chicago: University of Chicago Press.

Thompson, E.T. (1975) *Plantation Societies, Race Relations, and the South: The Regimentation of Populations, Selected Papers of Edgar T. Thompson*, Durham, NC: Duke University Press.

Turkel, S. (1967) *Division Street: America*, New York: Random House.

Turner, R. (1962) 'Role-taking: process versus conformity', in A.M. Rose (ed.) *Human Behavior and Social Process*, Boston: Houghton Mifflin, pp. 20-40.

Turner, R. (1967) 'Introduction', in *Robert E. Park on Social Control and Collective Behavior*, Chicago: University of Chicago Press (Heritage of Sociology), pp. ix-xlvi.

Valentine, C.A. (1968) *Culture and Poverty, Critique and Counter-Proposals*, Chicago: University of Chicago Press.

Valentine, C. and Valentine, B.L. ((1970) 1975) 'Making the scene, digging the action, and telling it like it is: anthropologists at work in a dark ghetto', in J. Friedl and N. Chrisman (eds) *City Ways: A Selective Reader in Urban Anthropology*, London: Harper & Row.

197

Van den Berghe, P. (1978) *Race and Racism*, New York: John Wiley.

Vidich, A.J. and Lyman, S.M. (1985) *American Sociology, Worldly Rejections of Religion and their Directions*, New Haven and London: Yale University Press.

Volkart, E. (ed.) ((1951) 1981) *Social Behavior and Personality: Contributions of W.I. Thomas to Theory and Social Research*, Greenwood, Conn.: Greenwood Press.

Wacker, F.R. (1985) *Ethnicity, Pluralism and Race: Race Relations Theory in America Before Myrdal*, Westport, Conn.: Greenwood Press.

Wallman, S. (1978) 'The boundaries of "Race": processes of ethnicity in England', *MAN* 13 (2): 200-17.

Wallman, S. (1979) 'Introduction: the scope for ethnicity', in S. Wallman (ed.) *Ethnicity at Work*, London: Macmillan.

Wallman, S. (1983) 'Identity options', in C. Fried (ed.) *Minorities: Community and Identity*, Dahlem Konferenzen Berlin, Heidelberg, New York: Springer Verlag, pp. 69-78.

Wallman, S. (1984) *Eight London Households*, London: Tavistock.

Wallman, S. (1986) 'Ethnicity and the boundary process in context', in J. Rex and D. Mason (eds) *Theories of Race and Ethnic Relations*, Cambridge: Cambridge University Press, pp. 226-45.

Washington, B.T. ((1901) 1956) *Up from Slavery*, New York: Doubleday.

Washington, B.T. (1909) *The Story of the Negro*, New York: Doubleday.

Washington, B.T. (1911) *My Larger Education*, New York: Doubleday.

Washington, B.T. with the collaboration of Park, R.E. (1912) *The Man Farthest Down: A Record of Observations and Study in Europe*, Garden City, NY: Doubleday, Page & Company.

Washington-Park: Correspondence. Booker T. Washington Papers, Library of Congress, Washington DC.

Waskow, A.I. (1967) *From Race Riot to Sit-In: 1919 and the 1960s*, New York: Doubleday.

Watson, J. (ed.) (1977) *Between Two Cultures, Migrants and Minorities in Britain*, Oxford: Blackwell.

Wax, M.L. (1971) *Indian Americans: Unity and Diversity*, Englewood Cliffs, NJ: Prentice-Hall.

White, M. and White, L. (1964) *The Intellectual and the City*, New York: New American Library (Mentor).

Wiley, N. (1979) 'The rise and fall of dominating theories in American sociology', in W.E. Shizell *et al.* (eds) *Contemporary Issues in Theory and Research*, Westport, Conn.: Greenwood Press, pp. 47–79.

Wiley, N. (1986) 'Early American Sociology and the "Polish Peasant"', *Sociological Theory '86* 4 (1): 20-40.

Wilson, J.Q. (1985) 'The rediscovery of character: private virtue and public policy', *The Public Interest* (Fall): 3–16.

Wilson, W.J. (1978) *The Declining Significance of Race: Blacks and Changing American Institutions*, Chicago: University of Chicago Press.

Wilson, W.J. (1987) *The Truly Disadvantaged: The Inner City, The Underclass, and Public Policy*, London and Chicago: University of Chicago Press.

Wirth, L. ((1928) 1956) *The Ghetto*, Chicago: University of Chicago Press.

Wirth, L. (1938) 'Urbanism as a way of life', *American Journal of Sociology* 44 (July): 1-24.

Wirth, L. ((1945) 1964) 'The problem with minority groups', in *Louis Wirth on Cities and Social Life*, ed. Albert J. Riess Jr, Chicago: University of Chicago Press, pp. 244-69.

Wirth, L. ((1948) 1964) 'Consensus and mass communication' reprinted from *Community Life and Social Policy*, ed. E.W. Marrick and A.J. Reiss Jr, Chicago: University of Chicago Press (1956), pp. 368-91; first published in *American Sociological Review* XIII (February 1948): 1-15; Presidential address to American Sociological Society, New York City, 28-30 December 1947; reprinted in *Louis Wirth On Cities and Social Life*, Chicago: University of Chicago Press (Heritage), pp. 18-43.

Wirth, L. ((1956) 1964) 'Human ecology', *Community Life and Social Policy*, eds. E.W. Marrick and A.J. Reiss Jr, Chicago: University of Chicago Press (1956), pp. 133-42; *American Journal of Sociology* 50 (May 1945): 483-8; reprinted in *Louis Wirth on Cities and Social Life*: 178–88.

Wirth, L. (1964) *Louis Wirth on Cities and Social Life: Selected Papers*, ed. Albert Reiss Jr, Chicago: University of Chicago Press (Heritage).

Wrong, D. (1961) 'The oversocialized conception of man in modern sociology', *American Sociological Review* XXVI: 184-93.

Yancey, W.L., Ericksen, E.P., and Juliana, R.N. (1976) 'Emergent ethnicity: a review and reformulation', *American Sociological Review* 41: 391-403.

Yancey, W.L. and Ericksen, E.P. (1979) 'The antecedent of community: the economic and institutional structure of urban neighborhoods', *American Sociological Review* 44 (April): 253-62.

Young, P.V. (1932) *The Pilgrims of Russian-Town*, Chicago: University of Chicago Press.

Zeitlin, I. (1973) *Rethinking Sociology: A Critique of Contemporary Theory*, New York: Free Press.

Zorbaugh, H.W. (1929) *The Gold Coast and the Slum*, Chicago: University of Chicago Press.

NAME INDEX

Abbott, E. 69
Ackerman, N.W. 176 n. 7
Adamic, L. 13
Addams, J. 2, 69
Adorno, T.W. 176 n.7
Ali, Muhammed 58
Amersfoort, H. van 8
Ames, E. S. 16, 30
Anderson, J. 177 n. 14
Anderson, N. 2, 25, 120
Angell, J. 16, 30

Baker, P.J. 18, 21, 22
Baker, R.S. 176 n.4
Baldwin, J. 40
Baldwin, J.M. 19, 24
Barth, F. 87, 169
Barth, G. 120
Bauer, A.H. 129
Bauer, R.A. 129
Becker, H. 2, 7, 38, 65–6, 79, 81
Bell, D. 115
Berger, B. 7
Berger, P.L. 7, 64
Bernstein, B. 174 n.4
Béteille, A. 44, 176 n.6
Bettelheim, B. 176 n. 7
Blau, P. 177 n.13
Blauner, R. 3, 121, 177 n.14
Blumer, H.: Chicago school 2, 159;
    quoted 30, 70, 90; works cited:
    Critiques of Research. . . 79; 'The
    future of the color line' 65; 'Ind-
    ustrialism and race relations' 65;
    'The methodological position . . .'
    85, 89, 163; 'Race prejudice as a
    sense of group position' 40, 85, 105,
    162–3; 'Reflections on theory of

race relations' 65; 'Social unrest
and collective protest' 47;
'Sociological analysis. . .' 65, 66, 82;
*Symbolic Interactionism, Perspective and
Method* 30, 71; 'Theories of race and
social action' 34, 65, 71, 86–7, 147,
163–7
Boas, F. 1, 69–70, 108, 152, 154, 169
Bowker, G. 5
Bramson, L 47–8
Breckinridge, S. 69
Brittan, A. 85
Bruce, B.K. 134
Bulmer, M., works cited: *The Chicago
    School of Sociology* 6, 8, 16, 17, 23, 25,
    29, 89–91; *Sociological Research
    Methods* 79
Burgess, E.W. 9, 17, 23–4, 40, 42–8, 80

Caplan, N. 153
Carey, J.T. 14, 16, 17, 172 n.7
Carmichael, S. 3
Carrier, J. 5
Castells, M. 4
Castles, S. 52
Cayton, H.: Chicago school 2; work
    cited *see* Drake, St Clair, *Black
    Metropolis* Chicago Commission on
    Race Relations 8, 17, 25, 34, 86,
    139–43, 161
Cicourel, A. 8, 83
Colfax, J.D. 4, 78
Collins, R. 64
Cooley, C.H. 24, 37, 54
Cox, O.C. 5, 42, 58, 64, 122
Cruse, H. 3, 13, 50, 177 n.14

Darwin, C. 24

200

NAME INDEX

Davidson, D. 5, 6
Denzin, N. 79
Dewey, J.: influence 18, 24, 30–1, 130, 132; pragmatism 16, 88, 169
Dicey, A.V. 24
Diner, H. 51
Diner, S.J. 3, 6, 14, 15, 16, 17, 30
Dinnerstein, L. 93–4
Douglas, J. 8
Doyle, B.W. 34, 81
Drake, St Clair: Chicago school 2; work cited: *Black Metropolis* 8, 59–60, 70, 81, 88, 143, 156–9, 161
Dreiser, T. 76
Driver, G. 167
Du Bois, W.E.B. 155
Dumont, L. 44
Dunbar, P.L. 149
Durkheim, E. 24, 62
Duster, T.: works cited: 'Review. . .' 153; 'Theories of race and social action' *see* Blumer, H.

Elliott, R.B. 134
Ellison, R. 4–5, 51, 121

Farberman, H. 2, 6, 36, 38
Faris, E. 90
Faris, R.E.L. 30, 89, 171 n.3
Filmer, P. 8
Finlay, M.I. 126
Firth, R. 87
Fisher, B.M. 56–7, 66
Flew, A. 158
Ford, F. 18
Franklin, J.H. 126, 140, 175 n.3
Frazier, E.F.: Chicago school 2, 158; on culture of poverty 83; works cited: *Black Bourgeoisie* 58–60, 81, 82, 88, 157; 'Certain aspects of conflict. . .' 156; 'The Negro Church in America' 54; *The Negro Family in Chicago* 161; *The Negro Family in the United States* 8, 158, 160–1; 'The new Negro middle class' 157; 'Race contacts and the social structure' 156; 'Tradition and patterns. . . 158
Friedrichs, R.W. 78
Furner, M.O. 15

Gandhi 37
Garfinkel, H. 8
Geertz, C. 110–11

Genovese, E. 53, 129
Gifford, Lord, 173 n.1
Glazer, N.: Cruse on 51; on culture of poverty 83; works cited: *Affirmative Discrimination* 3, 112, 115, 153; *Beyond the Melting Pot* 3, 29, 112, 160; *Ethnic Dilemmas* 3; *Ethnic Pluralism* 8; *Ethnicity, Theory and Experience* 3, 112, 160; 'Interests and passions' 172–3 n.1; *The Limits of Social Policy* 3
Goffman, E. 2, 7, 38, 66–8, 82
Gordon, M.M. 3, 64, 112
Gosnell, H. 23, 161
Gossett, T.F. 3
Gouldner, A.W. 6, 78, 173 n.2
Greeley, A.M. 110
Gusfield, J. 2

Hamilton, C. 3
Hannerz, U. 88, 173 n.1
Harlan, L.R. 20, 126, 130
Harper, W.R. 16
Henretta, J.A. 84
Henslin, J.M. 4
Higham, J. 3, 49, 94–5, 111, 153
Hofstadter, R. 12, 14–15, 154
Hollinger, D.A. 16, 89
Hughes, E.C.: Chicago school 2, 65–6, 159; works cited: *The Chicago Real Estate Board* 147–8; 'Dilemmas and contradictions of status' 38–9; 'The ecological aspect of institutions' 148; *French Canada in Transition* 81; 'Going concerns. . .' 66; *The Sociological Eye* 7; 'The study of institutions' 148
Hughes, H. 2

Isaacs, H.R. 110–11, 116.

Jackson, P. 8, 168
Jahoda, M. 176 n.7
James, W. 19, 20, 37, 73–4
Janowitz, M. 33, 66, 176 n.7
Johnson, C.S.: Chicago Commission 24; Chicago school 2, 157, 159; Fisk University 25; *Shadow of the Plantation* 80–1, 145, 161
Johnson, J.W. 148–9

Kallen, H. 13
Kantrowitz, N. 175 n.1
Katznelson, I. 139

201

Khan, V.S. 169
Killian, L. 2, 7, 159, 168, 170
King, M.L. 57
Kistiakowski, T. 19
Kolchin, P. 177 n.12
Kosack, G. 52
Kramer, D. 76
Kuhn, T. 158
Kurtz, L.R. 6, 88

Labov, W. 174 n.4
Ladner, J. 5
Lal, B.B. 7, 8, 41, 89
Langston, J.M. 134
Leavitt, M. 98
LeBon, G. 47
Lecky, W.E.H. 24, 46
Lee, A.M. 88
Leonardo, M. di 162, 170
Leopold, King of Belgium 19
Levine, D.N. 46
Lewis, O. 83, 158
Lieberson, S. 3, 156
Liebow, C. 88
Light, I. 3
Lipset, S.M. 5, 41, 65
Lofland, L. 70, 87
Lowie, F. 69, 70
Lubove, R. 14
Luckmann, T. 7, 64
Lyman, S. 5, 42, 58, 63, 171 n.2, 173 nn.5, 6

Makowsky, M. 64
Malcolm X 58
Mann, A. 14
Mannheim, K. 47, 78
Matthews, F.H., works cited: 'Cultural pluralism in context. . .' 13; Quest for an American Sociology 5, 6, 17, 18, 20, 41, 139, 152, 171 nn.3, 6, 177 n.16; 'The revolt against Americanism. . .' 95–6
Mayo, E. 62
McKay, C. 148–9
McKay, H. 17
Mead, G.H.: educational theory 130, 132; influence 7, 16, 17, 30, 72, 88, 169; Mind, Self and Society 33, 37–8, 172 n.5
Meier, A. 122, 142, 166
Meltzer, B.N. 85
Merriam, C. 17

Merton, R. 4, 6
Miles, R. 52
Miller, H.A., see Park Old World Traits
Mills, C.W. 72, 78, 161
Mirza, H. 167
Modood, T. 60
Moore, A.W. 16, 30
Moore, R. 8, 168
Morel, E.R. 19
Moynihan, D.P. 3, 29, 83, 112, 113, 115, 160
Muensterberg, H. 19
Myrdal, G. 5, 42, 128, 151, 176 n.6

National Advisory Commission on Civil Disorders 8
Norris, F. 76
Novak, M. 13

Oberschall, A. 17, 90
Ogburn, W. 90–1
Ortega y Gasset, J. 47
Osofsky, G. 84, 152, 177 n.14
Ovington 6

Park, C.C. 22
Park, R.E., works cited: 'Assimilation, social' 149; 'An autobiographical note' 20; 'The bases of race prejudice' 39, 45, 50, 126, 127, 135–7, 146, 151; 'Behind our masks' 25, 39, 118–19, 124, 135, 138, 149; 'Blood-money of the Congo' 20; 'The city as a social laboratory' 26, 69, 80; 'The city: suggestions. . .' 23, 29, 48, 70, 76; 'Community organization and the romantic temper' 122; 'The concept of social distance. . .' 138; The Crowd and the Public and Other Essays 36, 37, 43, 45; 'Cultural conflict and the marginal man' 33, 39, 52, 113; 'Culture and civilization' 11, 19; 'Culture and cultural trends' 28; 'Documents, letters collected. . .' 73; 'Education and the cultural crisis' 20; 'Education in its relation. . .' 150, 154; 'Experience and race relations . . .' 86; 'German Army' 173 n.5; 'Human migration and the marginal man' 35, 38, 52; 'Human nature and collective behaviour' 32, 75; 'Human nature, attitudes and

mores' 34, 145; *The Immigrant Press and its Control* 10, 24, 73–5, 79–81, 95–7, 99–102; 'Industrial fatigue and group morale' 62, 118; 'Introduction' in Doyle 34–5, 50, 128–9, 133–4; 'Introduction' in Young 35, 120; *An Introduction to the Science of Sociology* 23–4, 40–8, 172 n.4; 'A king in business' 20, 173, n.5; *The Man Farthest Down*. . . 39, 80; 'A memorandum of rote learning' 150; 'Mentality of racial hybrids' 153; 'Natural history of the newspaper' 119; 'The nature of race relations' 62, 137, 139, 173 n.5, 176 n.9; 'The Negro and his plantation heritage' 73, 80, 145; 'Negro home life and standards of living' 175 n.2; 'Negro race consciousness. . .' 136, 144–5, 148–9, 151–2, 177 n.15; 'News and the human interest story' 119, 175 n.8; *Old World Traits Transplanted* 10, 24, 33, 35, 39, 73–4, 79–80, 95–9, 103–4, 106–9, 117; 'Our racial frontier on the Pacific' 25, 39, 41; 'Personality and cultural conflict' 32–3, 37, 39, 52, 167; 'Politics and the man farthest down' 3, 130, 139, 142, 145, 148, 171 n.5; 'Race ideologies' 20, 144–6, 148; 'Race prejudice and Japanese-American relations' 67; 'The race relations cycle in Hawaii' 172 n.6; 'A race relations survey' 78, 138; 'Racial assimilation in secondary groups' 3, 6, 45, 119, 124, 130, 134, 137–8, 144–5, 147–8, 175 n.3, 176 n.8; 'Reflections on communication and culture' 28, 31, 34, 42, 172 n.1; 'The social function of war. . .' 35; 'The sociological methods. . .' 37, 72; 'Sociology and the social sciences' 27, 38, 95; 'Sociology community and society' 34, 36, 63; 'Symbiosis and socialization. . .' 28–9, 91; 'The terrible story of the Congo' 20, 173 n.5; 'The urban community. . .' 26, 32, 37, 117, 168
Parsons, T. 4, 6, 65, 111–13
Paulson, F. 19
Peach, C. 8, 168
Persons, S. 5, 42, 58
Petersen, W. 113

Petras, J.W. 85
Phillips, U.B. 129
Phillipson, M. 8
Philpott, T.L. 5, 94, 124, 140–1
Phizacklea, A. 52
Pickvance, C.G. 4
Pierson, D. 81
Pitt Rivers, W. 69
Plummer, K. 6, 8, 85
Polenberg, R. 152–3
Popper, K. 72

Quandt, J.B. 12, 122–3

Rainwater, L. 84, 88, 123, 162, 167, 175 n.9
Raushenbush, W.: assists Park 24, 73; Chicago school 2; *Robert E. Park*. . . 19, 21–2, 23, 25, 171 n.4
Redfield, R. 69
Reeves, F. 34
Revels, H. 134
Rex, J. 8, 168
Reynolds, J.M. 4, 78
Reynolds, L.T. 4, 78
Rivers, W.H.R. 28
Roach, J.L. 4, 78
Robinson, J.H. 94–5
Rock, P. 6, 8
Rose, A. 2, 7, 30, 172 n.3
Royce, J. 19
Rucker, D. 16, 30
Rudwick, E. 121–2

Santayana, G. 19
Sapir, E. 69, 110
Scarman, The Rt Hon Lord 8, 173 n.1
Schneider, D.M. 111
Schwendinger, H. 4, 5, 78
Schwendinger, J. 4, 5, 78
Scott, E.J. 21, 146, 149–50
Scott, M. 7
Scudder, V.D. 95
Shaw, C. 2, 17
Sherman, H.J. 53
Shibutani, T. 2, 7, 36, 64
Shils, E. 4, 12, 110, 158, 174 n.6
Shipman, M. 79
Sighele, S. 47
Simmel, G.: influence 24, 30, 42, 137, 162; Park studies under 12, 19; *The Sociology of Georg Simmel* 42, 176 n.9
Sinclair, U. 76

Small, A. 17, 154
Smith, A.D. 13, 116
Smith, D. 6, 42, 58, 64
Smith, S. 8, 168
Sowell, T. 3, 158
Spear, A. 141, 144, 152, 166
Spencer, H. 24
Stack, C. 88
Stampp, K. 53, 127
Steinberg, S. 13, 112, 116
Steiner, J. 2
Stocking, G.W. Jr 3, 108, 152
Stone, G. 2, 6, 36, 38
Stone, J. 5, 52
Stonequist, E.V. 52
Stouffer, S. 90
Strauss, A. 2, 56–7, 66
Strickland, A.E. 17
Sumner, W.G. 23, 174 n.1
Suttles, G. 2

Tarde, G. 47
Tauber, A.F. 173 n.3
Tauber, K.E. 173 n.3
Thomas, D.S. 35
Thomas, J. 83
Thomas W.I.: Chicago school 90–1;
    influence on Park, 22, 23, 89; Old
    World Traits Transplanted 24, 99,
    102–9, 117; Park's colleague 1, 3,
    10, 18, 30, 46, 49, 69, 82, 92, 95,
    114, 120; works cited: The Child in
    America 35; The Polish Peasant in
    Europe and America 10, 73, 79, 169;
    Social Behavior 55; Source Book for
    Social Origins 10; The Unadjusted Girl
    35
Thompson, E. 2, 80, 172 n.4
Thrasher, F. 2
Thurstone, L.L. 75, 90
Tufts, J.H. 16, 30
Turkel, S. 75
Turner, R. 2, 7

Valentine, B.L. 84

Valentine, C.A. 83–4, 158
Van den Berghe, P. 113, 115
Veblen, T. 23
Vidich, A.J. 63, 171 n.2, 173 nn.5, 6
Villard, O.G. 95
Volkart, E. 24

Wacker, F.R. 6
Wald, L.D. 95
Wallman, S. 38, 84, 87–8, 168–70, 173
    n.4
Warming, E. 24
Washington, B.T.: relationship with
    Park 20–2, 83, 153; strategy for
    black culture 134, 144, 153;
    Tuskegee Institute 20, 130–4;
    works cited: 'Documents, letters. . .'
    73; The Man Farthest Down 21, 39, 80;
    My Larger Education 20–1; The Story
    of the Negro 20–1; Up from Slavery 130,
    145
Waskow, A.I. 6, 152
Watson, J. 169
Wax, M.L. 113, 116
Wiley, N. 6, 69, 90
Wilson, J. 55
Wilson, W.J. 60–1
Windelband, W. 19
Wirth, L. 2, 17, 25, 29, 71, 81
Wissler, C. 28
Wood, J.L. 53
Wright, R. 76
Wrong, D. 6

X, M. 58

Yancey, W.L. 115
Young, K. 8
Young, P. 2, 79–80, 81, 120

Zeitlin, I. 78
Znaniecki, F. 2, 10, 73, 79, 169
Zorbaugh, H. 2, 120

SUBJECT INDEX

accommodation 5, 41–2, 43–4
acculturation 3, 107
affirmative action programmes 114,
153–4
African culture 150
Afro-Americans: class structure
59–62; colour bar 136–8; culture
building process 120, 147;
disabling attributes 67; economic
prospects 156; history in Chicago
141–4; image of 35; intelligence
154; literature 148–9; Park's
inquiries 3; Park's views 5, 154–5;
population statistics 139; underclass
84, 158
Afro-Caribbeans 60
altruism 50
American Federation of Labour 143
American Sociological Society 25
anthropology 70
'apperception mass' 102–3
assimilation 3, 5, 41–2, 44–5, 95, 103,
108–9
autobiographies 72

behaviourism 75
bi-racial organization 146–7, 163
Black Codes 63, 128
Black Jews 113
Black Muslims 58, 113
black: culture 13, 121, 153; ghetto 123,
124, 145, 156, 166, see also Chicago
('Black Belt'); institutions 144;
poetry 148–9, 157
Britain 60, 88
Bureau of Indian Affairs 116
bureaucracies 68

capitalism 53
Carnegie Corporation 24
case-study approach 69, 85–6, 89–91
caste 35, 129, 135, 145–6, 158
character 55
Chicago: 'Black Belt' 124, 141–2, 166;
black population 140–4;
Commission on Race Relations 4,
24–5, 142; community studies 75–6;
immigrants 94, 98, 106; School 4,
6–8, 65–6, 78–9, 88–91; school of
philosophy 16, 89; race riot (1919)
24–5, 86; study of 59; University 4,
16–17, 22–5, 30, 89–91; Urban
League 4, 17
Chinese-Americans 25
Christian fundamentalism 54, 117
churches 3, 51, 54, 118, see also
religious sects
civil rights movement 152–3
Civil Rights Act (1968) 61
Civil War 124–5
civilization 11, 13
class see social classes, status groups
collective: action 45–6, 49; behaviour
45–8, 57; definitions 49, 87, 163–4
colour 67, 124, 136–8, 149
Columbia University, New York 154
communication 27, 31–3, 35–6, 42, 49,
56, 62–3, 64, 90
comparative analysis 80
competition 5, 28, 41–2, 135, 152, 159
'concentric zone' theory 80
conflict 5, 41–3, 52–3, 151
Congo Reform Association 19–20, 22
Congress of Industrial Organisations
143

205

consensus 41–2, 56, 90
control *see* social control
conventions 43
crowds 45–8
cultural: consensus 117–18;
   nationalism 3; pluralism 96, 108–9
culture: acquisition of 49; black 121–2;
   Boas on 108; building 147, 167;
   city-wide shared 117–18; Negro 121;
   Park's concept 1–3, 9, 27–8, 49–50,
   52, 64, 69, 84, 90, 108, 120–2, 154,
   158, 160–2, 169–70; of poverty 83–5;
   Quandt on 122–3

Darwinism, Social 154
Debtors Anonymous 54
'democratic public' 56–7
Depression, Great 93
deviance 38
discrimination *see* racial discrimination
documents, human 72, 76, 77, 85–6,
   89–91
domination/subordination axis 163
dualisms 165–7

ecology, human *see* human ecology
education: black middle-class attitudes
   160–1; industrial 130–2; self-help
   149–50
empathy 50, 63
emulation 165
equality 134
ethnic: boundaries 88, 169; groups 92,
   111–12; revival 116
ethnicity: as genuine culture 110–11;
   by consent 13, 54, 96, 113;
   compulsory 13, 96, 114–15; paradox
   3, 96, 109, 117, 167; role of 168
ethnography, sociological 70–1
ethnomethodology 8, 83, 90
etiquette of race relations 34, 50, 128
evolution 31

field-work 69–72, 75–6, 90–1
Fisk University, Tennessee 25, 90
force 56, 62
Frederich-Wilhelm University, Berlin
   12, 19
freedmen 129–30, 133
funerals 99

German immigrants 101
ghetto: black 123–4, 145, 156, 166, *see*

also Chicago ('Black Belt'); Jewish
   80–1; revolts 57–8
government 65, 156
group: life 49; position 162
groups: dominant/subordinate 163;
   ethnic *see* ethnic; racial 164–5;
   sentimental 53–4

Hare Krishna movement 113, 117
Harvard University 19
Heidelberg University 19
hidden interests 51
holism, sociological 6, 82
human documents 72, 76, 77, 85–6,
   89–91
human ecology 28–9, 168
'humanist sociology' 88
Hungarian immigrants 94, 101–2

identity, ethnic/racial 3, 113–14
Illinois Commission on Race Relations
   17
immigrant institutions 98–108
immigrants to US from Europe 92–5
immigration, US urban 14, 74
individual: choice 15; requirements of
   11; socialization of 36
institutions: black 144–5, 166;
   immigrant 98–108; role of 147
integration 12–13, 107, 166
intellectuals, role of 13
intelligence 154
interpretations, variable 164
isolation of blacks 144–5
Italian immigrants 104

Japanese-Americans 25, 74, 104–5, 138
Japanese culture 150
Japanese Exclusion Act 25
Jewish: Americans 51, 73–5, 99, 103,
   105, 117; ghetto 80–1; orthodoxy
   54, 103
Jews, Black 113

labelling theory 38, 65
language 31, 33, 97, *see also*
   communication, press
legislation 61, 63, 65, 156
liberals, role of 136
life history materials 72
literature 148–9, 157
Local Community Research
   Committee 25

lodges, fraternal 54
London 88

'marginal man', 33, 38, 51–2, 113
'marginality' 3
Methodism 46
Michigan, University of 18
Minnesota, University of 18
mobs 46
Molokan community 79–80, 120
Montgomery bus boycott 57
Moonies 117
'moral brotherhood' 63
'moral density' 12

'naive realism' 83
National Committee for constructive
    Immigration Legislation 94
National Community Center 17
Native Americans 113, 116
naturalistic inquiry 85, 87
New York City 117
newspapers see press

'opportunity structure' 93, 115

parochial minority groups 116–17
participation 96, 107
philanthropists 51
plantations 53, 80–1, 126, 128–9
poetry 148–9, 157
Polish immigrants 104, 169
political: conflict 47; organization 3
power 62, 65–6
pragmatism 16, 89
press, foreign-language: importance of
    3, 97, 99–102; Park's studies 73–5,
    81, 100–2
press, role of 119–20
Progressive politics 14–16, 122–3
public opinion 47, 119

qualitative/quantitative techniques 79

race: dominant/subordinate 163;
    Park's perspective 2–3, 123;
    prejudice 50, 85, 87, 135–6, 162–3;
    riots 24–5, 34, 86–7, 152–3
race relations: Blumer (and Duster)
    on 65, 163–5; 'cycle' 5, 41, 58, 86;
    etiquette of 34, 50, 128; in the
    North 134–9; in the South 125–34;
    Park's emphasis 154–5

racial: antipathy 137; conflict 151–2;
    discrimination 15, 63, 143, 151–2,
    155, 159; groups 164–5;
    stereotypes 37; temperament
    154–5
racism 53, 145, 155
Rastafarians 113
Reconstruction 134, 156
religious sects 46, 54, 113, 117, see also
    Black Muslims, churches, Jewish
    Americans
Russia 62, 79–80

segregation 29, 63, 133–4, 152, 159,
    166
self, Goffman on 66
self-concept 37–8
self-consciousness 43
self-esteem 39–40, 103–6, 167–8
self-help 149–50, 156
self-restraint 56, 62
sentimental groups 53–4
Sicilian immigrants 98
'situational analysis' 35
slave trade 150
slavery 5, 35, 53, 63, 85, 125–31
slums 14
social: accommodation see
    accommodation; assimilation see
    assimilation; behaviourism 7;
    change (models of) 56–8; classes 52,
    59–62, 112, 115, 145–7, 157–8;
    conflict 52–3, 62–3; contact 42;
    control, 26, 27, 32–3, 55–6, 62–3, 90;
    Darwinism 154; distance 128;
    equality 134; forces 58; identity 67;
    integration see integration;
    interaction (typology of) 41–5;
    mobility 3, 133; movements 46;
    process 63–4; structure 63–8, 81–2,
    158; surveys 87–8, 91; systems
    approach 66
socialization 35
sociological ethnography 70–1
sociology: humanist 88; Park on
    16–17, 23, 26, 86, 90–1; role of 120;
    spatial 168
solidarity 165
Southern Christian Leadership
    Conference 57
specialness 165
status 38–41, 105–6, 159, 167–8
status groups 52–4, 59

207

stereotypes 149
stigma 66–7
Strasbourg University 19
structural analysis 64–5, 82
subjective dimension of social action 28
'subjectivist sociologies' 6–8, 75
symbiosis 28
'symbolic interactionism' 7, 30, 169
symbolic nature of group life 49
Syrian immigrants 101, 103–4

trade unions 51, 118, 143, 155
Tuskegee Institute, Alabama 20–2, 130–2

unions *see* trade unions
urban: ethnography 2, 85, 88–9; sociologists 76–7
urbanization 55

'variable analysis' 66

wages 140–1
war: Civil 124–5; First World 101–2, 142; Second World 152, 157
Weight Watchers 54
welfare policies 93

xenophobia 94, 96

Yiddish press 73–5

For Product Safety Concerns and Information please contact our EU
representative GPSR@taylorandfrancis.com
Taylor & Francis Verlag GmbH, Kaufingerstraße 24, 80331 München, Germany

www.ingramcontent.com/pod-product-compliance
Lightning Source LLC
Chambersburg PA
CBHW070418270326
41926CB00014B/2837

9 781138 036628